AF539853

ENVIRONMENTAL AWARENESS
A NEED OF THE HOUR

ENVIRONMENTAL AWARENESS
A NEED OF THE HOUR

Edited by

Dr. Lingaraj Patro

Professor & Head

Deptt. of Zoology & Biotechnology

K.B.D.A.V. College, Nirakarpur

Khurda (Orissa) (India)

DISCOVERY PUBLISHING HOUSE PVT. LTD.

NEW DELHI-110 002

Reprinted - 2019

First Published - 2010

ISBN: 978-81-8356-638-4

Environmental Awareness: ***A Need of the Hour***

Published by:

DISCOVERY PUBLISHING HOUSE PVT. LTD.

4383/4B, Ansari Road, Darya Ganj

New Delhi-110 002 (India)

Phone: +91-11-23279245, 23253475; 43596065

E-mail: discoverybooksindia@gmail.com

discoverypublishinghouse@gmail.com

web: www.discoverypublishinggroup.com

Printed at:

Infinity Imaging Systems

Delhi

Preface

The term 'environment' refers to the surroundings of a species to which it is in complete adaptation and continuous interaction for various activities of life and also for its survival. The environment consists of certain factors - social, economic, biological, physical and chemical etc. The largest number of any given species that a habitat can support indefinitely is its carrying capacity. The resource base becomes rickety when that maximum sustainable population level is surpassed. Not only our most basic requirements but also our levels of consumption of a whole range of resources, the amount of waste we generate, the technologies we choose and our success in mobilizing to deal with major threats determine the earth's capacity to support humans. Of late, ozone depletion and green house warming have underlined the danger of over-stepping the earth's ability to absorb our waste products. Because of our population size, consumption patterns and technology choice we have transcended the planet's carrying capacity. Thus, we are stripping the earth off its natural capital and its environmental assets now don't suffice to sustain our economic activity and life support system as well. If present trends continue and world population hikes it will lead inevitably to greater environmental devastation. In developing countries there is widespread water pollution - the very source of many diseases that kill myriad children every year. There is a need of clean water; it is high time we developed awareness among general public for the environmental hazards.

The role of ecologists and environmentalists is very vital. Unluckily, our economic growth is of a damaging variety based on extraction and consumption of fossil fuels, water, timber, minerals and other resources. Public awareness should centre round population growth, cropland destruction and degradation, depletion in the quality of soil and water, forest destruction etc. So, attention must be focused on the links between poverty, population growth and environmental decline and to devise strategies that simultaneously address the root causes. Efforts should be made to raise women's social and economic status, to give them equal rights to choose. Business leaders, religious communities and all have to join hands to halt earth's environmental deterioration. Then the scientists' "Warning to Humanity" may end and the human community may live sustainable on the earth.

Environmental Awareness: A Need of the Hour contains selected papers by eminent professors, researchers, scientists and academicians of different parts of India and abroad pertaining to various issues and dimensions of environment. It is hoped that the book will immensely aid the policymakers, researchers, environmentalists and general readers for policy implications.

Dr. LINGARAJ PATRO

Acknowledgements

I can't but gratefully acknowledge my indebtedness to all those who have extended unstinting assistance in the successful accomplishment of this indispensable work. It will be a serious blunder if I forget to mention some of my colleagues Prof. Dr. S.N. Padhi, Vice-Principal, Prof. Sarat Chandra Mishra, Head, Department of English, and Dr. Suresh Chandra Rath, Head. Dept. of Chemistry, K.B.D.A.V. College, Nirakarpur for their ardent encouragement and beacon-guidance in bringing out this work.

Last but not least my heart felt gratitude to my wife knows no bounds for her unblemished co-operation.

I am also much beholden to Mr. Tilak Wasan, Managing Director, Discovery Publishing House Pvt. Ltd., New Delhi for publishing the work in a record time.

Dr. LINGARAJ PATRO

Contents

1

Influence of Socio-demographic Factors on Environmental Education Awareness of People in and Around Kolkata City

Shreyashi Paltasingh[1]

ABSTRACT

Environmental education awareness of 120 respondents belonging to Kolkata city and its adjacent suburban areas were studied. Impact of socio-demographic factors such as age, sex, marital status, locality, educational background and income of family on it was examined by testing the hypotheses. It was observed that there was significant difference in awareness between two different categories of respondents due to age, sex, locality, parental education and income of family. But it was not significant due to marital status.

INTRODUCTION

Environment has been considered as sum total of all the factors that influence on an organism. It includes water, air, land

1. **Lecturer, S.I.E.T. (B.Ed. Training College), 5/B.R. Dasgupta Road, Kolkata.**

and their inter-relationships with different organisms. Human being derives all its needs, comforts and luxury from the environment. It is erroneous to say that environment is limitless with resources. Humanity depends on various living and nonliving elements of environment and not viceversa. This must be considered very essential for humanity to proceed ahead and it needs to be communicated to the public. Environmental problems cause disequilibrium in relationship between biotic and abiotic factors. Pressures due to rapid population growth, urbanization, lavish consumption, industrialization, advances in Science and Technology and its applications with huge energy utilization etc. had caused serious environmental problems (Santra, 2001). Human being cause such problems and in turn hurt by it. So, humanity needs to be educated for the understanding, solution and prevention of such problems.

Environmental problems may be global, national or local in nature. Global problems are depletion of ozone layer, exhaust of petroleum resources, extinction of wildlife species etc. National problems are exhaust of mines, deforestation, irregularity in climate etc. Regional problems are soil erosion, desertification, acid rain etc. Environmental education addresses such issues and foster environmental literacy among all citizens. It enables the public to make sound judgements and decisions and have ethical responbilities about environment and its related issues. The Hon'ble Supreme Court on its judgment delivered on 18th, December, 2003 directed NCERT to prepare model syllabus for environmental education to be taught at different grades and submit it to the court, so as to consider feasibility to introduce such syllabus uniformly through out the country. Accordingly, NCERT and SCERT of different States had developed environmental education in either science or social science curriculum in school level right from first grade standard. The UGC had also recommended introduction of compulsory foundation course on environmental education in Indian universities at Under-graduate level (Panigrahi, 2004).

The Ministry of Environment and Forests emphasise on promotion of non-formal environmental education and awareness among all sections of society through diverse activities using traditional and modern media of communication. Such initiatives are National Environment Awareness Campaign, Establishment of National and Regional Museums of Natural History, setting up eco-clubs in schools, production of popular publications on environmental issues, encouraging to organize seminars/symposia/conference on environmental issues etc. The Environmental Education Conference at Tbilisi(USSR) in 1977 identified its ultimate aim as:

> "creating awareness, behavioural attitudes and values directed towards preserving the biosphere, improving the quality of life everywhere as well on safe guarding ethical values and cultural and natural heritage, including holy places, historical land marks, works of arts, monuments and sites, human and natural environment including fauna and flora and human settlements."

Environmental awareness is an attitude towards environment which manifests itself in terms of awareness towards physical pollution, psychological pollution, social pollution and cultural pollution. It is the characteristic quality of man to understand and know the ins and outs of working forces and conditions of the environment. As the present society is witnessing more and more environmental crisis due to unscientific exploitation by human being, so there is urgent need to conserve, protect and nurture our environmental resources (Yadav and Bharati, 2007). Here, an attempt was made to find out impact of socio-demographic factors like age, sex, marital status, locality, education and income on environmental awareness of people in and around Kolkata metro city.

OBJECTIVE

The objective of present study was to study impact of socio-demographic factors such as age, sex, marital status, locality, educational background and family income on environmental awareness of people.

NULL HYPOTHESES

Different null hypotheses for the present investigation are as follows:

H-1: There is no significant difference in environmental awareness between sub samples due to age.

H-2: Awareness towards environment does not form normal distribution among males and females.

H-3: Environmental awareness does not differ significantly among married and unmarried people.

H-4: Awareness toward environment does not form normal distribution among residents of metro city and adjacent sub urban locality.

H-5: Educational background of respondents do not influence environmental awareness

H-6: Environmental awareness is not affected by parental education.

H-7: Income of family does not significantly influence environmental awareness.

METHODOLOGY

Sample: It comprised 120 respondents from urban and suburban areas of Kolkata city of West Bengal. Samples were selected in such a way that adequate coverage could be done under each category to test the hypotheses.

Tools: The questionnaire was developed by the researcher to measure environmental education awareness of people which included 20 items. Each item had five response category like strongly agree, agree, undecided, strongly disagree and disagree and they were scored for 5, 4, 3, 2 and 1 respectively. The tool had reliability of 0.84 and it had content validity.

Statistical Analysis: The data were tabulated as per requirement. Then mean and S.D. of each item was found out. The t-test was employed to test hypothesis at 0.05 and 0.01 level of significance.

RESULTS AND DISCUSSION

The mean, SD and t-value of different variables are presented in Table 1.1. The samples were divided in to two groups on the basis of age i.e. one group individuals with less than 25 years age and the other group with age 25 years and more than it. In such case the t-value was found as 2.654 which is significant at 0.05 level of significance and thus hypothesis H-1 is not accepted. It can be inferred that there was significant difference between sub samples due to age. The t-value between male and female awareness was found as 2.130 which was significant ($P<0.05$) and thus the hypothesis H-2 is rejected. It can be concluded that there was significant difference in environmental awareness of males and females. It is in agreement with earlier works of Abraham and Arjunan (2005) where a differential effect of gender in environmental interest was recorded. However, it differs from works of Sahaya Mary and Paul Raj (2005) who observed no significant difference in environmental education awareness between male and female teachers which can be attributed to upper social, educational and economic factors in comparison to ordinary individuals/respondents of present study. The t-value between environmental awareness of married and unmarried respondents was found as 1.657 which is not significant. So, the hypothesis H-3 is accepted indicating environmental awareness does not differ significantly among married and unmarried sample. The t-value between awareness of respondents belonging to metro city and adjacent suburban areas was recorded as 2.202 which was significant at 0.05 level of significance. Hence, the hypothesis H-4 is rejected indicating significant difference in environmental awareness of two different categories of sample. It resemble with earlier work of Abraham and Arjunan (2005) who recorded differential effects of urban and rural students in their environmental interest .It bears similarity with works of Sahaya Mary and PaulRaj (2005) who found significant difference in environmental education awareness between urban and rural teachers with the former having greater awareness. The awareness of respondents of two

Table 1.1: Mean. S.D. and t-values of environmental education awareness due to different socio-demographic factors

Sl No.	Category	Variable	Sample(N)	Mean	S.D.	t-value
1.	Age					
A		Below 25 years & 25	48	4.12	0.58	2.654**
B		More than 25	72	4.37	0.45	
2.	Sex					
A		Male	63	4.06	0.52	2.130*
B		Female	57	3.87	0.45	
3.	Marital Status					
A		Married	66	4.27	0.55	1.657 NS
B		Unmarried	54	4.09	0.64	
4.	Locale					
A		Metro	73	3.92	0.56	2.202*
B		Suburban	47	3.68	0.62	

(Contd...)

Sl No.	Category	Variable	Sample(N)	Mean	S.D.	t-value
5.	Education of respondent					
A		Below HS	56	3.83	0.52	2.075*
B		HS & more	64	4.05	0.63	
6.	Parental education					
A		Below Secondary	68	3.83	0.56	2.908**
B		Secondary & above	52	4.11	0.47	
7.	Income (P.M.)					
A		Below 3000	44	3.68	0.47	2.384*
B		3000 & more	76	3.87	0.39	

* Significant at $P < 0.05$.

** Significant at $P < 0.01$.

NS= Not Significant.

different educational background i.e one group with education less than HS (Higher Secondary) and the other with HS and more than it were considered. The t-value was found as 2.075 which was significant ($P<0.05$) and thus the hypothesis H-5 is discarded. Subsequently, impact of parental education on environmental awareness was considered. Here, two groups comprised with respondents whose parents (either father or mother or both) have less than secondary education and the other group with secondary and more than it. The t-value was found as 2.908 which was significant at 0.01 level of significance and thus hypothesis H-6 is rejected. It can be concluded that educational background of respondents and their parents have significant impact on environmental awareness. Respondents were divided in to two sub samples based on their monthly income i.e one group with monthly income of less than Rs. 3,000 the other with more than it. The t-value was found as 2.384 which is significant ($P<0.05$) and thus hypothesis H-7 is rejected. It implies that income of family has significant influence on environmental education awareness of individuals.

CONCLUSION

The uncontrolled and uncoordinated usage of environment resources causes several problems like deforestation, pollution, loss of biodiversity, ozone depletion, global climate change and over consumption of natural resources. The need of the hour is to utilize the resource by protecting the environment otherwise it will adversely affect the human society. Environmental education plays an important role in creating public awareness and enhancing protecting attitude towards environmental issues (Onder, 2006).

It empowers and develops a sense of ownership among people to address environmental problems and develop issues in their own communities. It touches beliefs and attitudes of people so that they live in sustainable manner and provide adequate information to support these beliefs and translate attitudes and values into actions. It was found in the present study that different socio-demographic factors influence the environmental education awareness of people. While designing such awareness programmes, these findings may be kept in mind to address the issues in order to achieve the target.

REFERENCES

Abraham, M. and Arjunan, N.K. (2005): Environmental Interest of Secondary School Students in Relation to Their Environmental Attitudes. *Perspectives in Education,* 21(2): 100-105.

Onders, S.(2006): A Survey of Awareness and Behaviour in Regard to Environmental Issues Among Selcuk University Students in Konya, Turkey. *Journal of Applied Sciences,* **6**(2): 347-352.

Panigrahi, S.K. (2004): Environmental Education: Need of the Hour. *Yojana,* 48(6): 13-22.

Sahaya Mary R. and Paul Raj, I. (2005): Environmental Awareness Among High School Students. *Edutrack,* 5(4):33-55.

Santra, S.C. (2001): *Environmental Science.* New Central Book Agency Pvt. Ltd., Calcutta.

Yadav P.S. and Bharati, A.(2007): A Study of Relationship Between Environmental Awareness and Scientific Attitudes Among Higher Secondary Students. *Indian Journal of Education,* 33(2): 59-84.

2

Periyar
A Model of Ecotourism Development

A.Vinodan[1] and C.H. Pramodini[2]

ABSTRACT

Ecotourism, one of the well-conceived tourism product as well as an approach to tourism development in the scenario of tourism history. Well-designed programme of action, to mitigate all negative impacts of conventional tourism operations. Conservation and community development are always aimed in all development programmes especially initiative which utilize natural resource as a prime product. Practically, meeting these two is the focal point of policy decisions. The principle of eco-tourism always speaks about the sustainability at all levels. Numerous eco-tourism programmes are underway globally but

1. Faculty in Tourism, Indian Institute of Tourism and Travel Management, Bhubaneswar, Orissa.
   E-Mail: vinodan_tt@yahoo.co.in vinodan.iittm@gmail.com

2. Senior Faculty in Commerce, Avaiyar Government College for Women, Karaikkal, Pondicherry. *Email:* sga5@rediffmail.com

hardly few meet the sustainability. This article presents the success story of Periyar Ecotourism Project, one of well-established tourism destination in India.

INTRODUCTION

Sustainable and equitable development is the challenge of these days. The consumption-poverty-environmental nexus are accelerating day-by-day. The traditional developmental approaches were not able to address these issues systematically because of different reasons like concentration of economic power in few hands, top down approach of planning and resource distribution, illiteracy, and many more. Same time discontents among communites are increasing worldwide. Though tourism is regarded as a smokeless industry, industrial operation of tourism is not free from negative impacts. It has lot of visible and invisible negative impacts which surpass its positive contributions to the society. In this inequitable and scarce resource scenario a well thought out programme or approach to development is the need of the hour, which keep the all dimensions of sustainability.

Ecotourism is new approach to tourism development, which make platform for harmonious existence of development activity with nature. As defined by the Ceballos-Lascurain (1996), a Mexican architect as well as environmentalist 'it is the traveling to relatively undisturbed or uncontaminated natural areas with specific objective of studying, admiring, and enjoying the scenery and its wild plants and animals, as well as any existing cultural manifestations (both past and present) found in these areas.

Goodwin (1996) has updated the concept of eco- tourism with changing scenario of tourism development and defined it as low impact tourism which contribute to the maintenance of species and habitat either directly through a contribution to conservation to conservation and/or indirectly by providing revenue to the local community sufficient for local people to value, and therefore protect, their destination as a source of income. The International Ecotourism Society (IES) define ecotourism as responsible travel that conserve the environment and sustain the well-being of local people. Recently Quebec City Declaration on Ecotourism (2002) and Oslo Statement on Ecotourism (2007) proposed five distinct criteria to define ecotourism, namely: nature based product, minimal impact management, environment education, contribution to conservation and community. As the traditional approach to conservation and impact mitigation measures are away from common man for his developmental needs the concept like eco tourism certainly integrating the conservation, livelihood and other developmental aspirations of the people.

ECOTOURISM IN KERALA

The State of Kerala, forming part of the Western Ghats, contains protected area of 2324 sq. km, 4 national park and 12 wildlife sanctuaries. All these eco-systems are form part of Nilgiri Biosphere Reserve one of the eighteen hotspots in the world and one of the two hotspots in India. These are special eco-system providing a natural advantage for development of Eco-tourism. In order to develop ecotourism products appropriate and destination specific strategies are needed in this area.

Development of Kerala is a model for other States of India and other developing countries; tourism development of this State is not an exemption. State is well-known in introducing innovative tourism products, such as back water tourism, medical tourism, monsoon tourism, poll tourism, helicopter tourism, baby moon tourism, diamond tourism and walking tourism. For the development of ecotourism in the State a separate directorate has been created and 47 destinations were identified to develop eco tourism programmes. Thenmala Ecotourism project developed in and around Shenduruni Wildlife Sanctuary managed by Thenmala Ecotourism Promotion Society, is the first planned ecotourism project in the country. Another world-wide acclaimed tourism project is Priyar Ecotourism Project is a paradise of nature lovers.

ECOTOURISM IN PERIYAR TIGER RESERVE - THEKKADY

The Periyar Sanctuary area was declared as reserved forest in the year 1899 to protect the catchments area of Periyar River. This river had been dammed in 1895, resulted small lakes and a reservoir. In 1934 the area declared as a sanctuary. The total area of the present sanctuary is 777 sq. km and it is located in the southern part of the Western Ghat with 70 per cent ever green and semi evergreen forest which make Thekkady as a unique destination in the tourism map meet distinct climate, landscape and possibility of wildlife watching. The lake artificially formed due to the submergence of low lying areas following the construction of Mullaperiyaar Dam in 1895 is the prime attraction of this place. In the year 1978, the area declared it as Tiger Reserve and witnessed tremendous increase in the number of tourist visitation (Table 2.1).

Tourist Arrivals at Periyar

Year	*Number of Visitors*		*Total*
	Domestic	*Foreign*	
1999-00	320973	24347	345320
2000-01	303895	37038	340933
2001-02	357690	26026	383716
2002-03	420960	31831	452791
2004-05	333882	37150	371032
2005-06	400686	40243	440929
2006-07	498636	49064	547700

Source: Periyar Foundation, Periyar Tiger Reserve, Kerala.

In 1996, forest management strategy introduced in India by Global Environment Facility (GEF) and World Bank (WB) for participatory biodiversity conservation at Periyar Wildlife Sanctuary in Thekkady under India Eco-Development Project (IEDP). The wildlife department decided to develop ecotourism programmes with local participation with an ecotourism component the Thekkady Tiger Trail. The project envisaged to the conservation of the biodiversity and creation of livelihood options to the people who are living the vicinity of the project area. The project envisaged by the GEF completed its operations on June 2004. July 2004 onwards Periyar Foundation is entrusted to continue the further programmes of the destination.

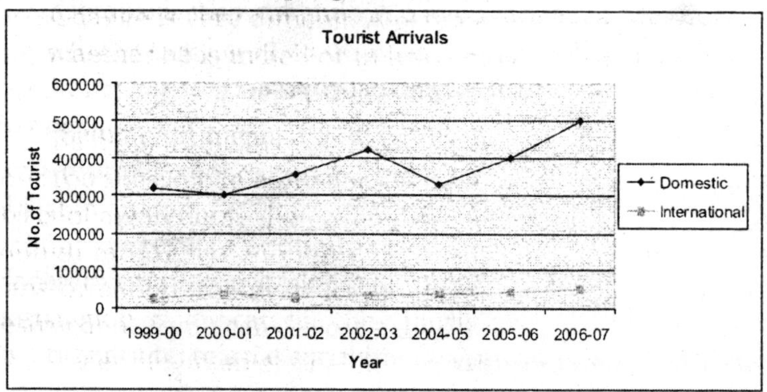

Fig. 2.1: **Tourist Arrivals at Periyar (1999-2000 to 2006-07)**

A committee of local people called Eco Development Committees (EDC) has been formed to actively participate in resource identification, maintenance based on traditional and modern technique of conservation. They have been asked to form EDC's at different parts of destination and mobilize human resource for the decent management of resource available with them for the livelihood requirements. The committee members are from five ethnically different tribal communities namely Mannan, Paliya, Urali, Mala-araya, and a small nomadic group called Malampadaram. There are following three types of EDC's in this destination:

1. *Village EDC*; consists of EDC in tribal settlement and hamlets created for socio economic upliftment of the Village;
2. *User Group EDC*; For Graziers, fuel wood, Thatching, Grass collection and assisting pilgrimage especially to Sabarimala for the purpose of reducing the negative impact of pilgrims' activities at the destination; and

3. ***Professional Group EDC***; formed for establishment of long-term interaction in the protected area , consists of Ex-Cinnamon Bark Collectors, Tribal Trekker cum Guides and Watchers Welfare.

The identified objective of the Eco Development Committee are to actively participate in decision making with regards to local requirements, identifying the local resources, suggesting ways and means of conserving the resources including all floral and floral varieties, reinstating cultural and ritual practices of the community, actively participate in tourism development programmes of the area, identifying the new options for the livelihood, restrict all kinds of illegal activities in the project area with the support of local people. The project area occupies around 2,50,000 people most of them belong to below poverty line category of Government of Kerala. In the project area de barking of Cinnamon trees (Vayana) as well as Sandal wood smuggling poaching was very common. While forming eco development committees these people were also included as members. They were asked actively participate in the all conservation measures including protecting the resources from other illegal poachers from outside forest area. Today they are acting as the backbone of the conservation programme of the Periyar Tiger Reserve like other local people. They have started Bamboo Rafting programme for the tourist in November 2002, with a groups of 20 members who belongs to tribal community and its major part of earnings are going to the community development fund of EDC's. Another group of 70 members who were employed as watchers in the forest department formed Periyar Tiger Samrakhan Samiti (tiger protection force) also involved in tourism product development. They undertake day treks through forest, arranging nature camps, and other special tailor made programmes for tourist. Along with forest and wildlife department, the tribal trekkers also contribute in spotting and surveying the species varieties at the destination hence a significant increase in the animal and birds checklist of protected area. Presently 73 Eco Development Committees covering forty thousand people are formed under PTR for meeting the different needs such as conservation, livelihood and other resource management programmes.

ECO TOURISM PRODUCTS IN PERIYAR TIGER RESERVE

Tiger Trial

Adventurous trekking and camping programme arranged in the dense forest with two packages consists of one night and two night stays, depending on the preference of visitors. Trekking in peak seasons usually limited to two occasions n a week. Each trekking is unique in selection of path ways randomly. Under the scheme maximum five tourists will be accompanied by five guides and one armed forest guard. The guides who recruited from local people are well acquainted with every nook and cranny of Thekkady forest reserve. Visitors feel a lap of Mother Nature at the bio diversity slots of the destination. The number of tourists who are allowed to participate in trekking programme is restricted in anticipation of proper management of guest as well as the natural areas. This is the core of ecological sustainability by limiting the resource consumption based on the carrying capacity of the destination. The tiger rail gives impetus to other tourism development initiative to the outside world in mobilizing the people who were committed many mistakes in their yesterdays due to variety of socio economic reason in conservation and management of natural resources for meeting their own needs with out impairing the ability of future generations to meet their own needs. There by number of species increased substantially in these days. Due to this outstanding performance in tourism product development and conservation innovation government of India awarded national award for excellence in environmental concern and the state of Kerala awarded for innovation in tourism to Periyar.

Bamboo Rafting

Local people who were associated with Cinnamon trees (Vayana) collection initiated an innovative tourism product at the destination - Periyar in the year 2002. A full day nature package is offered to the visitors to enjoy the pristine beauty of the Periyar Lake and surroundings. Number of tourists allowed undertaking bamboo rafting is ten who are accompanied by five guides and one escort, one group per day. The participants are allowed to two-hour long trekking, one and half hour long rafting and sightseeing with a component of education and interpretation of the ecological and cultural importance of the area.

Day Trekking

Trekking programme conducted by eco development committee members; consists of tribal trekkers and guides formed by 20 youths from the near by places. The programme offers unique experience to visitors through tropical ever green forest for duration of three hours. One group consists of five guests and an accompanying one tribal youth who is the member of eco development committee.

Wild Adventure

This unique programme involves close interaction with nature at Gavi a place 40 km away from Thekkady. The eco development committees at Gavi, Meenar and Kochupanpa are regularly conducting this programme. The package consists of vehicle Safari from Thekkady to Gavi and trekking in the dense forest. Provision for sight seeing also incorporated and a night stay is also permitted. Bird watching, Rowing, Outdoor camping in the forest, Tree top stay and night safari will be designed as a tailor made package.

Jungle Inn

Staying inside the dense forest areas is a unique selling proposition in all most tailor made tour programme for nature tourist. For this purpose, in Periyar a well-furnished accommodation provision is arranged near by expanse of wetland area of the destination, open to the overnight visitors. Provision for two visitors and an accompanying guide for experiencing the pulse of the nature.

Tribal Heritage

Culture is always form part of ecotourism programme, the 'authentic' experience of the 'real' life situation is a fascination for tourist. Different cultural presentation are common n tourism scenario like exhibition of culture in an authentic plat form, real contact with the people for first hand experience, museums and showcasing of cultural practices. Under tribal heritage programme of Periyar Ecotourism destination tribal life are exhibited for two hours at the same time the visitor can directly interact with people and experience the real life situations of the local people.

Learning Programme in Bamboo Grove

Education and interpretation of the natural and cultural value of the destination is considered as a one of the condition of sustainability in ecotourism management. For the learning programme locally initiated tribal huts were erected in the bamboo grove at Anavachal Vayal for learning. The programme includes interactive session, experience local cuisine and stay in tents etc.

Cruising

The lake offers boating facilities to the visitors. Facility available early morning and afternoon for two hours offers sightseeing. The programme is managed by the Kerala Tourism Development Corporation (KTDC) and Kerala Forest Department.

Other Products

The destination also offers variety of value added services to the visitors to make their visit memorable. Major such initiatives include Elephant Ride, Jungle Patrol, Bullock Cart Discoveries, Watch Tower at Edappalayam and Manakkavala, Major proposed products are Organic Village Visit, Dreamscapes, Border Hiking and Windy Walks at Vallakadavu, Mannan and Paliyan Tribal Dance. A visitor's centre as well as an interpretation centre at Rajive Gandhi Centre for Nature Education which preserves varieties of flora and fauna and a reference library is also form part of the product profile of the destination.

Is Periyar a 'Model of Ecotourism'?

Policy formulation and projectwise implementation at the respective areas definite the output at a desired level. However in reality there may be variation in the reach of the programme to the targeted people according to the policy formulated. Tourism programmes are not an exemption especially a programme which seeks the support of people who has no precedence of participation, and decision-making. The people who are targeted under ecotourism are always excluded in other developmental initiatives. In the case of Periyar Ecotourism Project, the targeted group is tribal people who have no access in main stream developmental programmes and no option for further development except their natural and cultural heritage. Such an environment ecotourism is advised as an appropriate tool for livelihood. Fennel (2003) gives more practical meaning for the concept of eco tourism 'is a sustainable form of natural resourced based tourism that focus primarily an experiencing and learning about nature, and which is ethically managed to be low impact, non consumptive, and locally oriented (control, benefit, and scale). It typically occurs in natural areas, and should contribute to the conservation or preservation of such areas.'

Study concludes by revisiting the destination in terms of application of ecotourism principle suggested by Quebec City Declaration (2002), as result of first international conference on ecotourism held at Quebec City Canada. The same year is declared as International Year of Ecotourism jointly by United Nations World Tourism Organization (UNWTO) and United Nations Environment programme (UNEP).

Distinct five criteria attributed by Quebec City Declaration to ecotourism are:

- Nature Based Product;
- Minimal Impact Management;
- Environmental Education;
- Contribution to Conservation; and
- Contribution to the Community.

The Oslo Statement on Ecotourism (2007) also reiterated the adherence of these five criteria for developing ecotourism destinations worldwide.

Assessment of these criteria in the context of Periyar Ecotourism Project will bring a motivation to the policy makers and decision makers in the area of eco tourism, conservation and management of natural resources especially in the present scenario tourism is considered as a tool for poverty eradication, community development, local level resource management and livelihood alternative for an inclusive growth. The examination also gives impetus to the measurement of impact of the destination development in the given society. The reviews are as follows:

Nature Based Product

All activities at the destination are nature based. Programmes such as Tiger Trail, Trekking, and Bamboo Rafting are performed in the interiors of the reserve. Each trekking is made it different by choosing different path. No alteration is made inside the forest area, the trekkers has to carry for their basic belongings. Other outside intervention is strictly prohibited; only limited trekkers are allowed to undertake the activities inside the forest.

Minimal Impact Management

In Periyar, precautionary measures like minimizing the number of participant in every programme, proper direction to the visitors, instant supply of guides, escorts with all programmes at the destination, and use of eco friendly products itself minimize the negative implications of the tourist activity.. Beside these, the initiative of Periyar Foundation's Ecosystem Protection and Management deployed Tiger Monitoring Protocol at range levels, studies on human-wildlife conflict also help to mitigate negative impact of human intervention at the destination. More over, eco tourists their concerned consumption style also contribute the sustainability.

Environmental Education

Education and correct interpretation is one of the requirements for sustainability. An informed society can only contribute for further development of the area through judicious use of scarce resource. Periyar eco development programme regularly arrange programme for eco tourist, trekkers, local people who are the members of eco development committees and other conservation groups. Content of the course mainly covers the peculiarity of the destination; the unique selling proposition of the products offered at the destination, important do's and don'ts, environmental ethics and preferred behavior. Apart from this firsthand experience can be derived by participating programme such as tiger trail. Special interpretation programmes of Rajive Gandhi Centre for Nature Education and Research is a unique experience to the visitors. They use traditional and modern methods of teaching and interpretation tools in a natural setting. Besides these, environment education programme, Nature Sensitization Camp at Thekkady and Vallakkadav by students and non-governmental organizations (NGOs), *Vanampadikal;* folk group who actively engaged in stage shows or street plays, the observation of Plastic Free Day on the 28th of every month wildlife week celebration, Capacity Enhancement, *Kilikkoottam;* a summer camp for school students and the issue of news letters of PTR are contributing to the conservation of the area.

Contribution to Conservation

The eco development committees usually operationalise the subject of conservation at the destination. In Periyar, Tiger Samrakshan Samiti (tiger protection force), and EDC's are undertaken the invigilation of the forest area. The force consists of seventy members. Three EDCs viz., Malampandaram EDC, Thelli (Black Dammar) Collectors EDC and Fishermen EDC are being proposed to be constituted to strengthen protection in the core and buffer zones of PTR A certain percentage of the revenue around *ten* percent is transferred to the conservation fund for regeneration of the vegetation due to other issues like forest fire, flood etc.

Contribution to the Community

No project will be successful unless the basic needs of the local peoples are satisfied. Ecotourism always address the issue of local livelihood issue as primary target of the programme development. World wide nature based tourism programmes call for an equitable use of resource for the welfare of the respective society. The communities in the Periyar Ecotourism project area are the members of eco development committees of the programmes. Notorious poachers are also now members of the eco development committees who are actively working with their local people for the conservation and waged employment programmes of the tourism operations. Their transformation is the ideal and inevitable change in the history of conservation and resource management not only for India but for whole world. Through tourism related operations the local people mobilizing a substantial amount for their livelihood. A common pool called Community Development Fund (CDF) has created to mobilize the income derived from all tourism activities at the destination and the members are earning a daily wages of Rs. 163 *i.e* monthly wages of Rs 4,238 (October 2008).

The benefit covers around 5540 families consist of forty thousand people. The Community Development Fund (CDF) is distributed as follows:

- Ten per cent for Government of Kerala;
- Ten per cent for Marketing of the Destination;

- Ten per cent for Conservation;
- Seventy percent for Local Community Members as Wages and Welfare Funds.

Evaluation shows Periyar Ecotourism Programme initiated at Thekkady fulfils the basics criteria proposed by the Quebec City Declaration, reaffirmed by Oslo Statement on ecotourism. Numbers of initiatives are also underway; to give a value addition to these criteria, certainly this will be a well sited trend setter in ecotourism as well as eco development initiatives of the world.

CONCLUSION

Visitation to the Periyar Eco development Programme clarifies the concern of balancing the conservation and resource use strategies for the welfare of the local community. The community participation in developmental programme is not new in the world scenario. Practically, such initiative are relatively undervalued or underestimated to some extent in tourism related operations. Some of the community based tourism programmes are not able to attain the fundamental ideas like resource and benefit sharing in real terms. The initiative under PTR eco development programme made the tourism development possible according to the aspirations of all stakeholders by fulfilling the all relevant requirements of successful eco tourism. Really Periyar is a model for all people who argue for equity in resource sharing and inclusive growth.

REFERENCES

Ceballos-Lascurain (1996) *Tourism, Ecotourism and Protected Areas* IUCN.

Department of Public Relations (1999) *Ecotourism in Kerala,* Government of Kerala.

Fennel (2003) *Ecotourism: An Introduction* Routledge London.

Goodwin (1996) 'In pursuit of Ecotourism' *Biodiversity and Conservation* 5(3) 277-292.

www.departmentoftourism.org

www.ecotourismkerala.org

www.oslodeclaration.com

www.periyarfoundation.org/pdf/pf_annualreport06-07

www.periyartigerreserve.com

www.quebeccitydeclaration.com

www.thenmalaecotourism.org

www.ties.org

3

Water
The Elixir of Life

Dr. Lingaraj Patro[1]

ABSTRACT

Adequate quantity and acceptance quality of water is essential to human existence. Survival of man on earth depends on the environment of the planet. With rising population and consequent demand for food, water, shelter and consumer goods, our environment is under serious stress. Recognition of the importance of water quality developed slowly in early days, quality of water was divided based on physical sense of sight, taste and odour. Due to the development in chemical, biological and medical fields the water quality with respect to all character like physical, chemical and bacteriological characteristic to ascertain its suitability for consumption. The need for additional food necessitated much greater application of chemical inputs

1. **Environmental Toxicology Lab., Department of Zoology and Biotechnology. K.B DAV Collage, Nirakarpur, Orissa (India),** ***E-mail:*** **dr.lrpatro@rediffmail.com**

to the soil, which in many areas has degraded the soil to an almost irrevocable way. The green house effect causing a slow rise in temperature due to production of excess carbon dioxide, oxides of sulfur and nitrogen needs to be tackled. With over 30% of the population in India living in the urban areas, the question of supply of safe drinking water, disposal of different kinds of waste has become highly problematic. The waste water from each house and storm water finds its way through drains and finally gets collected at the nearby pit. The waste water contains solids, plant fertilizing nutrients such as nitrogen and phosphorous compounds, many micro-organism including pathogenic types as well as viruses. They are easily passed through soil and pollute the open well water. We need qualitative water to drink conforming to the standards of portable water with respect to physical, chemical and bacteriological parameters because water is the other name of life. No living entity can survive, grow and develop without water.

INTRODUCTION

Life cannot be possible without water. So water is the other name of life living entity can survive, grow and develop without water. No other material is as widely used in agriculture and industry as water. It is not only used as above and drinking purpose to over comes thirsty, but also it acts as a great solvent.

Among the different components of our environment, water has played the major role in human activity, as unlike many other components. The distribution of water in space and time has been widely variable.

Water is precious natural resource for sustaining life and environment. It is in continuous circulatory movement between land, ocean and atmosphere. India is gifted with natural water resources by the presence of many large rivers with its numerous tributaries and distributaries. Similarly the availability of ground water in most of the places in the country is very high. Also being very rich with major mineral deposits like coal, iron ore manganese, bauxite, chromites, dolomite and limestone etc. in addition to water country has become the destination of intensive industries like thermal power iron and steel, pulp and paper, and other metrological industries. Further India is expected to be the major metal producer in the world. Costal area with high concentration of population and economic activity are particularly vulnerable to multiple whether hazards like flood, drought, cyclone etc. the saucer shaped land forms, high rainfall due to south west monsoon, poor drainage condition makes the costal region susceptible to water logging and flood prone and area remains submerged for about 2-3 months under water. No cropping is possible due to excess water.

India has long tradition of water management. Many of the traditional water harvesting systems have either gone under disuse due to a variety of physical, social, economical, cultural, political factors which have caused the deterioration and decline of institution which have natured them (Agarwal and Narain, 1997) or have lost their relevance in the modern day context due to their inability to meet the desires of the community. While the first dimension of the decline water harvesting tradition has been well researched and documented, the second dimension is much less understood and appreciated. The lake of resistance to appreciate the fact that different periods in history are marked be genesis, rise and fall of some new water harvesting tradition is also very clear.

AVAILABILITY AND REQUIREMENT OF WATER

With rising population and consequent increase in demand for goods, the demand of water is on the rise. Agricultural irrigation is in fact a highly water requiring process. An urban-dweller in a developing country and one in village would require annually approximately 10 cum and 3 cum of water respectively.

For bleaching and dyeing a ton of cotton, about 250 cum of water is required. Another estimate shows that out of India's total expenditure on water 53% is for irrigation and drainage, 20% is for hydro power and 18% is devoted to municipal and industrial water supply.

In some cities there is an acute scarcity of water even for drinking. Water resource development and proper maintenance of water bodies are of at most importance in view of the fact that by turn of the century when our population may touch a billion plus water availability will reduce to 1900 cum per capita per year from the current rate of 2355 cum per capita per year. According to one estimate the total ground and surface water development potential in India is 92.7 mham ($927 \times 109\ m^3$) per year which would account for use of all available water by about the year AD 2005.

Fortunately for mankind there is plenty water on this earth. In nature water is continuously in cyclic process. Solar radiation vapourises water from the water bodies forming clouds. From clouds the rainfall reaches the ground in process of precipitation and flow back to water bodies, partly over ground and partly underground. Thus the surface and subsurface water sources are in component phase of natural hydrological cycle.

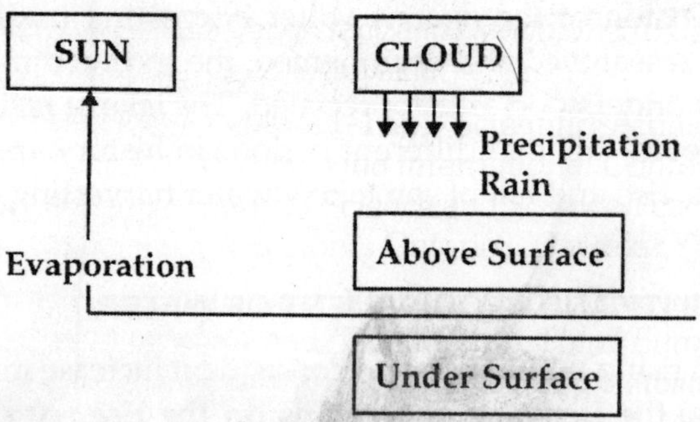

Fig. 3.1: Hydrological Cycle

In spite of this plenty availability, 80% of the mankind suffer water scarcity in varying magnitude. This paradox is due to two factors:

1. Water is not available at the place of need.
2. Water is not available at the time of need.

At the time of need thus to utilize the available natural water resources, storage and transportation is necessary.

Normally the purest form of water is rainfall and seawater is the worst. Of course to meet the demand seawater is now-a-days made portable after desalination. It is wise required to save rainwater in the way of water harvesting for use.

According to a study, India receives 400 million hectare meter (mham) of rain and snowfall. Another 20 mham flow in as surface water from outside the country. This total 420 mham provides the country with river flows of 180 mham, another 67 mham is available as ground water about 173 mham is lost as evaporation or becomes soil moisture which can captured directly as rain water or as run-off from small catchments, in and near villages or towns.

POLLUTION OF WATER

Water pollution especially in urban and semi-urban industrial areas, has become a matter of serious concern. The sacred river Ganga is all along polluted by untreated sewage roughly from 140 cities each with a population of half a lakh and above, besides receiving affluent of toxic chemicals from factories, paper and pulp mills, rubber manufacturing units and tanneries. An approximate 150 km stretch of the Hoogly river along Kolkata-Howrah and adjoining industrial belts receives untreated effluents from 150 major factories and raw sewage from 361 outfalls and it is reported that fish yield on which thousand of fisherman depend for their livelihood has gone down to one-sixth of that in the unpolluted zone of the river. Even bathing in the river water would be injurious to health.

Population growth, urban expansion and industrial development have persistently raised the demand for water supply and consequently increases the exploitation of ground water and disposal of domestic and industrial effluent poses threat to the ground water resources of the area both in term of quantity and quality.

Surface and subsurface water resources is at risk from contamination due to rapid and unplanned urbanization, industrialization and indiscriminate disposal of domestic, industrial, agricultural and mining wastes at many part of the country.

Mining is one of the major activities causing water pollution and threatens the quality and quantity of ground and surface water resources in many part of the country. Dumping of over burden and spoil or spreading of over burden through rolling and washing may cause the chemical pollution. As there is no proper water management plan in most of the mines, major part of the water discharged into the open channel. There it pollutes the channel and become unused. Not only this, the mining and related activities also damage the aquifer make the area as water scare. Mine water can vary greatly in concentration of contaminates present and in some cases it may not even meet the drinking water specification.

The quality of water available for human consumption is a direct measure of the health of the population/community and that of the country is over populated like India, the quality water is very poor due to heavy contamination of soil and water with biological waste and chemical pollutants. Each year water born diseases transmitted mainly through drinking unclean water, kill on estimated 4 million children under the age of 5 and make adult sick enough to lose billions of hours of work productivity.

WATER POLLUTANTS

The signs of water pollution are:

1. Bad test of drinking water.
2. Offensive odour from lakes, rivers and ocean beaches.
3. Unchecked growth of aquatic weeds in water bodies.
4. Decrease in number of fish in fresh water, river water and sea water.
5. Oil and grease floating on water surface etc.

Table 3.1: Water Pollution due to Mining and its Preventive Measures

Nature of mining	*Activity/Source*	*Pollutants*	*Preventive/Mitigative measures*
Opencast mining	Removal of Vegetation	1. Suspended Solids	1. Catchments/garbage drains around the mines
	Removal of top & Sub Soil Drilling & Blasting	2. Dissolve solids 3. Heavy Metals 4. Oil & Grease 5. Change in pH	2. Sedimentation pond 3. Minimum removal of vegetation in rainy season 4. No blasting in rains
	(Overburden (OB dumps, soil and coal stacks)	All Above Plus Bacteria	5. Proper of machine maintenance 6. Dumps and stack managements 7. Treatment of mine water before discharge
Underground Mining	Strata water	1. Suspended Solids 2. Dissolve solids 3. Heavy Metals 4. Change in pH	1. Plugging of surface cracks 2. Proper surface drainage 3. Proper of machine maintenance 4. Cleanliness in underground working 5. Provision of toilets at underground 6. Treatment of mine water before discharge

(Contd…)

Nature of mining	*Activity/Source*	*Pollutants*	*Preventive/Mitigative measures*
	Water from storing	1. Suspended solids 2. Dissolve solids	
	Water from surface	1. Suspended solids 2. Dissolve solids 3. Chemical and fertilizers 4. Bacteria 5. Change in pH	
	Other underground sources	1. Suspended solids 2. Dissolve solids 3. Oil & grease 4. Bacteria 5. Organic Matter	

These disturb the normal uses of water supply for domestic, agricultural and industrial purposes. Different types of water pollutants may be broadly classified as follows:

1. **Organic pollutants:** Pollutants like disease causing agents, plant nutrients, oxygen demanding wastes, sewage, synthetic organic compounds, pesticides and insecticides, fungicides, herbicide, detergents, dyes and oils.

2. **Inorganic Pollutants:** These includes inorganic salts, trace elements, inorganic metallic compounds, complexes of metals with organics in natural water, finely divided metals or metal compounds, mineral acid, phosphates, nitrates, sulfates, bicarbonates, hydrogen sulfides, chlorine etc.

3. **Sediments:** It represents most extensive pollutants of surface water. In organic matters in streams, fresh water, estuaries and oceans, the bottom sediments are subjected to anaerobic reduction and under goes continuous leaching. The level of solid loading reaching natural water is about 700 times as large as solid loading from sewage discharge. Sediments and suspended particles are important repositories for fresh metal such as Cr, Mn, Cu, Ni, Co etc. Sediments destroy aquatic organisms.

4. **Radioactive materials:** Various compounds of radioactive fuels, low-grade radioactive liquid wastes, liquid and gaseous wastes from fuel elements, fission products, radionuclides etc. includes in the category. Traces of radioactive materials in water may cause cancer, leukemia, eye cataract, DNA breakage and carcinoma in men.

5. **Thermal pollution:** In many industrial processes generally water is used as coolant. Sometimes temperature rises by 10° or more during operations. The rising temperature decreases dissolved oxygen in water and adversely affects the fish and other aquatic life. The mortality of fishes is affected directly. There appears to be particular temperature ranges that are tolerated by fish and other related species. Thus thermal death of fish may occur due to that action of

heat on nervous system, inactivation of enzymes and coagulation cell protoplasm. Some bacteria such as chondrococous grow rapidly with rising water temperatures.

Permissible for the pollutants for the various uses of water and effluent discharges have been defined by Bureau of India Standard under 10500 for drinking water, IS 2490 for effluent discharges on inland surface and water for different purposes and IS 2296 for sewage discharge.

In most countries, particularly in developing ones nearly 70% of industrial waste dumped untreated into water bodies resulting in heavy pollution in both surface and groundwater. The share (%) of organic water pollutants by various industrial sectors in OECD countries and low-income countries are given (1990) in figure below:

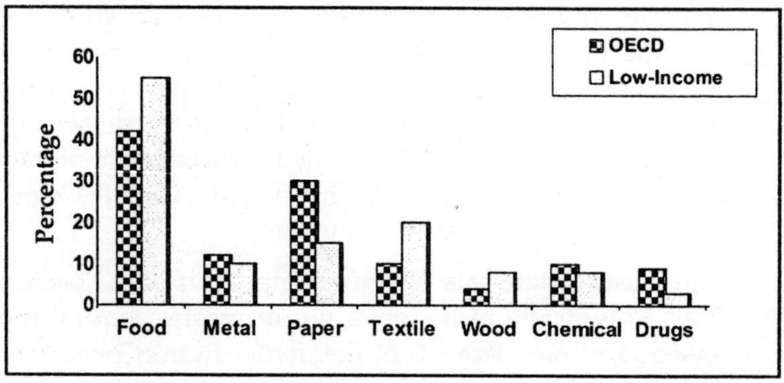

Fig 3.2: **Percentage of organic water pollutant in industrial sectors**

WATER MANAGEMENT

In order to supply sufficient amount of portable water it is required to take proper remedial measures with regard to insufficient water use, hydrological alterations, desertification, pollutants and pathogens.

Poor water management is reflected in poor pattern of water delivery, wasteful application process, pollution and water losses through seepage, leaks and evaporation. It may be worthwhile to economize the water consumption in different household purposes other than that used in the kitchen for cooking and drinking.

The water used for toilets, which comprises the major fraction of the total water i.e, used for household purpose, can and should be replaced by water of an inferior quality; for example, that obtained from the treatment of sewage water.

Hydrological alterations of the landscape along with dam constructions very often lead to water quality degradation and rendering the water unusable for domestic purposes. Therefore, it is necessary to protect the landscape and avoid construction of large dams. It should be our goal to preserve water and carefully use it to produce electricity.

Desertification is equally responsible for shortage of water on the planet. It is therefore essential to take necessary steps to prevent land desertification and degradation.

Due to intensive modern agriculture practices a rapid industrialization, both the surface and ground water are getting polluted rapidly resulting in dearths of portable water. In the monsoon rain still evades dams and run into the sea. It would be wiser to try to collect the rain in ponds, tanks and lakes at their sites than to carry water across the country. Harvesting rainwater through small and medium sized projects seems to be a wiser scheme.

Modern methods of irrigation systems, such as drip irrigation and use of sprinklers should be popularized.

CONCLUSION

Proper water pricing is essential in conserving and managing our water resources and also discouraging people from unnecessarily wasting water. Wastage of water must be prevented and any leakage from open pipes & broken taps must be controlled. Because water is essential for our very survival and sustainable economic progress with rapid urbanization, rise in population and development of industries. The water requirement for mankind is likely to soar high. We adopt drastic measures to polluting water resources. Nature has given enough water and will continue to give in the form of rain. We should make best use of rainwater & properly harvest to meet our requirements.

REFERENCES

Agarwal, Anil and Sunita Narain (1997). *Dying Wisdom: Rise and Fall of Traditional Water Harvesting System*, Centre for Science & Environment, New Delhi.

Bokina (1965) *Guideline for Drinking Water Quality*, WHO, 1984, p. 333.

Cosgrove , W.J. and F.R. Rijsberman (2000) *World Water Vision*, Making Water Everyday Business.

Jebidi, H. (1993): Effects of Desertification & Surface Hydrologic System, Water Availability and Water Quality Paper Presented at the U.N. Convention to Combat Desertification, Nairobi, May 1993.

Reference vander Run, (1995). *The Toilet Paper: Recycling Waste & Conserving Water*. Ecological Press, Sansalito, California.

The United Nations Environment Programme, 1999: The State of Environment Chapter 2 in UNEP.

4

Conservation and Restoration of Wetlands in India

A Strategic Approach for Sustainable Management

Chiranjibi Pattanaik[1], Debadatta Swain[2]
S.B. Choudhury[3] and S. Narendra Prasad[4]

ABSTRACT

Conservation of wetlands is a global concern throughout the world. Wetlands are under increasing threat from the adverse impacts of human development activities tied with natural causes such as reclamation, altered hydrodynamic conditions, dredging and changed water quality. Moreover, there is an

1. Salim Ali Centre for Ornithology & Natural History, Deccan Regional Station, 12-13-588/B, Nagarjuna Nagar Colony, Tarnaka, Hyderabad – 500017, A.P. *E-mail:* chiranjibipattanaik@gmail.com

2. Vikram Sarabhai Space Centre, Thiruvanathapuram – 695022, Kerala.

3. Oceanography Division, National Remote Sensing Centre, Hyderabad – 500625, Andhra Pradesh.

alarming threat from accelerated sea level rise and changes in the hydrological cycle due to global warming, further contributing to loss of coastal wetlands. The major issues affecting wetlands generally result from a lack of recognition of the wide range of benefits – ecological, economic and scientific – which they provide. This paper is an attempt at presenting a comprehensive view of the typical problems confronted in the wetlands, their present environmental status and outlines a strategic approach towards conservation and management efforts being made to make them environmentally sustainable. The conservation of wetlands can only be achieved by the combined efforts of individuals, community participation and effective government policies.

INTRODUCTION

The term "wetlands" refers to transitional lands (site) between aquatic and terrestrial systems where the water table is at or near the surface of the land where plants and animals have become adapted to temporary/permanent flooding by saline brackish or fresh water. The Ramsar convention on wetlands defines wetlands as areas of marsh, fen, peatland and water, whether natural or artificial, permanent or temporary, with water that is static or flowing, fresh, brackish or salt, including areas of marine water the depth of which at low tide does not exceed 6 m', thus encompassing a whole variety of ecosystems ranging from sea grass meadows, salt marshes, mangroves, mudflats and coastal lagoons to upland peat bogs, rivers and floodplains, oxbow lakes, reed beds, shore of mountainous lakes and rain fed ponds. Wetlands compromise only three to six percent of the earth's land surface area, but they provide human populations with a host of goods and services, including water quality maintenance, agricultural production, fisheries, and recreation (Acreman and Hollis, 1996). The interaction of man with wetlands during last few decades has been of concern largely due to the rapid population growth accompanied by intensified industrial, commercial and residential development further leading to pollution of wetlands by domestic, industrial sewage, and agricultural run-offs as fertilizers, insecticides and feedlot wastes (Prasad *et al.*, 2002; Rao *et al.*, 1999). India, by virtue of its geographical extent, varied terrain and climatic conditions, supports a rich diversity of inland and coastal wetland ecosystems. Although the significance of wetlands has been known for a long time, their role in maintaining ecological balance is less understood.

STATUS OF WETLANDS IN INDIA

Total area of wetlands (excluding rivers) in India is 58,286,000 ha, about 18% of the country, 70% of which comprises areas under paddy cultivation (Sinha, 2002), distributed over 9 coastal states and four Union Territories (Anon., 2001a). There are 67,429 wetlands in India, covering about 4.1 million hectares. Out of these, 2,175 wetlands are natural, covering about 1.5 million hectares, and 65,254 wetlands are man-made, occupying about 2.6 million hectares (Ramachandra, 2001). Most of the wetlands in India are directly or indirectly linked with the major river systems like the Ganga, Brahmaputra, Narmada, Tapti, Godavari, Krishna and Cauvery. Broadly the Indian wetlands can be categorized into three distinct types: (a) Himalayan zone; (b) Indo-Gangetic plains; and (c) Southern Peninsula. The country's wetlands are generally differentiated by regions into 8 categories (Scott, 1989):

1. The reservoirs of the Deccan Plateau in the south, together with the lagoons and the other wetlands of the Southern west coast.

2. The vast saline expanses of Rajasthan, Gujarat and the Gulf of Kutch.

3. Freshwater lakes and reservoirs from Gujarat eastwards through Rajasthan and Madhya Pradesh.

4. The delta wetlands and lagoons of India's east coast (Chilika lake).

5. The fresh water marshes of the Gangetic plain and the flood plains of the Brahmaputra.

6. The marshes and swamps in the hills of northeast India and the Himalayan foothills.

7. The lakes and rivers of the mountain region of Kashmir and Ladakh.

8. The island areas of the Andamans and Nicobars.

The eastern coast of India consists of the deltas of Ganges-Brahmaputra, Krishna-Godavari, Mahanadi, and Cauvery, which support large area of estuaries and excellent growth of mangroves. According to the mapping of wetlands (coastal included), carried out by Space Applications Centre (SAC, ISRO) in 1998, a total of 3960 sites of coastal wetlands have been mapped and classified under various types, covering an area extending to a total of 40, 230 sq km (Figs. 4.1 and 4.2) (Garg *et al.*, 1998). The study has mapped 97 major estuaries, 34 major lagoons and 241 creeks that are in urgent need of conservation.

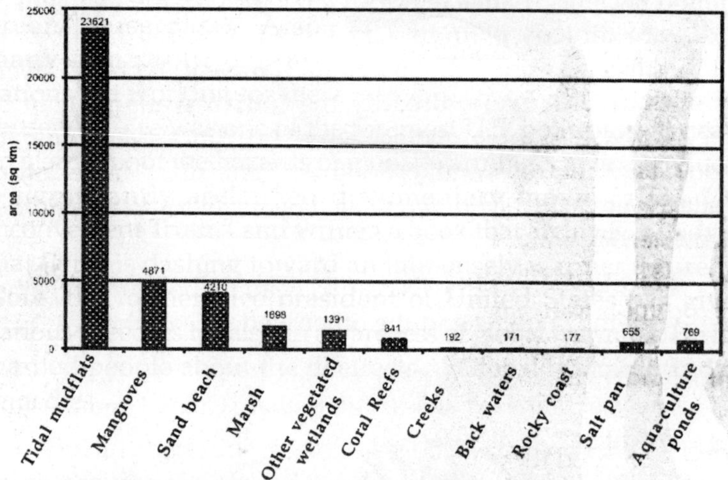

Fig. 4.1: Wetland types and their spread in India

Mangroves, a vital component of wetlands, play a critical role as regulators of water regimes in protecting coastlines and riverbanks against erosion, thus ensuring shoreline stability and contribute to biodiversity conservation. The total area of tidal

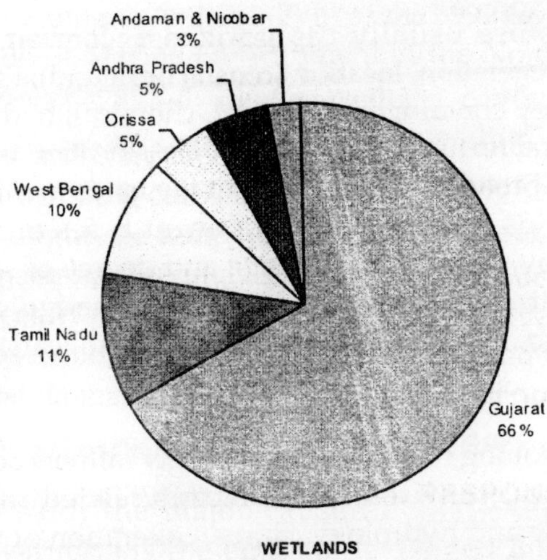

Fig. 4.2: Wetland distribution in India

forests in India was about 6,740 sq km (~ 7% of the world's area under mangroves) (Anon., 1987). The area under mangrove cover was estimated by remote sensing to be ~ 4,482 sq km in 2001 by FSI, Dehradun (Anon., 2001). The main land's coast covered by mangrove line is ~ 380 km (6% of entire coast of India). forty per cent of coasts (~ 260 km) of Andaman & Nicobar Islands are lined with mangroves (Singh, 2000). Out of the 35 true species from Indian subcontinent (Naskar and Mandal, 1999), 13 species are found in the west coast of India (Singh, 2002). Vast expansion of logging operations in the Andaman Islands, aquaculture, reclamation of swamps, paddy cultivation on the east coast of India and salt production on the west coast are the main reasons for degradation of mangroves in India, resulting into shrinking of tidal forests throughout the Indian coast. Though accurate results on wetland loss in India are not available, the Wildlife Institute of India's survey reveals that 70-80% of individual fresh water marshes and lakes in the Gangetic flood plains have been lost in the last five decades. Indian mangrove areas have decreased by half from 7,00,000 ha in 1987 to 4,53,000 ha in 1995.

TYPES OF WETLAND

Wetlands are usually categorized according to their characteristic vegetation, location (coastal or inland); the salinity of the water they contain; or biological, chemical, hydrological, and geographical features. The scientific classification of wetland consists of two broad categories: Inland wetlands and Marine & Coastal wetlands. Some of the prominent types of wetlands characterized by vegetation, soil type and degree of saturation or water cover are aquatic bed, marshes, sedge or "wet" meadows, scrub/shrub and forested, also called Peatlands.

WETLAND FUNCTIONS

The functioning of wetlands is strongly influenced by local and regional-scale environmental factors related to climate, geomorphology and hydrology. Human alteration of wetlands and the surrounding landscape can have considerable influence on wetland functioning. Wetland ecosystems are amongst the most productive in the world both biologically and economically and they and their products have been a constant lure to humankind. Coastal wetlands that support mangrove growth are particularly important as marine nurseries and as sources for the harvesting of shellfish apart from ensuring coastal stability. The plants supported by wetlands contribute to the earth's biodiversity and provide food and shelter for many animal species at critical times during their life cycles.

Natural Functions of Wetlands

(i) ***Shoreline Protection***: wetlands protect the shorelines from erosion by acting as a buffer against wave action by absorbing the force of waves and currents and by anchoring sediments. Roots of wetland plants bind lakeshores and stream banks, providing further protection.

(ii) ***Flood Protection***: wetlands reduce the effect of floods on coastal areas by acting as a sponge and slowing down floodwaters, thus acting as natural flood controls.

(iii) ***Sediment Trap***: sediment produced by erosion from upland areas settles out when the water flow slows upon entering wetlands, helping in preventing silting up of rivers, thus preventing flooding of adjoining areas. As a sediment trap, wetlands also protect marine resources such as coral reefs and sea grass beds from being smothered by silt brought down by rivers and streams.

(iv) ***Fishery, Wildlife Habitat & Nursery Area***: support a rich indigenous flora, and fauna, with several of the species being endemic. Wetlands support various species of animals, birds, crabs, fish, shrimp by acting as critical habitat for feeding, breeding, resting, nesting, escape cover or travel corridors.

(v) ***Vegetation and Land Building (mangrove wetlands)***: because of their submerged root system, mangroves retard water movement and trap suspended materials and the remains of organisms associated with the mangroves. The accumulations of this organic material contribute to raise the soil level.

(vi) ***Water Quality Protection***: wetlands act as natural filtration systems as they "trap and absorb" pollutants before runoff can mix with deeper waters.

ISSUES AFFECTING WETLANDS

The world's wetlands are fast disappearing causing havoc to the environment and jeopardizing long-term food production and thousand of human lives. Irrational and conflicting over-uses of wetlands are destroying the wetland ecosystem. Much of the wetland losses have resulted from the unsustainable developmental activities carried out by human interference. Forested wetlands, inland marshes and wet meadows have been drained for agricultural uses and intense pressure on land has led to the conversion of coastal wetlands/mangroves with no attempt to replace these resources at other sites.

The issues affecting wetlands result from lack of recognition of the wide range of benefits - ecological, economic and scientific that they provide, some of the main causes being:

(i) Pollution (direct and indirect from point and non-point sources).

(ii) Land reclamation (draining and filling).

(iii) Reduced flood control.

(iv) Disruption of wildlife habitat.

The major activities responsible for wetlands loss are urbanization, drainage for agriculture, and water system regulation (Shine and de Klemm, 1999). Apart from these, there has been direct exploitation of wetlands by human beings through:

- Timber cutting: wood for making charcoal, fish pots, racks for oyster farming.
- Fishing/shrimp farming.
- Recreation/tourism: sight seeing, boating, swimming and sport fishing.
- Scientific/educational: wetlands are like living laboratories providing opportunity for education and research concerning the ecological, and possibly medicinal value of various species of plants and animals.
- Agriculture/building.

CONSERVATION AND RESTORATION OF WETLANDS

Restoration means re-establishment of pre-disturbance aquatic functions and the related physical, chemical, and biological characteristics with the objective of emulating a natural and a self-regulating/perpetuating system that is integrated ecologically with the landscape and the functions the wetlands perform (Cairns, 1988; Lewis, 1989). The goals for any restoration program should be realistic and tailored to individual regions, specific to the problems of degradation, and based on the level of dependence. The restoration program should mandate all aspects of the ecosystems, including habitat restoration; elimination of undesirable species, and restoration of native species, from the ecosystem perspective with a holistic approach designed at watershed level, rather than isolated manipulation of individual elements. To sustain and restore wetlands, their respective resources and biodiversity, there is a need to work through proper planning. A strategic approach to be followed, therefore, must include:

1. ***Evaluation and Monitoring:*** The monitoring of wetland development is essential in order to safeguard wetland from sedimentation and extinction, register the rapid increase in population which threatens the forest environments, and monitor the amount of polluted water from various sources that can have a disastrous effect on the ecosystem of lakes, ponds and rivers found in the area. Advanced technology like remote sensing and GIS could help in mapping and monitoring the wetlands in a cost effective manner.

2. Productive acquisition of information, ideas, thoughts from the local communities in order to deliver recommendation aimed at creating a community based wetland management plan.

3. Specific identification of sites and choice of management prior to action being implemented.

There could be conflict between various aspects of wetland development and environmental causes, but this need not be a threat if developers and conservationists make adjustment to accommodate one another and compromise wherever necessary. Wetlands require collaborated research involving natural, social, and inter-disciplinary study aimed at understanding the various components, such as monitoring of water quality, socio-economic dependency, biodiversity, and other activities, as an indispensable tool for formulating long term conservation strategies (Kiran & Ramachandra, 1999). The management policies for the conservation of coastal wetlands, thus:

- be directed towards sustaining resources utilizing the area.
- promote the long-term health and productivity of wetland habitats for the marine species utilizing the area.
- generally not be impounded, although it is recognized that this may be necessary at times to control adverse impacts resulting from natural or human-induced hydrologic changes.
- strive to balance the benefits to all forms of indigenous marine resources and plant communities currently utilizing the area.
- provide adequate ingress and egress for marine species.
- allow adequate nutrient and sediment exchange as well as other important physical and chemical interactions with adjacent areas.
- support the necessary planning and implementation to ensure adequate freshwater inflows to sustain coastal wetlands.

STRATEGIC APPROACH FOR SUSTAINABLE MANAGEMENT

Management may be defined as the manipulation of a system to ensure maintenance of all functions and characteristics of the specific system. A wetland management program generally involves activities to protect, restore, manipulate, and provide for functions and values emphasizing both quality and acreage by advocating their sustainable usage (Walters, 1986). The loss or impairment of a wetland ecosystem is usually accompanied by irreversible loss in both the valuable environmental functions and amenities important to the society (Zentner, 1988). There is a general lack of awareness of the richness and importance of wetlands and their resources for people. So, there is a need for formulating certain policies and implementing them on a priority basis. The management of wetlands for better use could be made possible by keeping the following policies and goals in view:

- Establish the guidelines by which wetlands can be developed in order to ensure their continued existence.

- Bring to an end all activities carried on in wetlands that cause damage to these resources.
- Maintain the natural diversity of the animals and plants found in wetlands.
- Integration of wetland functions in planning and development of other resource sectors such as agriculture, forestry, fisheries, eco-tourism, and waste management.
- Provide protection against dredging, filling and other development.
- Designate wetlands as protected areas.
- Protect wetlands from pollution particularly industrial effluent sewage, and sediment.
- Ensure that traditional uses of wetlands are maintained.

Goals and policies should be formulated with an aim to:

- Improve the information base on Indian wetlands.
- Promote education and awareness about wetland values.
- Facilitate better wetland management.
- Contribute to the Govt. of India's National Programme on wetlands, mangroves and coral reefs.
- Support the Ramasar Convention and other relevant environmental treaties.
- Act to halt wetland destruction and degradation.
- Demonstrate the wise use of wetland resources.

Thrust Areas in Wetland Management in India

In order to sensitize human societies about wetlands and their values, it is critical to improve the quality of information available on these ecosystems. Much remains to be done, particularly in redressing historic damage to wetlands in recognizing legitimate indigenous interests in the cultural heritage of these and often environments and linking approaches to the management of cultural and natural heritage in such areas. The thrust areas include:

- Production of resource materials.
- Training, development and use of hydrological modeling tools in support of wetland conservation and restoration efforts.
- Facilitating participatory management planning and implementation (ensuring peoples' participation)
- Providing technical support to the Government of India.
- Propagating environmental education and awareness.

Any draft policy formulated for wetland management must include:

- A mechanism for leveraging resources expertise and authorities.
- A collaborative problem-solving focus that expedites initiatives.
- A consensus building process that avoids conflicts.

A holistic approach to develop and implement a coordinated strategy for the allocation of environmental, social, cultural, and institutional resources to achieve the conservation and sustainable multiple use of the coastal zone needs to be followed. Conservation of wetlands can be achieved only by sustainable development that means wise-use. Dialogue with rural population is a vital prerequisite to identifying local needs, possible resource use conflicts and defining the level at which resource should take place. The importance of community participation in wetland conservation cannot be over-emphasized. Tying the economic interests of local populations to sustainable natural resource management on the principles of local control, equitable distribution and collective responsibility are keys to effective conservation action. In fact programmes must evolve in consultation with communities – building upon the understanding they already possess about the wetland resources.

CONCLUSION

Wetlands are the most threatened ecosystems on account of a mix of social, economic and political factors. An understanding of the functions and uses of wetlands as well as the issues affecting wetlands is necessary in order to ensure the sustainable management of these resources. There are many reasons for the over-use, misuse and destruction of wetlands: the high dependency on wetlands of an ever-growing human population for food, water, fodder, fuel, fibre, shelter or intensification of resources exploitation, sometimes aggravated by technology, sometimes by commercial interests, and often promoted by prevailing policies or the lack of any; inadequate institutional mechanisms for management; and ignorance about conservation needs and methods.

It is essential to educate people about the need for the conservation of wetlands, and their economic utility, as well as promoting scientific and application-oriented research into their productivity. A national and international wetlands development committee should be constituted comprising the experts of various disciplines related to wetland conservation and sustainable use. Multidisciplinary-trained professionals, who can spread the understanding of wetland importance at local schools, colleges, and research institutions by initiating educational programs aimed at raising the levels of public awareness and comprehension of aquatic ecosystem restoration, goals, and methods, should be involved. Appropriate management and restoration mechanisms need to be implemented in order to regain and protect the physical, chemical, and biological integrity of wetland ecosystems. In this context, a detailed study of wetland management and socio-economic implications is required from biological and hydrological perspectives. Protecting and preserving wetlands must involve building a partnership among various agencies, working in co-ordination, and addressing the common goal of minimizing human-induced changes that affect the hydrology, biogeochemical fluxes and the quality of wetlands.

REFERENCES

Acreman, M.C. and Hollis, G.E. 1996. *Water Management and Wetlands in Sub-Saharan Africa*. IUCN, Gland, Switzerland.

Anonymous 1987. *Mangroves in India: Status Report,* Government of India, Ministry of Environment & Forests, New Delhi, December, 1987, pp. 1-150.

Anonymous 1999. *The State of Forest Report* 1999, Government of India, Forest Survey of India, Dehradun.

Anonymous 2001. *The State of Forest Report* 2001, Government of India, Forest Survey of India, Dehradun.

Anon. 2001a. *India 2001 – A Reference Manual* Compiled and Edited by Research, Reference and Training Division. Ministry of Information and Broadcasting, Govt. of India. 873 p.

Cairns, J. (Ed.). 1988. *Rehabilitating Damaged Ecosystems*. Boca Raton, FL: CRC Press.

Garg, J. K., Singh, T. S. and Murthy, T. V. R. 1998. Coastal Wetlands of India Nation-wide Wetland Mapping Project. Space Application Centre (ISRO), Ahmedabad: 6-125: 166 pp.

Kiran, R., and Ramachandra, T.V. 1999. Status of Wetlands in Bangalore and Its Conservation Aspects. *ENVIS Journal of Human Settlements,* 16-24.

Lewis, R. R. III. 1989. Creation and Restoration of Coastal Plain Wetlands in Florida. In J. A. Kusler, & M.E. Kentula (Eds.), *Wetland Creation and Restoration: The Status of the Science* (US EPA/7600/3-89/038) (Vol. 1, pp. 73-102). Corvallis, OR: U.S. Environmental Protection Agency, Environmental Research Laboratory.

Naskar, K., and Mandal R. 1999. *Ecology and Biodiversity of India Mangroves,* Daya Publisher House, Delhi, Part-I, p. 359.

Prasad, S.N., Ramachandran, T.V., Ahalya, N., Sengupta, T., Alok Kumar, Tiwari, A.K., Vijayan, V.S. and Vijayan, L. 2002. Conservation of Wetlands of India – A Review. *Tropical Ecology,* 43(1): 173-186.

Ramachandra, T.V. 2001. Restoration and Management Strategies of Wetlands in Developing Countries. *Electronic Green Journal, 15, Dec. 2001.*

Rao, B.R.M., Dwivedi, R. S., Kushwaha, S.P.S., Bhattacharya, S.N., Anand, J.B. and Dasgupta, S. 1999. Monitoring the Spatial Extent of Coastal Wetlands Using ERS-1 SAR Data. *International Journal of Remote Sensing,* 20(13): 2509-2517.

Scott, D.A. 1989. A Directory of Asian Wetlands, IUCN, Gland.

Shine, C., and de Klemm, C. 1999. *Wetlands, Water, and the Law: Using Law to Advance Wetland Conservation and Wise Use* (IUCN Environmental Policy and Law Paper No. 38). Gland, Switzerland: IUCN.

Singh, H. S. 2000. Mangroves in Gujarat – Current Status and Conservation Strategy. Gujarat Ecological Education and Research (GEER) Foundation, Gandhinagar. p. 128.

Singh, H.S. 2002. *Marine Protected Areas of India – Status of Coastal Wetland Conservation*, Gujarat Ecological Education and Research Foundation, Gandhinagar.

Sinha, P.C. and Mohanty, R. 2002. *Wetland Management Policy and Law*, Kanishka Publishers, Distributors, New Delhi, p. 436.

Walters, C.J. 1986. *Adaptive Management of Renewable Resources*. New York: Macmillan.

Zentner, J. 1988. Wetland Restoration in Urbanized Areas: Examples from Coastal California. In J.A. Kusler, S. Daly, & G. Brooks (Eds.), *Urban Wetlands: Proceedings of the National Wetland Symposium, June 26-29, 1988, Oakland, California*. Berne, NY: Association of Wetland Managers.

5

Environmental Impact on Human Health
A Review

Dr. Ram Prasad Panda[1]

INTRODUCTION

The environmental has always been critical to life but concerns over the balance between human life and the environment assumed international dimensions only during the 1950s. In the years that followed supposedly unconnected pieces of a global jigsaw puzzle began to fit together to reveal a picture of a world with an uncertain future. At the end of 1960s the voice of environment concerns was heard almost uniquely in the west. In the communist world, the relentless destruction of the environment in the name of industrialization continued unabated. In developing countries, environmental concerns were regarded as western luxuries. "Poverty is the worst form of pollution", held India's then Prime Minister, Indira Gandhi, who played a key role in orienting the agenda of the UN Conference on the Human Environment, held in Stockholm in 1972, to wards

1. **H.O.D. Zoology, A. Sc.College, Kshatriyabarpur (Ganjam).**

the concerns of the developing countries. This Conference established the United Nations Environment Programme (UNEP) as the environmental conscience of the UN system.

Human health and quality of life are strongly influenced by the environment. Both environment and genetic factors, however, are involved in the production of diseases and environmental factors to acquired ones. Such combinations of genetic and environmental factors in disease are frequently encountered among populations with high incidences of genetic anomalies inhabiting geographical areas in which communicable diseases are endemic (WHO 1980).

Epidemiological differences between and within countries can serve as pointers to the role of environmental factors in different regions of the world. These differences may also reflect variations in life style or cultural practice. Studies of people who are ethnologically related but live in different parts of the world have strongly incriminated environmental factors in a number of diseases. For example hardening of coronary and cerebral arteries (arteriosclerosis) and high blood pressure (hypertension).

Environmental narrations are reflected in seasonal differences in the incidence of diseases in many parts of the world. Some communicable diseases are transmitted much more easily during the rainy season. Temperature, humidity, soil, rainfall and atmospheric conditions are all important factors in the ecology of certain infective and infections diseases, especially they control the distribution and abundance of their vectors. Control of these ecological factors therefore provides an important means of interrupting the spread of ill health.

Health demands a sound mind in a sound body. The socio-economic implications of impaired mental health in any population group cannot be ignored. Impaired mental health can be caused by genetic or environmental factors. During the past decade, evidence of the role of biochemical changes in the causation mental health has increased. Exposure to heavy metals such as mercury or lead and certain synthetic compounds also create a predisposition to brain tumours or abnormal behaviour. The environment therefore has a broad and highly significant influence on the health profile of its inhabitants.

Several inter-governmental bodies are involved in formulation policies for the effective monitoring and control of the environment and with the interactions between the environment and health. These include World Health Organization (WHO), United Nations Environment Programme (UNEP), the United Nations Development Programme (UNDP), the Food and Agriculture Organization of the United Nations (FAO) and the United Nations Children's Fund (UNICEF).

Child mortality and life expectancy figures could be used as an indication of the effectiveness with which health care is provided. That will differ from once country to another and even within a country.

In the world as a whole there are three broad groups of diseases that account for a highly significant proportion of illness and death:

1. Communicable diseases.
2. Degenerative diseases.
3. Neoplastic diseases (Cancers).

Communicable diseases account for a large proportion of illness and death in developing countries. The degenerative diseases such as those of the heart and circulatory system and Neoplastic diseases account for a large proportion of illness and death in developed countries.

ENVIRONMENTAL DETERMINANTS AND COMMUNICABLE DISEASES

The transmission of any infection in influenced by four factors:

1. Immunological status of the host.
2. Characteristics of the environment.

3. Biology of organisms causing the infection.
4. Relationship between those Organisms and the host.

The environmental factors likely to be critical vary according to the route or mode of transmission which can be direct from skin to skin (Sexually–transmitted diseases) via soil, air, food or water through a vector etc. All infecting organisms are part of the human environment.

The most important environmental factor in the transmission of infectious disease is water. It is the habit of the larval stages of the mosquito vectors of such diseases as Malaria, Yellow fever and Dengue, and of the snails that are alternate hosts of schistosomiasis. It is the medium of transmission of Cholera and numerous organisms causing diarrhoeal diseases. The second major factor us the quality of the urban and residential environment (and especially excreta disposal system) and the third, the pattern of human movements and contacts. The risk of epidemics has been enhanced, and the difficulties of disease control increased. The climatic conditions are important to the spread of air born diseases, while changes in agricultural practices and techniques of animal husbandry can effect the distribution of pathogens.

THE EFFECT OF SURFACE WATER RESOURCE DEVELOPMENT

The health of the population was affected both during the construction and the operation of a scheme. Sometimes the workers were exposed for the first time to locally prevalent diseases. (Filariasis, Malaria, Japanese fever etc.)

THE EFFECTS OF IMPROVED WATER SUPPLY AND EXCRETA DISPOSAL

The task of providing improved water supplies because increasingly difficult due to population growth, particularly in an around cities. An annual urban growth role of four per cent implies doubled water needs every 18 years event at constant per capita use. Many infectious agents, including those that cause diarrhoea, escape from man via excreta and infect others by ingestion.

THE IMPACT OF HUMAN MIGRATION AND BEHAVIOUR

International travel contributed the rapid spread of sexually transmitted diseases like gonorrhoea and non-specific urethritis etc. Rural-Urban migrations also increased hazards. Abandoning of breast feeding causes the loss of resistance power in children.

MAJOR TRENDS

During the decade communicable diseases continued to cause a high proportion of the sickness and deaths in developing countries. Respiratory infections remained a major cause of illness all over the world. In most developing countries, environment conditions such as warm climate, food deficiencies, poverty, insufficient and unsuitable water supplies poor sanitation cause the spread of the disease. Although there were effective measures for the control of communicable diseases, poverty and other socio-economic constrains limited their global application.

TRENDS IN PARTICULAR DISEASES

The five bacterial diseases that are of particular epidemiological importance and whose transmission is dependent on human activities and environmental factors are gonorrhoea, leprosy, tuberculosis, meningitis and cholera.

Malaria continued to be the most important single disease in Africa and else where in sub tropic (UNEP 1978). In Africa approximately 50 per cent of children up to the age of three were infected. And one million children died from Malaria every year (WHO, 1980). In India the incidence of infection rose from 40,000 in 1966 to 1.4 million in 1972 and 6 million in 1976 (UNEP 1978). This situation is created by the development of resistance to insecticides by Anopheles mosquitoes, the continuous use of insecticides like DDT created other serious environmental problems. To control the disease it is advised to clean sanitation, and go for biological and genetic control.

Schistosomiasis is occurring in Africa and Western Asia. The causative agent is *Schistosoma harematobium*. It is usually effects the urinary tract and intestinal tract. The transmission of infection depends on ova from human excreta reaching water containing the intermediate host (snail). Any developments that facilities contact between people and water will therefore make the transmission of this disease more likely. Irrigation schemes increase its transmission most of all both by creating ideal snail (*Bulinus truncates rohifsi*) habitats and by increasing human contacts with water.

Onchocerciasis is s widerspread disease in Africa especially in west Africa. The vector a black-fly *(Simulium damnosune)* bread rapid to rivers. The disease caused by a nematode worm parasite *Onchocerca volvulus,* which produces cresting itching and skin changes and progressive blindness in the Volta river basisn 79,000 individuals lost their sight (WHO, 1980).

Six major Viral diseases such as Yellow fever, Measles, Rabies, Small-pox, Tick-borne encephalitis and Right valley fever have been encountered in many parts of the world.

POLLUTION AND HEALTH

Concern over the impact on human health of chemicals in the environment has increased in recent years. (UNEP 1980, 1981). It has become clear, for example that a number of chemicals act specifically on heart diseases. Relationship with environmental factors has also come to light, such as that between soft water and the incidence of heart disease, fluorine deficiency and excessive dental decay or increased arsenic in soil and water and the enhanced occurrence of cancer. In evaluating human exposure to potentially hazardous chemicals it is therefore necessary to consider all pathways – air, water, soil and food, and both the home and working environment – and to estimate values for whole-life exposure and exposure at work, as well as does over short period exposure under various circumstances.

The rate of circulation of may elements through the environment has been greatly increased by man's activities. In 1950, world production of organić chemicals was 7 million tonnes while in 1985 it was 250 million tonnes.

CHEMICALS IN THE WORKING ENVIRONMENT

Acute lead and mercury poisoning, pneumoconiosis (a lung disease caused by lung inhalation), slowing in verve conduction velocity due to heavy metal pollution, and occupational causes of cancer were reported.

AIR POLLUTION

Air pollution is not a new problem; it has been around for centuries. Over three centuries ago, the noted scientist John Evelyn described with great accuracy many of the effects of the air pollution arising from the combustion of coal, morbidity and mortality from respiratory aliments, dust fall etc. According to WHO air pollution may defined as "Substances but into air by the activity of mankind into concentration sufficient to cause harmful effect to his health, vegetables, property or to interfere with the enjoyment of his property".

Air pollution may exist in three district categories:-

1. **Personal Air Pollution**

   It refers to exposure to dust, fumes and gases to which an individual exposes himself when indulges in Cigarette, Cigar or Pipe smoking.

2. **Occupational Air Pollution**

   It represents the type of exposure of individuals to potentially harmful concentrations of aerosol, vapours and gases in their environment.

3. **Community Air Pollution**

   It represents the most complex of the three varieties since it involves a varied assortment of pollution sources and contaminates, metrorologic factors, and a wide diversity of adverse social, economic and health effects. It can exert a significant impact of mans total environment, including plants, animals, property and the weather itself.

One of the most visible alterations of the biosphere to human activities is air pollution. Air pollution occurs when these chemicals affect the visible quality of air, human health, the welfare of ecosystems and the processes that are important to protecting life on earth.

Air pollution is associated with documented episodes of human mortality; is suspected of contributing to high rates of Urban lung carrier; causes rainfall to become acidic affecting sensitive aquatic ecosystems for from pollution series, and involves the release of less reactive chemicals that have spread to sphere, affecting the shield of ozone that protects the earth from ultraviolet radiation.

NOTABLE AIR POLLUTION EPISODES

The London Smog

First incident happened in the year Dec. 1952. Truly it was a major air pollution disaster. The smog lasted 5 days (December 5-9), caused 4000 deaths. Shown acute respiratory syndrome to 60 cows.

Second incident occurred in the year 1962 (Dec. 3-7). Reported deaths were 340.

The Donora Smog

Occurred in Donora in Pennsylvania during the year 1984 (Ocotober 27-31). Many persons were hospitalized and 20 died.

Meuse Valley, Belgium

A strong a atmospheric inversion got settled over the Meuse Valley on Dec 1, 1930 and remained until December 5. 63 persons died and several hundred others become ill. Sulfur oxides and hydrofluoric acid were suspected by many, the actual lethal substance could not be proved.

Ducktown, Tennessee

For the early 1900's gases from two copper smelters near Georgian border of Tennessee caused widespread damage to vegetation in the surrounding countryside. Damages extended 30 miles into the forests of Georgia.

Pittsburgh, Pennsylvania

Prior to 1948 the nickname 'smoke city' had been appropriate for Pittsburgh. A black pall of smoke often turned day into night, blackened the brightest building in few months. The dieselization of locomotives and extinguishing burning helped to prevent this.

Los Angeles, California

The most publicized smog problem in U.S. In 1947 they restricted the emissions of smoke and sulfur dioxide.

Bhopal MIC Gas Tragedy (1984)

It has been regarded as the worst industrial accident which is related to air pollution. Around 2,00,000 Bhopal residents were affected by the leak of poisonous MIC gas from the Union Carbide Pesticide plant there. At least 5000 people were killed and doctors estimated that some 50,000 people have been seriously affected and many go blind.

Bhopal victims continue to die our of every three children born to women who were pregnant on the might of the disaster, only one survived. Out of 1350 new born babies 16 were physically deformed and 60 premature births. Deformities include children suffering from congenital hearts, holes in arms and impaired eye sight. High levels of thiocyanates were detected in water in Bhopal and continued exposure to this may cause adverse functioning of Organs like thyroid which in turn may effect pregnancy.

Factors responsible for increasing the air pollution is population growth, Expansion of industry and Technology and social changes include Urbanization and rising standard of living.

AIR POLLUTION FOLLOWED WATER POLLUTION

About 50 year ago, the rivers and lakes began to show signs of deterioration from human and industrial waste. The pollution eventually become so intense that drastic action has to be taken to protect human health and well-being. By using effective sanitary engineering measures, including waste treatment and water purification, it become possible to meet the needs of an expanding population without serious incident.

POLLUTION FOOD AND WATER

Food and drinking water may be contaminated:

1. When metals and other airborne particles settle out on crops.
2. When chemicals are applied to crops as fertilizers and biocides and are retained within them.
3. When fungi grow on badly – stoned food stuffs and produced toxins there in.
4. When potentially toxic substances enter water sources in sewage or industrial discharges.

Cadmium, mercury and lead were the most publicized metallic contamination of found and water (UNEP 1980). Cadmium had previously been incriminated in the out break of Itai-Itai disease in Japan – when rice paddy was irrigated with river water containing cadmium (WHO 1977). Mercury poisoning has occurred from two main causes; the consumption of grain treated with mercurial fungicide (the largest recorded instance of which caused 500 deaths and 6,000 hospital cases in Iraq in the winder 1971-72) (WHO 1976), and the accumulation of methyl mercury in Fish. This later phenomenon was the cause of the well-known outbreaks of poisoning at Minamata and Nigata in Japan. It was accident following research that inorganic mercury is readily accumulated by fish, posing a potential hazard to communities with a high component of Fish in their diet. A number of governments accordingly ruled that fish containing more than 1.0 or 0.5 PP mercury may not be sold.

In certain countries were lead water tanks and pipes used to carry acid water and pose a potential hazard (WHO 1977). Another problem created by the use of PCBs (polychlorinated biphenyls) used as dielectrics in transformers and capacitors and as plasticizers in paints and plastics. It was estimated that 1 million tones of PCBs had been produced since 1930 and that more than half of this had entered the general environment, where the compounds are extremely persistent. The highest concentration of PCB residues occur in fish. The recorded serious episode resulting from the contamination of food with PCBs occurred in Japan in 1968, when more than 1000 people who had eaten rice oil contaminated with PCBs developed dark pigmentation of the skin, discharging eyes and respiratory symptoms. The disease affected some newborn children since PCBs readily cross the placenta.

Nitrate in drinking water, which has the potential to cause health problems, may enter the supply either from sewage effluent or from agricultural land, due to the increasing use of nitrogen fertilizer and changing farming practices. Nitrate itself may cause methemoglobinoemia (a blood disorder) in bottle – fed infants if present in excessive quantities in drinking water. Nitrate also caused concern because of its possible conversion of nitrosamines, which is carcinogenic.

Those that caused most concern as far as human health is concerned were the organochlorine compounds. Like HCB (Hexachlor benzene) DDT (Dicloro diphenyl trichloro ethane) and DDE (Dichlorodiphenyl dichloro ethaylene).

CANCER AND ENVIRONMENTAL EXPOSURE

Human exposure to environmental factors such as ionizing radiation, carcinogenic chemicals in air food or water or through smoking, alcohol and drugs (Chemotherapeutic agents) creates a predisposition to the development of cancer.

ENVIRONMENTAL CARCINOGENS

Environmental carcinogens may be physical, chemical or viral.

Physical Carcinogens

The use of X-ray in diagnosis and therapy continued to be the main source of exposure to radiation. The effect includes high chances for leukemia, sqnamous cell carcinoma, soft tissue and bone sarcomas, thyroid carcinomas etc. Some ultraviolet (UV-B) radiation penetrates the atmospheric ozone screen and is capable for causing both benign and malignant skin cancers in people exposed to the sun for long periods.

Chemical Carcinogens

It includes nitrosamines, fungal toxins, pyroholizdine alkaloids, Drugs, biological agents (Vitamins, bile acids and fats) and Industrial Chemical Compounds.

Viral Carcinogens

A number of viruses that occur in the environment have been suspected of producing human cancer. The two identified of them are the Epstein – Barr virus, which produces

Burkittt lymphoma and the hepatitis B virus, which produces liver cell cancer (WHO 1980).

CONCLUSION

Health is a fundamental resource to individual and community and is a prerequisite for their social, spiritual and physical well-being, the protection and preservation of which is dependent on the ecological status of the environment and sustainable development. It is heartening to note that children suffer from intergenerational and inter-generational health problems due to stress and environmental deterioration, which they pass on to the next generation. This is a grave situation and it is reiterated that development efforts should be environment friendly to perpetuate development itself. After all human survival depends on *Development without Destruction of Environment*.

REFERENCES

Radha, S. and Amar Singh Sankhyan, *Environmental Challenges of the 21st Century*, Deep and Deep Publications, New Delhi, 2002.

Sinha, A.K., R.P. Singh and K.M. Rastogi, *Human Health and Environment*, APH Publishing Corporation, New Delhi, 1997.

Swarup, R., S.N. Mishra and V.P. Jauhari, *Envrionment an Assessment*, Mittal Publications, New Delhi, 1992.

UNEP, *Global Environmental Outlook 3. Past, Present and Future Perspective.* Earthscan Publication. London. 2002.

Vinoli, Jeffry, W., *Lewis Dictionary Occupational and Environmental Safety and Halth.*

6

The Myth of a Burning Earth and its Legal Policy Acts

Mamini Kumari Maharana[1]
Binod Kumar Maharana[2]
Dr. Lingaraj Patro[3]

ABSTRACT

The 21st century's millennium boon is that more that 1,50,000 people died every year because of Global Warming. The 21st Century's Millennium boon can call as the environmental threat, living with Global Change one has to pay the price of pollution i.e. not in respect of money but by loosing ones valuable life in coaly age. According to Al Gore: "This is the era of consequence ness global warming is inspiring scientist philosopher to fight

1. Lecturer in English, Deccan College, Berhampur, Orissa, India, *E-mail:* mamini.maharana1@gmail.com

2. Environmental Lawyer, Berhampur,Orissa,India. *E-mail:* binod.maharana1@gmail.com

3. Environmental Toxicology Lab, Department of Zoology & Biotechnology,KBDAV College, Nirakapur, 752019 (Khurda), Orissa, India, *E-mail:* dr.lrpatro@rediffmail.com

for to bring awareness and to consciences to protect and preserve the outer environment which possible if and only if we will known how to improve are inner environment fist so, as to become whole with nature". The various effects of global changes directly or indirectly linked to the unlimited greedy of man, weapon and technology used vigorous for shape of their own need and benefits. Population and poisonous are every where, i.e. not only in air, water, land fruit, vegetable, drinks, berating every where. Certain legislation environment law and act should enforce strongly to the polluter pays principle to build in the vision of healthy and a better world for future.

Key words: Environment, Global Warming, Environmental Management Systems (EMSS), Disasters, Health hazards, Environmental havoc and its Legislations.

INTRODUCTION

The end of the world is here screamed the placards during public rallies to shock everyone about looming disasters for over 64 years. These protests started in the fifties after the Atom Bomb was dropped on Hiroshima and Nagasaki in 1945 and continued as more and more lethal atomic and nuclear weapons were tested, developed and stockpiled. With the end of the Cold War, and 64 years of not using the nuclear weapons despite many crises, the protests against nuclear weapons have subsided these days. Now a more dangerous threat is facing man and the earth: our depleting environment. The alarm sirens have been strident in the past years as we suffer from heat waves, tornadoes, advancing deserts, melting polar caps and suffocating pollution, among other hazards. At the same time, an increasing number of animals, plants and marine species are decimated. The air we breathe, the water we drink, the fruits, vegetables and meat we

eat are polluted, if not poisonous. All these horrors that we have inflicted upon ourselves by abusing this earth are now threatening our lives on this planet.

Who is to blame? The unlimited greed of man. Cutting down forests, polluting water bodies, poisoning air and generally damaging eco-systems is the work of individuals, cartels or corporations in their pursuit of money. Why are they so destructive for the environment? Because their inner environment is disturbed with greed. First, our inner environment needs to be changed so that we can look after our outer or physicalenvironment. Once we connect with our inner environment, we can connect better with our outer environment as we become whole with Nature, and indeed the Universe. And how can we connect and improve our inner environment? To protect and preserve the outer environment, let us improve our inner environment first.

The 1000-year climatic and environmental history of the Earth contained in various proxy records is examined. As indicators, the proxies duly represent or record aspects of local climate. Questions on the relevance and validity of the locality paradigm for climatologically research become sharper as studies of climatic changes on timescales of 50-100 years or longer are pursued. This is because thermal and dynamical constraints imposed by local geography become increasingly important as the air-sea-land interaction and coupling timescales increase. Because the nature of the various proxy climate indicators are so different, the results cannot be combined into a simple hemispheric or global quantitative composite. However, considered as an ensemble of individual observations, an assemblage of the local representations of climate establishes the reality of both the Little Ice Age and the Medieval Warm Period as climatic anomalies with world-wide imprints, extending earlier results by Bryson *et al.* (1963), Lamb (1965), and numerous other research efforts. Furthermore, these individual proxies are used to determine whether the 20th century is the warmest century of the 2nd millennium at a variety of globally dispersed locations. Many records reveal that the 20th century is likely not the warmest nor a uniquely extreme climatic period of the last millennium, although it is clear that human activity has significantly impacted some local environments.

Over the past two decades, the Indian judiciary has fostered an extensive and innovative approach to environmental rights in the country. Complex matters of environmental management have been resolved and consequently a series of innovative procedural remedies have evolved to accompany this new substantive right. The new environmental right is therefore championed as a legal gateway to speedy and inexpensive legal remedy.

The national expansion of right to life was recognized even in the absence of a specific reference to direct violations of the fundamental right. Placed in a nutshell, the human right culture has percolated down to Indian human right regime within a short period of time. An inter-disciplinary approach to environmental protection may be another reason for the operation of the right to healthy environment. This has been undertaken through international environmental treaties & conventions, national legislative measures and in judicial responses. On undertaking a comprehensive study of environmental law, it can be found that the Indian scenario is replete with examples of preserving the environment from degradation.

Environmental Threat: A Boon?

Is global warming a wake-up call?

"Sometimes, without warning, the future knocks on our door with a precious and painful vision of what might be" - said Al Gore in his Nobel Prize acceptance speech, pointing out at the humanity is sitting on a ticking time bomb.

If the vast majority of the world's scientists are right, we have just ten years to avert a major catastrophe that could send our entire planet into a tail-spin of epic destruction involving extreme weather, floods, droughts, epidemics and killer heat waves beyond anything we have ever experienced.

The human mind in its mindless quest to grow has tilted nature's balance and unleashed its fury. "This is the era of consequences" Al Gore points out rightly as we all stand witness to unprecedented climate changes and destructions across the globe the recent one being the devastating earthquake in China which left more than 40,000 people dead.

"Neglect in protecting our heritage of natural resources could prove extremely harmful for the human race and for all species that share common space on Planet Earth," said Dr. Rajendra Pachauri, Chairman IGPCC, in his Nobel Prize acceptance speech. Environmentalists and scientists are alarmed enough about the situation to release facts and figures to common man hoping that somewhere it will make an impact on the politicians who have been aware of these facts much before.

How imminent and immediate is the danger? One asks. Well, here are a few pointers:

Last September 21, as the Northern Hemisphere tilted away from the sun, scientists reported with unprecedented distress that the North Polar ice cap is "falling off a cliff." One study estimated that it could be completely gone during summer in less than 22 years but a new study, warns it could happen in as little as 7 years.

It was thought the entire Greenland ice sheet could melt in about 1,000 years, but the latest evidence suggests that could happen much sooner. It implies that sea levels will rise a great deal faster as well; the comprehensive analysis found that the amount of ice dumped into the Atlantic Ocean has doubled in the last five years. If the Greenland ice sheet melted completely, it would raise global sea levels by about 7 meters.

Even as scientists are struggling to work out solutions which can reverse the process, a majority of human race prefers to ignore the issue. But the issue will not go away, it only grows worse.

As we stand at the brink of a major climate catastrophe - a thought arises - this may be the worst of times but also this maybe the best of times. As a threat of a total wipe-out stares us in the face the humanity has no choice but to wake-up.

The threat is so real and immediate we have no choice but to act. This is the time when the Einstein has to wake up to his Buddhahood.

Interestingly, Al Gore's speech talks about the situation demanding a new consciousness. This new consciousness requires expanding the possibilities inherent in all humanity. "When we unite for a moral purpose that is manifestly good and true, the spiritual energy unleashed can transform us," he points out, reflecting the message of all enlightened masters through the ages. "Science now needs great mediators, otherwise this earth is doomed. Science now needs people who can use their minds, who are masters of their being, who can use science in a conscious way. Otherwise we are on the verge of committing universal suicide".

Osho points out that so far the scientists have not been masters of their minds:

> "They neither used nor abused the mind; the mind used them, abused them. That's my work here, my basic fundamental work: to help you be free of the mind so that you can use it. And if you are the master, you cannot abuse it; that is impossible. When you are alert, conscious, meditative, abuse is not possible."

AN INCONVENIENT TRUTH

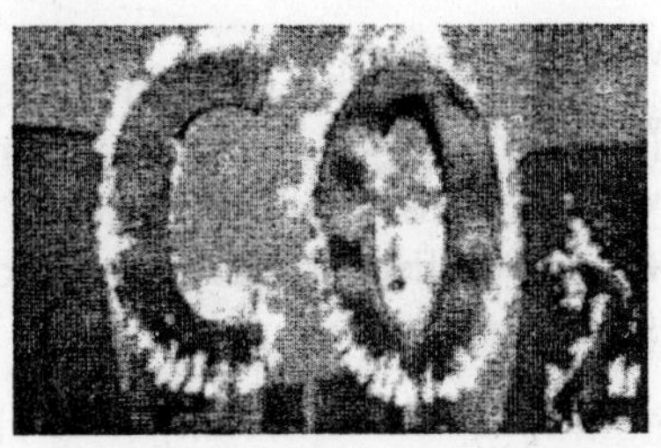

Humanity is sitting on a ticking time bomb. If the vast majority of the world's scientists are right, we have just ten years to avert a major catastrophe that could send our entire planet into a tailspin of epic destruction involving extreme weather, floods, droughts, epidemics and killer heat waves beyond anything we have ever experienced.

If that sounds like a recipe for serious gloom and doom think again. A global hit film, An Inconvenient Truth, offers a passionate and inspirational look at one man's fervent crusade to halt global warming's deadly progress in its tracks by exposing the myths and misconceptions that surround it.

That man is former Vice President Al Gore, who, in the wake of defeat in the 2000 election, re-set the course of his life to focus on a last-ditch, all-out effort to help save the planet from irrevocable change. In this eye-opening and poignant portrait of Gore and his "traveling global warming show", Gore also proves himself to be one of the most misunderstood characters in modem American public life. Here he is seen as never before in the media-funny, engaging, open and downright on fire about getting the surprisingly stirring truth about what he calls our "planetary emergency" out to ordinary citizens before it's too late.

Interspersed with the bracing facts and future predictions is the story of Gore's personal journey: from an idealistic college student who first saw a massive environmental crisis looming; to a young Senator facing a harrowing family tragedy that altered his perspective, to the man who almost become President but instead returned to the most important cause of his life-convinced that there is still time to make a difference.

With wit, smarts and hope, An Inconvenient Truth ultimately brings home Gore's persuasive argument that we can no longer afford to view global warming as a political issue rather; it is the biggest moral challenges facing our global civilization.

Gore has screened the film personally all across the DSA and in many parts of our depreciating globe. The film has shaken audiences and has been screened on global TV channels to arouse human awareness about the plight of our home planet. Anyone who loves this earth cannot miss to be shocked, awakened and inspired by this inconvenient truth.

SAVE THE EARTH TO SAVE YOURSELF

The population of the world is growing so fast that just the growth of population will be enough to kill half of humanity out of hunger and thirst.

Such is the situation of humanity. At least you have to come out of it and you need a constant hitting on your head to remind you that the times are no longer ordinary. And there have never been, in the whole history of man, such dangerous moments as those through which we are passing. It is no time for quarrelling, arguing about theological matters; it is not intelligent to console yourself that some miracle will happen and the world war will be postponed. It is not only the world war, the attack is multidimensional.

The ecology of the earth is breaking down. There are thousands of submarines moving around the earth in the ocean, and each submarine is carrying nuclear weapons so powerful that even the whole energy that was used in the II World War is nothing compared to the energy of one submarine carrying nuclear missiles. The Soviet Union has its own submarines; America has its own submarines. Just by accident two submarines can collide, and the whole life on the planet will evaporate into smoke. And the politicians of the world are continually piling up more and more nuclear weapons.

The population of the world is growing so fast that just the growth of population will be enough to kill half of humanity out of hunger and thirst.

Sexual perversions have become so rampant that Gomorrah and Sodom seem outdated.

Ten million people around the earth already have AIDS, which has no cure. And this number of ten million people is not accurate, because many countries have not yet declared how many people there have AIDS; they don't have any way to find it out. For example, India is not aware how many people are suffering from AIDS. Muslim countries are bound to have a very large number of people suffering from AIDS, because homosexuality has existed there for thousands of years. Even according to very moderate estimates, by the end of this century there will be one hundred million people suffering from AIDS. And when one hundred million people suffer from AIDS that means at least one billion people must have been involved in homosexuality.

We have cut so many forests, a thick layer of carbon dioxide has gathered on top of our atmosphere, miles away from the earth, where the air ends. The layer is so thick that it has already increased the temperature more than it has ever been on the earth; and that rise of temperature is melting the ice of the north and south poles.

These are the multi-dimensional ways that death is approaching the earth. Because we have cut so many forests, a thick layer of carbon dioxide has gathered on top of our atmosphere, miles away from the earth, where the air ends. The layer is so thick that it has already increased the temperature

more than it has ever been on the earth; and that rise of temperature is melting the ice of the north and south poles. If that ice keeps melting, and there is no way to prevent it, all the oceans of the world will rise four feet higher. And all your big cities are ports; they will be flooded with water, will become unlivable. If this carbon dioxide becomes a little thicker then the Himalayas and the Alps which have eternal snow which has never melted will start melting. The Himalayas alone have so much ice that if it melts completely it will raise all the oceans of the world forty feet higher. All your cities will be drowned and this is not a flood that is going to recede.

One of the most dangerous things happening is that carbon dioxide is going to accumulate more and more. The trees go on inhaling carbon dioxide. If you cut the trees you are cutting two things: the supply of oxygen for your life and the place for carbon dioxide to be absorbed. It is a double-edged sword and absolutely unnecessary.

Man has been trying to reach the moon and Mars, and before that, we were never aware that where the air ends, miles above earth, all around the earth there is a thick layer of a certain gas, ozone, O_3, which is a very protective layer.

Because of that ozone, life has been possible on earth. That ozone has only one function: it does not allow any sunrays which are destructive to life; it returns them. It allows only those rays which are life giving.

Because of our rockets moving towards the moon and towards Mars we have made holes, for the first time, in the layer of ozone.

Now those holes are allowing in all the rays of the sun towards the earth and death-rays are also included.

So when I say the end is not very far away, it is not like when Jesus says it just a device. By the end of this century, you will see all these dimensions bringing death to you. It has to be emphasized: unless you become absolutely clear about death, you are not going to concentrate your whole energy on transforming your being.

People change with difficulty; they find it easier to remain as they are just like stones, like rocks. Change means a determined effort, a commitment to transform your energies, to take your being in an absolutely serious manner, it has not to be wasted or fritter away in idle pursuits.

A famous playboy dies, and his best friends decide to celebrate with a mourning party. Late at night someone suggests calling Hell in order to find out where he is. "But how can you call Hell?" someone asks.

"Well," the man answers, "I guess it is just a long distance call."

So they check the telephone book and find out all about outer space calls and then dial Hell. A few seconds later a very hoarse voice answers, "This is Hell. What do you want?"

Terrified by the devilish voice, they say,
"We are looking for a friend."
"What is his name?" "Peter Thompson."
"He is not here." And the devil hangs up.

Totally amazed and having dropped all reference to logic, they decide to call Purgatory. They dial Purgatory, and to their relief, the voice on the phone does not sound so terrible, more businesslike. They explain that they are looking for a dead friend who is not in Hell and who just died.

"Well," the voice answers, "he is not here, either. Try Heaven."
"But he was a playboy!" his friends reply.
"He has to be somewhere. Try Heaven."

So they dial Heaven, and a heavenly voice answers very softly and slowly, "Hello. This is Heaven. This is Virgin Mary. Can I help you?"
Very shy, they explain the whole story.
"No," says the beautiful voice, full of echo: "He is not here. Thank you for calling. Call again."

So every day they call Heaven, and every day they get the same answer. So they call again and again; and one week later, on Sunday morning, a very sexy, foxy, quick voice answers, "Hey, this is Mary. What do you want, guys?"

Looking at each other and laughing, the friends agree: "He has arrived!"

Change is very difficult. A playboy will be a playboy, whether he is in hell or in heaven; he will stick to his repetitive style of life.

Being alert means you have to stop being robots. Change your routines, move more consciously; let every act become an object of awareness. Then even these few years that are left are enough more than enough. If you put your total energy into transformation, the destruction of the earth will not be your destruction. If you can die consciously, you have found the key to a higher life, to an eternal life, to a divine life.

Man is so asleep he is almost in a coma, and all his actions are arise out of this state of coma otherwise, there is no necessity for the world to end. But we are carrying nuclear weapons within our souls. The end is going to come because of our own ignorance, our own deep sleep.

A Remarkable Story of the Sorry Planet in the Universe

Five Looming Disasters

There is only one hope: that life does not follow logic, that it is irrational. If it was rational, mathematical and logical, then you could not give more than twenty years to life on this earth.

The future remains always unknown and takes strange turns which-no one would have ever conceived. Moreover, my approach to life is to not be bothered with the past and future. The past is no more, the future is not yet all that we have got in our hands is this moment. The past is dead and the future is unborn.

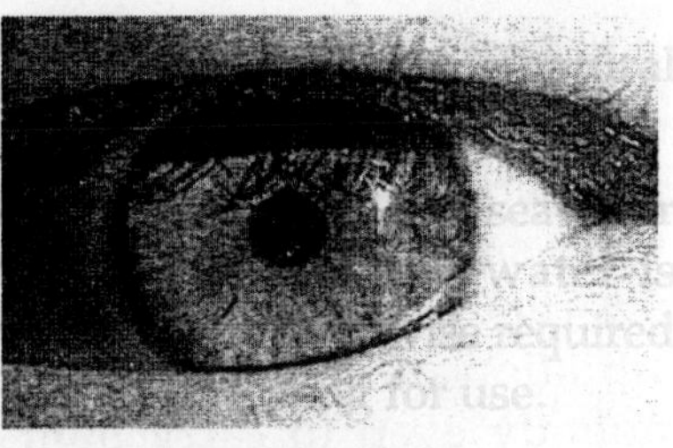

Keeping this approach in mind, I would like to say a few words. First, there is every possibility that there will be no future as far as life is concerned. We are coming closer to a dead-end street. It is sad to recognise the fact, but it is good to recognise it, because then there is the possibility of taking a different turn. As things are moving today, the logical conclusion is a global suicide.

There is only one hope: that life does not follow logic, that it is irrational. If it was rational, mathematical and logical, then you could not give more than twenty years to life on this earth.

The reasons are five:

First - Nuclear Weapons

First, the nuclear weapons are piling up every day. Right now, only five countries are nuclear powers. Within twenty years, twenty-five more countries will have joined the nuclear club. Thirty countries will have nuclear weapons. Already we have so much nuclear power that the whole earth can be destroyed seven times. And this will show you the insanity of man. Now what is the point of piling up more and more nuclear weapons?

Everybody is not a Jesus Christ, and everybody is not going to be resurrected again and againseven times. The truth is, even Jesus himself was never resurrected, because in the first place he never died. The President of the Soviet Union, Gorbachev, said, "It is not possible to calculate how much destructive energy is already available." Just one submarineand there are thousands of submarines moving underwater carrying nuclear weapons - just one submarine is equal to hundreds of second world wars. So the first problem is nuclear weapons.

Second - Population Growth

The second problem is the immense rate of population growth. By the end of this century, we will have seven billion

people on the earth. And the earth is so heavily exploited that it cannot support that much population. Fifty per cent of the population has to die simply of hunger. And just think, if fifty per cent of the people die, what will be the situation of the living ones? There will be nobody even to carry their corpses to the graveyard; they will be rotting in your streets, in your neighborhood, even in your own house. The whole world will have become a vast graveyard, stinking of death.

No effort is being made by the politicians to prevent the population growth. On the contrary, a few rich countries of the West, for example, Germanywhere people are intelligent and can see that more population means more death, more population means more poverty, more population means more diseasehave stopped producing children. And the politicians of those countries are giving incentives to produce more children because their population is decreasing.

They are not worried about the whole world. Their whole worry is . . . for example, Germany is losing three thousand people every day and thirty thousand immigrants are entering into Germany. The politician is not worried about the world; he is worried about his power, his country. If this continues for twenty years — that their population keeps decreasing and immigrants go on coming more and more — the immigrants will be in the majority, they will be the rulers. So before it becomes a problem, the Germans have to start producing as many children as poor countries are doing. And the same is true of a few other Western countries.

Third - Disease AIDS

The third problem is the disease AIDS, which is spreading like wildfire. And there seems to be no possible at least in the coming twenty years, of finding a cure for it. Scientists are more or less certain that there is no cure.

But no country is making celibacy a crime, and celibacy is the cause of the disease AIDS. It is the monks, the soldiers, the students, who live separately from women, who become homosexuals and homosexuality has created the disease. But homosexuality is only a symptom; the real problem is celibacy, brahmacharya.

And it is not that the ecology is being disturbed from one direction alone. It is being destroyed by multi-dimensional methods. For example, because of the accumulation of carbon dioxide and manmade chemicals, the heat of the atmosphere has risen as it has never risen before.

Mahatma Gandhi has written a book, *Celibacy is Life*. Now somebody has to write a book, Celibacy is Life. And every country is trying to hide the facts: how many homosexuals they have, how many people suffer from AIDS, because no one, no country, wants to be exposed to the world as homosexual. But you can see that every day people die from AIDS, all over the world. And AIDS takes time to ripen, it can take years - and then for death, at least two more years. If so many people are dying, millions around the world must be practicing homosexuality.

But it seems nobody has the guts to say that celibacy should be made a crime, and that those who are homosexuals should not be punished, but trained again to become heterosexuals. Every college, every school, every hospital, every institution that is concerned with human welfare should teach homosexuals, uncondition their mind from homosexuality and turn it to the natural way, the well-trodden way of heterosexuality.

All the religions are suffered from it, because they all teach celibacy. But no religion is ready to accept it, and whenever you don't accept enemies you are give more power to the enemy. Recognize it, so that you can find ways to fight with the enemy.

Fourth - Ecology

The fourth great problem that man will face in the coming twenty years is a collapse of the ecology. We are unaware of how we are destroying our own sources of life in different ways. Life needs an ecological balance, and that balance is being disturbed. For example, around the earth is a layer of air. And just on top or that layer is the ozone layer, which is a protective seal for the earth. But we have made holes in it by sending rockets to the moon and to Mars, which was absolutely unnecessary. You cannot manage the earth and you are attempting to manage the whole universe.

The rockets, going out and coming in, have made holes and those holes are now turning out to be one of the most dangerous things - because the sun sends rays and all the rays are not life-giving. That layer, the ozone layer, returned those rays which would bring destruction and disease to the earth, and allowed only life-giving rays. But we have made holes, not only with rockets, but by other means also. Suffer all those destructive rays are entering the atmosphere. Our atomic explosions have destroyed that layer; and there are many gases which scientists are producing those gases have also created holes. Now the whole protective seal is no longer protective.

And it is not that the ecology is being disturbed from one direction alone. It is being destroyed by multi-dimensional methods. For example, because of the accumulation of carbon dioxide and man-made chemicals, the heat of the atmosphere has risen as it has never risen before. For the first time there is a possibility that the ice on both the poles, north and south, has started melting. It has never melted before. If all the ice from the north and south poles melts, then all the oceans will rise by four feet. Cities which are ports, like Mumbai, New York, or London, will be filled with water. But four feet, perhaps we can manage somehow.

The Himalayan ice has never melted, it has been eternally there. If the heat of the atmosphere rises a little more, then the Himalayan ice will start melting, and that is the greatest danger. And the heat is rising because nobody is listening, nobody is caring about anything. What happens to future humanity is nobody's concern they are concerned with their power, their politics.

Atomic experiments continue, nuclear experiments continue. And it is a really horrible picture if the whole Himalaya melts; all the seas of the world will rise by forty feet. Perhaps four feet somehow we can protect ourselves by creating walls or something, but forty feet higher. The oceans will drown all your big cities, all your wealth, because they are all near the ocean.

A forty-foot rising of the oceans has immense implications. All the rivers will start moving backwards, because the oceans will not absorb them. The land will be flooded with water, and a flood will happen exactly like the one we read about in the Old Testament, which happened in Noah's time, when all life and everything got drowned. It has been, up to now, only a story; but the coming twenty years will see it happen as a fact. And there is nobody, and no way. In that small story it was possible to create an ark, because sooner or later the floods would subside. But this is not a flood that is going to subside.

Fifth - Man

And the most dangerous thing is the fifth, which is man himself, with all his discriminations between black and white, between East and West, and a new discrimination has suddenly arisen between North and South. Humanity is divided by religions, by nations, by color, by race, and they are at each other's throats. To avoid these five dangers, which man has never faced before, seems to be almost impossiblc - unless a miracle happens. But miracles happen only in stories, not in real life. And the most disturbing factor is that the intelligentsia of the world, the politicians of the world, the philosophers of the world are ignoring all these facts.

It happens in times of danger, that the only way to protect your peace of mind is to ignore the danger. This is called the "ostrich logic." The ostrich lives in the desert, a beautiful animal with a long neck, very colorful. Whenever the ostrich sees its enemies, other animals who can kill it, it has a strange logic but very human. It simply digs a hole in the sand of the desert and puts its head inside the hole, because then it cannot see the enemy. And its logic is: if you cannot see the enemy, the enemy does not exist.

People are concerned about trivia, very stupid things, when great dangers are ahead. Hope that some sanity comes to humanity and life can be saved, but we will have to encounter all these five factors very carefully.

LIVE NOW FOR TOMORROW

It is restless as it has never been before. It has forgotten the language of relaxation, it has forgotten the language of totality, it has forgotten the language of intensity. And all those qualities are needed to make your meditation a revolution in your being.

Why am I insisting that there is, for the first there will not be any tomorrow at all? There is an old proverb: 'Tomorrow never comes'. But the old proverb has been only a proverb and in spite of that proverb, tomorrow has kept coming. It may not come as tomorrow; it will always come as today, in that sense the proverb is right. But today the situation is totally different: Tomorrow really may not come. I want it to sink deep into your being that we have come to the very end of the road and there is nothing left except dancing and rejoicing. To make it now, I am destroying your tomorrow completely. I am taking it away from your mind which is deeply involved with tomorrows. Even if you say you understand that perhaps tomorrow the world wit end, deep down your mind keeps on saying, "There have been thousands of wars, and the world has survived. One war more is not going to make much difference."

The mind is very clever in finding excuses, that something or other will prevent the destruction. And I am not saying that the destruction should not be prevented. What I am saying is that in your mind, there should be no excuse left for postponement — so your whole energy gathers in the now; it is not spread in the future. And if the whole energy is concentrated in this point, then this moment can become the moment of enlightenment.

Enlightenment is nothing but your consciousness being concentrated on a single point - now and here.

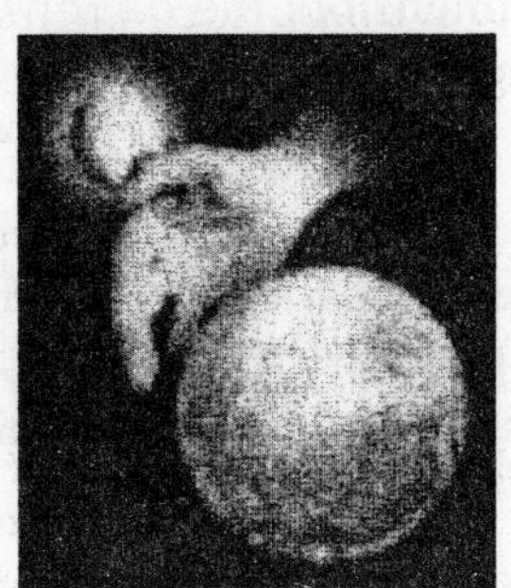

Looking at the human mind, nothing is enough. People will go on living in their old unconscious ways hoping against hope that although there have always been people like Jesus and Buddha predicting the end of the world, the world is still there. But this time the situation is totally different. I am not predicting the end of the world; it is simply becoming so certain, so logically certain, that there seems to be no possibility to avoid it.

But my interest is not in avoiding it if it can be avoided, it will be avoided my interest is to make it so clear to you that it cannot be avoided, and that you don't have any future to invest your energy in, that you have to pull all your energy back to the present moment. And the moment the whole energy becomes a pool, here and now, the explosion of light happens and you are, for the first time, absolutely yourself an eternal being, an immortal being, who knows nothing of death, who has never come across any darkness.

On the surface it seems everything is going perfectly well but deep down there is great turmoil in the unconscious layers", human beings. You are not even aware of your own unconscious nightmares, but humanity is suffering as it has never suffered before.

It is restless as it has never beer, before. It has forgotten the language of relaxation, it has forgotten the language of totality, it has forgotten the language of intensity. And all those qualities are needed to make your meditation a revolution in your being. It is not a question of morality, not a question of character, not a question of virtue religions have been concerned with all those things for thousands of years, and they have not been successful in changing man. It is a totally different approach, a different dimension: the dimension of energy and the concentration of energy.

And just as atomic energy is the explosion of a small atom into its constituent of electrons, protons and neutrons, it is not visible to the eyes, but the explosion is so vast that it can destroy a great city such as Nagasaki or Hiroshima exactly parallel is the inner explosion of the living cell.

The atomic energy is outside and destructive, objective and destructive. The inner energy, the subjective cell of your being, has the same qualities, the same tremendous power once it explodes but it is creative.

It is a chain reaction: one cell inside you explodes, and then other cells inside you start exploding in a chain. The whole life becomes a festival of lights. Every gesture becomes a dance; every movement becomes sheer joy. My emphasis that there is no future has nothing to do with gloom; it has something to do with you. If you can drop the idea of the future completely, your enlightenment becomes immediately possible. And it is a good opportunity to drop the idea of the future because the future itself is disappearing. But don't even in any comer of your mind; keep carrying the idea that perhaps this too is a device. These are the strategies of the mind to keep you the same old zombie.

This is your home; this very moment is your paradise. It all depends on you. You do not need to be virtuous to dance totally; you do not need to be learned to dance totally; you do not need to be pious to dance totally. To dance totally, all that is needed is that we accept the reality only of this moment.

The mind is clever. If you want to rise early in the morning, you put on an alarm clock, and you hear the alarm, the mind is so clever; it may start dreaming that you are in a church and church bells are ringing. The poor alarm clock cannot do anything more than that; the mind has created a dream and made it possible for you to go on sleeping.

The old religions were basically insistent on one thing, and that was the future. You should note it: not only the future in this life, but after life; their whole program me was to take your whole energy as a project for a future life, after death, in paradise far, far away. This strategy worked; it took away the very juice of human life.

All the religious scriptures say this world is nothing but a waiting room; your real home is far away, above the clouds. There is real living; here is only waiting.

I am trying to change the whole pattern of religious thinking. I am trying to say to you: This is your home; this very moment is your paradise. It all depends on you. You do not need to be virtuous to dance totally; you do not need to be learned to dance totally; you do not need to be pious to dance totally. To dance totally, all that is needed is that we accept the reality only of this moment. We will accept the reality of the next moment when it arrives, but we will not be waiting for it.

All the religions have been teaching you to wait. I am teaching to live, to love, to dance, to sing and don't wait.

THE MAJOR ENVIRONMENTAL DILEMMAS

Human Population Explosion is challenging the ecological balance. Will Earth's population continue to grow as fast as the last 100 years? This is an alarming question. Human population growth is the primary source of environmental damage. Of course, this is not a comparison to natural catastrophes that eventually result in a natural change of life and ecosystems, but rather it is a statement about the challenges human population poses for nature. The world's populations may still double again by the end of the century to 12 billion persons. Several questions have emerged due to over population like:

1. Is this too many people for the size and resources of the planet?
2. Will our natural resources run out?
3. Will natural habitat vanish?
4. Will starvation increase?
5. Will we all live in large cities?
6. What are barriers to decreasing human population growth? and
7. and what are we doing and can we do to prevent overpopulation?

The current world population increases at a rate of 76,570,430 people every year.

EI NINO: IMBALANCE IN THE ENVIRONMENT

The 1997-98 EI Nino produced the most extreme climate event of the 20th century. Many areas suffered heavy flooding, severe tornadoes, major droughts and wildfires, and devastating floods worldwide. El Nino is a recurring phenomenon that cyclically threatens and temporarily alters the balance of life and ecosystems. EI Nino is a significant warming of the Pacific Ocean in the area of the equator and extending north, south and west across the ocean, resulting in a radical redistribution of lower food chain supplies (like phytoplankton) and wreaking havoc on many climates around the world. These changes have caused starvation and deaths of animals that relied on the relocated food chains and were unable to pursue them like seals and otters. Other species like whales and birds are able to follow their food supplies and survive fairly well. But as the El Nino cycle ends, the food chains return, the malnourished and depleted seal populations gradually bounce back, and the whales and birds go back to their normal range.

What is Pollution?

Water, Air, or Soil pollution means the introduction of materials that harm the health or survival of plants, animals and humans - too often, only those of economic importance to humans. An upstream chemical company that pollutes a river by discharging wastes into it harms not only people downstream who drink river water but also fish in the river, birds who eat the fish, and thousands of other organisms that live in or near the river. People changing their own car oil cause pollution of nearby lakes, rivers, or bays when they dump used oil in storm drains.

Air is significantly polluted after releasing taxies in gas and particle emissions from automobile exhaust pipes and the smokestacks of power plants, refineries, and factories. Winds carry industrial emissions hundreds of miles away, where they come down as acid rain, snow, and dust, making lakes too acid to support fish and damaging the health of forests. Smog, which forms when sunlight hits automobile and industrial emissions, hurts the lungs of humans and other animals. It causes billions of dollars worth of damage to pine trees, grapevines, citrus trees, and many other plants. It corrodes paint and tires, shortening their lives.

The impact pollution can be short-term if the Biosphere possesses enough capacity to absorb and transform pollutants. Sometimes humans assist in this process. Sewage treatment facilities sometimes make use of artificial marshes to purify wastewater, remove most pollutants, reoxygenate water, and destroy disease organisms. More often we simply dilute pollutant wastes in rivers or lakes, or hide them in landfills, from which they slowly leach out into nearby waters.

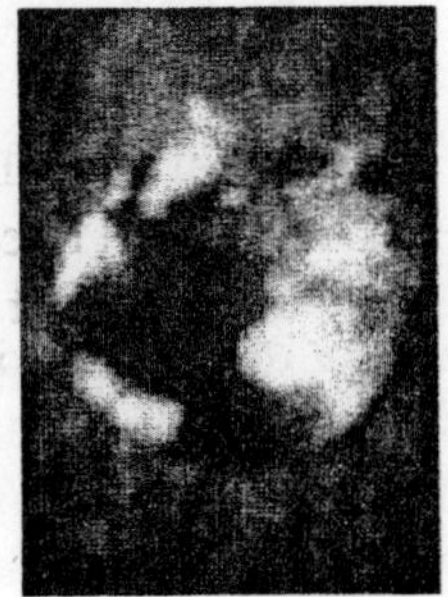

Pollutants increasingly overwhelm the biosphere's capacity to deal with them, and often have long-term consequences. Fish in the Great Lakes, in about 20 per cent of all our other lakes, and in 5 per cent of America's rivers, contain too many pollutants to be safely eaten. Widespread lead, from decades of using gasoline whose lead content was dispersed through exhausts, remains distributed over our soil. Lead is dangerous, especially for children, because it reduces brain development when it gets into the blood. Persistent residues· of pesticides, plastics, and other materials accumulate in body fat and disturb human's and other animals' hormone systems. Some radioactive wastes from nuclear bomb testing, power plants, and other sources will remain dangerous for tens of thousands of years. Long-continued pollution even affects evolution: it will eliminate organisms that cannot tolerance certain pollutants and favor others who can eat, use, or tolerance them.

Public pressure has led to regulations limiting certain industrial pollutant emissions. However, new unregulated polluting substances are constantly being developed, and the government agencies responsible for policing pollution regulations are weak and under funded. Companies often save money by continuing illegal pollution and paying minor, tax-deductible fines responsible go unpunished. Such economics harm thousands of people, not to mention their dire effects on other species, but because individual victims can seldom be identified with certainty, existing law does not threaten corporate economically with prison. Recently, green taxes on pollution as well as energy use have been proposed as a more workable means of reducing emissions. If citizens want a less polluted world, we must use political pressure to bring about such changes.

MODERN ENVIRONMENTALISM

The undesirable effects of pollution probably have been recognized at least as long as those of forest destruction. In 1273, King Edward I of England threatened to hang anyone burning coal in London because of the acrid smoke it produced. In 1661, the English diarist John Evelyn complained about the noxious air pollution caused by coal fires and factories and suggested that sweet-smelling trees be planted to purify city air. Increasingly dangerous smog attacks in Britain led, in 1880, to formation of national Fog and Smoke Committee to combat this problem.

The tremendous industrial expansion during and after the II World War added a new set of concerns to the environmental agenda. Silent Spring, written by Rachel Carson and published in 1962, awakened the public to the threats of pollution and toxic chemicals to humans as well as other species. The movement she engendered might be called environmentalism because its concerns are extended to include both environmental resources and pollution. Among the pioneers of this movement are activist David Brower and scientist Barry Commoner. Brower, while executive director of the Sierra Club, Friends of the Earth, and more recently, Earth Island Institute, introduced many of the techniques of modem environmentalism, including litigation, intervention in regulatory hearings, book and calendar publishing, and using mass media for publicity campaigns. Commoner, who was trained as a molecular biologist, has been a leader in analyzing the links between science, technology, and society. Both activism and research remain hallmarks of the modern environmental movement.

GLOBAL CONCERNS

Viewing the earth from space provides a powerful icon for the fourth wave of ecological concern that might be called global environmentalism. These photos remind us how small, fragile, beautiful, and rare our home planet is. We all share a common environment at this global scale. As our attention shits from questions of preserving particular landscapes or preventing pollution of a specific watershed or air-shed, we begin to worry about the life-support systems of the whole planet.

ENVIRONMENTAL MANAGEMENT SYSTEMS (EMSs)

Recognizing that environmental excellence is a good business strategy and a source of new opportunities, many organizations are implementing environmental management systems (EMSs) to improve economic and environmental performance. A new international EMS standard, ISO 14001, sets up an accepted model for an EMS. This article will describe the principles of an EMS and the elements of the ISO 14001 model. Following Figure illustrates, five major components comprise the

ISO 14001 EMS model. This model follows the total quality management cycle of Plan-Do-Check-Act that leads to continued improvement. Most organizations already have certain elements of an EMS in place, although their system may not be structured to follow the 14001 models. How can your organization implement or improve upon an existing EMS? ISO 14004 guidance document will accompany the standard, and many courses and workshops are currently being offered.

PRINCIPLES OF EMS

According to the draft ISO 14001 standards and ISO 14004 guidance, an EMS should be based upon the following principles:

1. Rank environmental management among corporate priorities;
2. Emphasize pollution prevention;
3. Establish communication within the organization and constituents;
4. Enhance management and employee commitment to environmental protection;
5. Encourage environmental planning throughout the life cycle of the product and/or process; and
6. Improve the EMS by proper auditing and review procedures.

EMS BENEFITS

Potential benefits of implementing an EMS include:

1. Demonstrated commitment to environmental goals;
2. Improved public/community relations;
3. Adherence to vendor certification requirements;
4. Enhanced market shares;
5. Improved operational efficiency;
6. Reduced environmental liabilities;

7. Conservation of resources;
8. Favorable insurance and loan status; and
9. Better industry-government relations.

MICROCLIMATE AND HABITAT

Microclimates on a larger scale, such as slope position and aspect (position relative to the sun), are of minimal influence to most plants and animals. What does affect them is the microclimate on an even smaller scale-what conditions are like on the side of shrubs and trees, in tree cavities and logs, beneath logs, stones, and leaf litter, and in caves.

Plants respond to microclimatic conditions. Unable to move, they depend on colonization of most favorable microclimatic sites. Herbaceous growth in a dense forest, for example, may be limited to micro-sites that are flooded with large flecks of sunlight. Some of the most pronounced micro-climatic effects on plants occur in areas of convex slopes and low concave surfaces. These places have much lower temperatures at night, especially in winter, much higher temperatures during the day, especially in summer, and a higher relative humidity. The concave surfaces radiate heat rapidly on still, cold nights, and air flows in from surrounding higher levels. The air temperature may be 8°C lower than surrounding terrain, causing a temperature inversion on a small scale. Because low ground temperatures in these areas tend to result in late spring frosts, early fall frosts, and a subsequent short growing season, these depressions are called frost pockets.

CLIMATE NEAR THE GROUND

On a summer afternoon the temperature under a calm, clear sky may be 28° C at 1.83 m (6 ft), the standard level of temperature recording. On or near the ground-at the 5 cm level—the temperature may be 5° C higher; and at sunrise, when the temperature for the 24 hour period is the lowest, the temperature may be 3° C lower at ground level.

The chief reason for the great differences between temperature at ground level and at 1.83 m is solar radiation. During the day in an open field, the soil, the active surface (where most solar energy is absorbed), absorbs solar radiation, which comes in short waves, and radiates it back as long waves to heat a thin layer of air above it. Because air flows at ground level is almost nonexistent, the heat radiated from the surface remains close to the ground. Temperatures decrease sharply in the air above this layer and in the soil below. The heat absorbed by the ground during the day is reradiated by the ground at night. This heat is partly absorbed by the water vapour in the air above. The drier the air, the greater is the outgoing heat and the stronger is the cooling of the surface of the ground and the vegetation. Eventually the ground and the vegetation are cooled to the new point, and water vapour in the air may condense as dew on the vegetation and ground. After heavy dew a thin layer of chilled air lies over the surface, the result of rapid absorption of heat in the evaporation of dew.

INFLUENCE OF THE SEA ON CLIMATE

Gardeners on the coast are often grateful for the sea breeze which cools their gardens in the afternoons. Holiday-makers are less appreciative, for what promises to be a fine day in the morning so often clouds over and becomes cooler later in the day. These changes occur because water, unlike land, is slow to heat and equally slow to cool. As the day advances the sun heats the land quickly while the sea remains cool. The hot air rises and draws in a cold sea breeze. In addition the rising air cool and condenses into cloud, giving relief to the gardener but disappointment to visitors.

ATMOSPHERIC MOISTURE OR HUMIDITY

Atmospheric moisture consists of both visible and invisible water vapours. The visible atmospheric moisture consists of fog, mist and clouds. The weight of water vapour per unit volume of air is absolute humidity and is measured in grams per cubic meter.

Atmospheric humidity is the amount of water vapours present in a unit volume of the air. It is expressed as relative humidity of R.H. Relative humidity is the percentage of water vapours actually present in the unit volume of the atmosphere at that temperature. Humidity is influenced by a number of factors like temperature, precipitation, latitude, wind velocity, soil moisture, soil cover and proximity to water bodies. Nearness to water bodies increases atmospheric humidity. Vegetation also does the same through transpiration, regular precipitation and higher altitude enhance humidity. Dry wind reduces the same.

The capacity of the atmosphere for holding water vapours doubles every 200° F. If the temperature is lowered, the humidity may increase to 100 per cent or even beyond saturation point. At this temperature the water vapours get condensed. Therefore, with the same humidity the warmer areas.

What is Global Warming?

Scientists have discovered that concentrations of minor greenhouse gases in the atmosphere, particularly carbon dioxide (CO_2), are rising. Theoretically, these gases could trap more heat in the atmosphere, leading to a gradual warming of the Earth's atmosphere and, again theoretically, global warming could be harmful to the environment and to human health.

Since the stakes are high, careful research and a deliberate response are called for. In 1997, representatives of the United States and other nations met in Kyoto, Japan, to negotiate a treaty to address the possible threat of global climate change. That treaty, called the *Kyoto Protocol,* would require the U.S. to reduce its greenhouse gas emissions—primarily carbon dioxide (CO_2), methane (CH_4), and nitrous oxide (N_2O) - to 7 per cent below 1990 levels by the year 2012.

Global warming has emerged as the most serious environmental threat of the 21st century. Most countries on earth are discussing environmental problems and how to limit them. Environmental problems on a global scale can originate from any corner of the world and affect all ecosystems on earth. Such problems directly or indirectly can affect human beings.

Global climate has large natural variability at all time and space scales and under natural normal conditions; farmers on earth can tune to the current climate and produce food sufficient for society. Climate change is greatest environmental challenge, which is facing mankind on earth. This climate change is rapid, continuous, and irreversible. It is called Global Warming.

CAUSES OF GLOBAL WARMING

The main cause of global warming is green houses gases. These are carbon dioxide, methane, nitrous oxide, chlorofluorocarbon (CFC's) and ozone. Generally, these gases are present in rather small amounts but play the major role in the heat balance of atmosphere due to their capacity to absorb infrared radiations. By preventing long wave thermal radiation from radiating out of the atmosphere, the temperature of the atmosphere thus increases considerably. The naturally occurring green house gases keep the earth warm enough to be habitable. Prior to the industrial revolution, the amounts of these gases remained constant over thousands of years. But amount of these gases is increasing due to increased industry and agriculture. A major factor of green house gases is their longevity in the atmosphere. Once they are emitted into atmosphere, they will persist for several decades as shown in table. In case of CFC's and nitrous oxides it takes over a century for them to degrade.

Another main cause of global warming is ozone depletion in outer atmosphere. Ozone layer protects biosphere from life-damaging high energy ultraviolet radiation. Ozone layer is depleting by gases such as CFCS. The CFCS are commonly used in spray cans, refrigerators, air conditioners, foam producing equipment, etc. Deforestation is also major problem. The major causes of deforestation are shifting cultivation, changing patterns of land use by conversion of forest areas to cash crops, building of infrastructure and land settlement.

IMPORTANT ASPECTS OF GLOBAL WARMING

1. Most scientists do not believe human activities threaten to disrupt the earth's climate;
2. The most reliable temperature data show no global warming trends;
3. Global computer models are too crude to predict future climate changes;
4. The IPCC did not prove that human activities are causing global warming;
5. A modest amount of global warming, should it occur, would be beneficial to the natural world and to human civilization;
6. Quickly reducing our greenhouse gas emissions would be costly and would not stop global warming; and
7. The best strategy to pursue is one of no regrets.

EARTH'S CLIMATE AND OPINION OF THE SCIENTISTS

Over 17,000 scientists have signed a petition saying, in part, there is no convincing scientific evidence that human release of carbon dioxide, methane, or other greenhouse gases is causing or will, in the foreseeable future, cause catastrophic heating of the Earth's atmosphere and disruption of the Earth's climate. A remarkable 89 per cent agreed that current science is unable to isolate and measure variations in global temperatures caused only by man-made factors. The most reliable temperature data show no global warming trend.

GLOBAL COMPUTER MODELS AND GLOBAL WARMING

Predictions of global climate change are based on general circulation models (GCMs), complex computer programs that attempt to simulate the Earth's atmosphere. The GCMs help scientists learn more about atmospheric physics, but they cannot predict future climates. The Intergovernmental Panel on Climate Change (IPCC) did not prove that human activities are causing global warming.

EFFECTS OF GLOBAL CHANGES

Climatic Effects

Work done with different climatic models shows there is scientific uncertainty about the effects of global change. However, work on these simulation models has agreed on many common things, including:

1. There will be a warming of the earth's surface and lower atmosphere and a cooling of stratosphere;
2. The warming trend over the earth's surface is varied. Warming in the tropics is smaller than the global mean by about 2-3° C depending on seasonal changes, which in other latitudes the average warming might account for 5-10° C increase in temperatures;
3. Precipitation patterns will be changed. Some areas will become wetter and some areas dryer;
4. Seasonal patterns will change due to the changing of temperature and precipitation patterns;
5. Soil moisture regimes will be changed due to the changes in evaporation and precipitation;
6. With the decrease in cloud cover over Eurasia in summer, which will enhance the solar heating of the surface and increase the land-sea temperature contrast, tropical monsoons will be driven with more severity and intensity; and
7. Wind direction and wind stress over the sea surface will be changed, which will alter ocean currents and cause change in nutrient mixing zones and productivity of the oceans.

RISE IN SEA LEVEL

In the absence of efforts to cut greenhouse-gas emissions, sea levels will rise by between 10 and 30 cm by the year 2030 and 30 to 100cm by the end of next century. The direct effects are:

1. Recession of shorelines and wetlands;
2. Increased tidal range and estuarine salt front intrusion; and
3. an increase in salt-water contamination of coastal fresh-water aquifers.

All the above effects have profound implication for human society, especially in the many coastal areas that are densely populated.

IMPACTS ON FORESTS

The Inter-governmental Panel on Climate Change or IPCC (a group of more than 2,500 of the world's leading scientists) has concluded that forests are highly sensitive to climate change and that up to one third of currently forested areas could be affected in some way. Conservation of forest habitats in a rapidly warming world will present us with new challenges, and is likely to be hardest in the places where these ecosystems are fragmented, polluted or under development pressure. Rapidly rising emissions of carbon dioxide and other greenhouse gases, such as methane, are having a dramatic impact on climate, both by raising average temperatures and by increasing extreme events such as droughts, floods and storms.

BIOTIC EFFECTS

The most important effect has been assumed to be the stimulation of the fixation and storage of carbon by terrestrial plants through the increase in carbon dioxide in the atmosphere. The hypothesis is that the CO_2 in the atmosphere speeds photosynthesis. The data show that increasing 'Concentrations of carbon dioxide often, but not always, increase the rate of growth of young plants. The most important consideration of biotic feedbacks is the ratio of grass production to total respiration globally. The effect of such transitions is to reduce the capacity of the Earth for supporting life, including people. The species favored in such transition are, first, those that are normally recognized as success ional, those that occur following disturbance. As the disturbance continues, these species are replaced by smaller-bodied, rapidly reproducing species of wide distribution.

EFFECTS ON HUMAN SETTLEMENTS AND SOCIETY

Worldwide, hundreds of millions of people would be displaced by the inundation of low-lying coastal plains, deltas, and islands in the next century if efforts to reduce greenhouse-gas accumulation in the atmosphere were unsuccessful. These would be jointed by countless millions displaced from the land as aridity and biotic impoverishment spread.

EFFECTS OF HUMAN HEALTH

Temperature-change may have an impact on several major categories of disease, including cardiovascular, cerebrovascular, and respiratory diseases. Climate may affect the respiratory tract in following three ways:

1. Seasonal effects;
2. Direct effects of specific weather-conditions, such as thunder-storms and cold fronts;
3. Combined effects of weather with other environmental or topographical factors.

The other diseases in tropics are malaria, trypanosomiasis, leishmaniasis, amoebiasis, ilariasis, onchocerciasis, schistosomiasis, and various worm infestations. The potential impact of climatic change on communicable disease is not likely to be limited to Third World. Even in an affluent country such as Australia, mosquito-borne disease may pose considerable threats to health, which will probably increase as a result of the greenhouse effects. Ultraviolet radiation is known to have effects on the immune system.

OTHER DISASTERS

In 1972, for instance, a dam collapsed in the U.S.A. leading to the deaths of 125 people and causing 4,000 to be homeless.

Traumatic neurotic reactions were found in 80 per cent of the survivors, and there was persistent evidence of unresolved grief, survivor shame, and feelings of impotent rage and hopelessness. Disabling psychiatric symptoms included anxiety, depression and changes in character and life-style. Over 90 per cent of the children who were interviewed had developmental problems more than two years after the disaster.

How Much One has to Pay?

It has also been suggested that quickly reducing our greenhouse gas emissions would be costly and would not stop global warming. The cost to only one country say for USA, for reducing and stabilizing only one greenhouse gas CO_2 to 93 per cent of 1990's levels would range from 2.4 million to 3.1 million jobs lost and an annual reduction in gross domestic product of between $177 billion and $318 billion.

CARRYING CAPACITY OF THE EARTH

An extreme estimate of the human carrying capacity of the Earth would consider only enough land and resources per person to provide basic necessities-food, water, clothing, and treatment of human wastes-and would not allow for amenities-wilderness, wildlife, scenery, recreational space. We can also imagine an *optimal carrying capacity*, which would provide a high standard of living for each individual and an environment that would enable the persistence of all other species present on the earth. An optimal carrying capacity would include ample areas for recreation, wilderness, wildlife, and other features that people enjoy. Between these extremes are many intermediate choices. Which do we want? What are we willing to accept?

Scientists try to determine which future carrying capacities are possible and what the environmental costs will be. What we choose is a matter of values. However, an intelligent, rational choice must not be based simply on feelings but on knowledge of what is likely, what is possible, and what the trade-offs are. Do we want those who follow us to live short lives in crowded, unhealthy surroundings, 'without the chance to enjoy the Earth's scenery and great diversity of life? Or do we hope that our descendants will have a life of high quality and good health?

Determining the earth's carrying capacity requires that we pursue topics from many fields of knowledge. In the past, calculations about the carrying capacity of the earth for people often ignored the ecological requirements for survival and, in a sense, focused simply on the physical space required for people to sleep. As discussed in detail, we now realize that any population is sustainable only if its habitat and its life requirements are available and in good condition.

PLACING A VALUE ON THE ENVIRONMENT

How do we place a value on some aspect of our environment? How do we choose between two different concerns? Environmental values can be based on four categories of justification: utilitarian, ecological, aesthetic, and moral. Two of these, utilitarian and ecological, concern practical reasons that have to do with our own survival or economic benefit. A utilitarian justification sees some aspect of the environment as valuable because it provides individuals with economic benefit or is directly necessary to their survival. For example, fishermen obtain their livelihood from the ocean and need a supply of fish so that they can continue to earn a living. An ecological justification is based on the value of some factor that is essential to larger life-support functions, even though it may not benefit an individual directly. For example, there is ecological value in dealing with the problem of burning lignite and poor quality coal in Eastern Europe. The polluted air that has resulted in parts of Poland, eastern Germany and the former Czechoslovakia may have shortened human life spans. As another example, burning coal and oil adds greenhouse gases to the atmosphere which may lead to a change in climate that could affect the entire earth, These ecological reasons form a basis for the conservation of nature that is essentially enlightened self-interest.

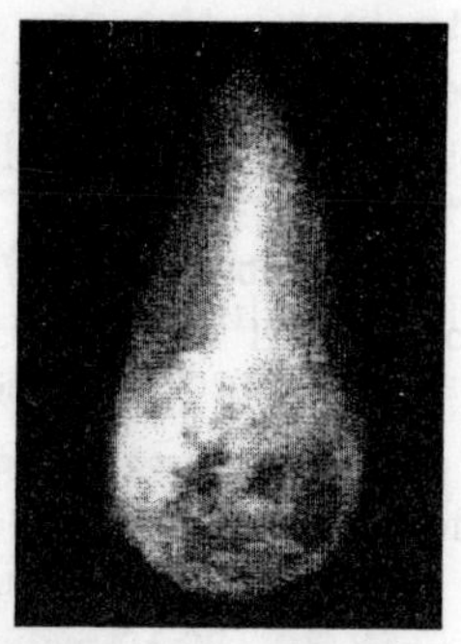

Aesthetic arguments have to do with our appreciation of the beauty of nature; For example, many people find wilderness scenery beautiful and would rather live in a world with wilderness than without it. The aesthetic justification is gaining a legal basis, the state of Alaska acknowledges that sea otters have an important role related to recreation people observe and photograph the otters and enjoy viewing them in a wilderness setting and many examples illustrate the importance of the aesthetic values of the environment. When people grieve following the death of a loved one, they typically seek out places with grass, trees, and flowers, and thus we decorate our graveyards, although popular discussions of environmental issues might make aesthetic justifications seem superficial in fact, beauty in their surroundings is of profound importance to people. Frederick Law Olmsted, the great American landscape planner, argued that plantings of vegetation provide medical, psychological, and social benefits and are essential to city life.

Moral justification has to do with the belief that aspects of the environment have a right to exist and that it is out moral obligation to allow them to continue or help them to persist. An example of a moral justification is the assertion that Nine Mile Prairie, located near Lincoln, Nebraska – one of the few remaining prairie preserves – has a right to exist. Moral arguments have been extended to many nonhuman organisms, to entire ecosystems, and even to inanimate objects, For example, the historian Roderick Nash has written an article entitled "Do Rocks Have Rights?" which discusses such moral justification. And the United Nations General Assembly World Charter for Nature, signed in 1982, states that species have a moral right to exist.

A new discipline known as environmental ethics analyzes these issues. Another concern of environmental ethics is our obligation to future generations – do we have a moral obligation to leave the environmental in good condition for our descendants, or are we at liberty to use environmental resources to the point of depletion within our own lifetimes?

In Czechoslovakia, poor air pollution controls and use of high pollutant fuels have created severe air pollution problems, at times requiring school children to wear masks.

How Do We Place a Value on a Piece of Nature?

Mount Monadnock, which stands alone in southwestern New Hampshire, provides a commanding 3600 view of the surrounding countryside. Sculpted by glaciers, its rocky slopes, except for the summit, are covered with spruce trees. In the early 1880s, a fire destroyed all vegetation at the summit, which remains bare rock to this day.

In the nearly 300 years since Europeans settled that part of New Hampshire. Mount Monadnock has been burned, logged, mined, and climbed. Hikers, including Hemy David Thoreau and Ralph Waldo Emerson, have always been attracted to Mount Monadnock, but in recent years it has become so popular that, at times, as many as 500 people can be found at the summit. Its attraction is its accessibility-a 2-hour drive from Boston and a 2-hour hike to the top and its wilderness character; its facilities are relatively primitive.

Overuse has caused erosion and damage to vegetation in and around the trails. In response, worried park officials and people from the nearby town of Jaffrey have proposed a controlled-use plan to be phased in over a 3 year period. This plan includes expanded parking areas, with a surface of gravel instead of soil new ranger stations, a campground, and possibly, a visitors' centre. Although the planners hope these improvements will not change the natural character of the park, some people fear that the very things that attract people to the park will cease to exist.

THE ATMOSPHERE, CLIMATE, AND GLOBAL WARMING

Earth's atmosphere is a dynamic system that is changing continuously while undergoing complex physical and chemical processes. After reading this chapter, you should understand:

- How urban areas affect local climate and produce an urban dust dome or heat island.
- How the climate has changed in major ways during the last million years, including an increase in the global mean annual temperature by approximately 0.5° C (0.9° F) over the last 100 years.
- Why there is considerable controversy and debate concerning whether we are now in or are entering a period of human-induced global warming.
- How human activity has resulted in increased emissions of greenhouse gases, such as carbon dioxide, chlorofluorocarbons (CFCs), methane, nitrous oxide, and ozone.
- How positive and negative feedback cycles in the atmosphere might affect global temperature change.

GLOBAL WARMING

The Greenhouse Effect

Global warming is defined as a natural or human induced increase in the average global temperature of the atmosphere near the earth's surface. The temperature at or near the surface of the earth is determined by four main factors:

1. The amount of sunlight the earth receives;
2. The amount of sunlight the earth reflects;
3. Retention of heat by the atmosphere; and
4. Evaporation and condensation of water vapour.

The sunlight that reaches the Earth warms both the atmosphere and the surface. The Earth's atmospheric system then reradiates the heat as infrared radiation. Water vapour and several other gases, including carbon dioxide, methane, and CFCs, warm the Earth's atmosphere because they absorb and reemit radiation. They trap some of the heat energy radiating from the Earth's atmospheric system. The trapping or warming is somewhat analogous to a greenhouse, which also traps heat: thus the process has been called the greenhouse effect. Actually, the process of trapping heat in the atmosphere might better be called the atmospheric effect, because the dominant process responsible for heating the air in a greenhouse is quite different from that which heats the lower atmosphere. Although some infrared radiation is trapped in a greenhouse, the dominant process responsible for warming the air is the restriction of cooling by air circulation (wind) because of the glass enclosure. Nevertheless, greenhouse effect has become the accepted term for the trapping of heat by the atmosphere. It is important to understand that the effect is in fact a natural phenomenon that has been occurring for millions of years on Earth as well as on other planets in our solar system. The majority of natural greenhouse warming is due to water in the atmosphere. On a global level, water vapour and small particles of water in the atmosphere produce about 85% and 12%, respectively, of our total greenhouse warming significantly

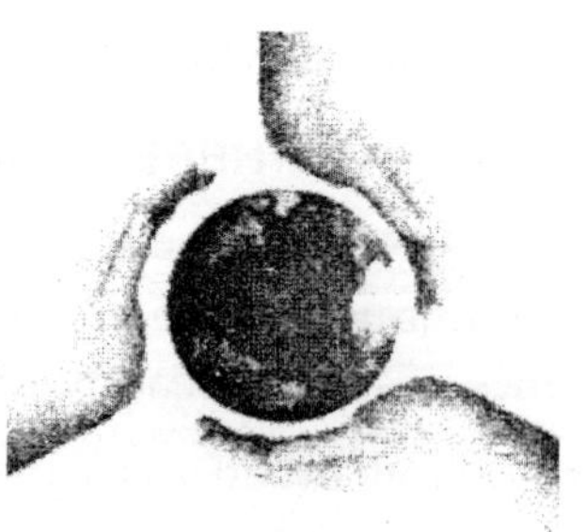

increasing in the atmosphere as a result of human-induced processes. The gases we are concerned with are those that result in part from anthropogenic processes-that is, those that result from human activities. These include carbon dioxide, CFCs, methane, nitrous oxides, and ozone, all of which have increased significantly in the atmosphere in recent years. CFCs are a group of inert, stable, human-made chemicals that are used as propellants in spray cans (deodorants, paints, etc.) and as the working fluid in appliances such as air conditioners and refrigerators. Use of CFCs as propellants for spray cans was banned in the United States in 1978 (CFCs are discussed in detail in, which addresses stratospheric ozone depletion).

We are not particularly worried about water vapour in the future because it is not because carbon dioxide, CFCs, methane, nitrous oxides, and ozone absorb infrared radiation emitted from the Earth it has been hypothesized that the Earth may be warming because of the increases of these anthropogenic greenhouse gases. Approximately 200 billion metric tons of carbon in the form of carbon dioxide enters and leaves the Earth's atmosphere each year as a result of a number of biological and physical processes. What we are concerned about in the following discussion is the anthropogenic greenhouse effect as it relates to two factors:

- The burning of fossil fuels adds 6 billion metric tons of carbon each year to the atmosphere, increasing the concentration of atmospheric CO_2; and
- Human activities that emit other greenhouse gases, such as CFCs, ozone, methane, and nitrous oxides.

A highly idealized diagram showing some of the important aspects of the greenhouse effect is presented in. The three arrows labeled "energy input" represents the energy from the sun absorbed at or near the surface of the Earth. The four arrows emitted from the upper atmosphere and the surface represents the energy output. Which balances the input consistent with the Earth's energy balance. The highly contorted lines near the surface of the Earth represent the absorption of infrared radiation occurring there and providing the 15° C (59° F) near surface temperature. Following many scatterings and absorptions and reemissions, the infrared radiation emitted from levels near the top of the atmosphere (troposphere) corresponds to a temperature of approximately -18°C (0°F). The one output arrow that goes directly through the Earth's atmosphere and is emitted represents the amount of outgoing radiation through what is called the *atmospheric window* wavelengths where natural greenhouse gases do not absorb very well. However, anthropogenic CFCs do absorb in this region. In other words, the atmospheric window (8-12μm) is centered on a wavelength of 10 μm and denotes the region where outgoing radiation from the Earth is not absorbed by water vapour or carbon dioxide, but is absorbed by CFCs. Therefore, CFCs significantly contribute to the greenhouse effect.

CHANGES IN GREENHOUSE GASES

The major anthropogenic greenhouse gases are listed in. The table also lists the recent growth rate in percent per year and the relative contribution in percent to the anthropogenic greenhouse effect.

CARBON DIOXIDE

Carbon dioxide has received a lot of attention with respect to global warming; 50% to 60% of the anthropogenic greenhouse effect is attributed to this gas. In order to evaluate recent changes in atmospheric carbon dioxide, we need to have a broader perspective of Earth's history. Ancient air may be sampled in glacial ice, which contains air bubbles, small samples of the atmosphere when the glacial ice formed. Measurements of carbon dioxide trapped in such air bubbles in the Antarctic ice sheet suggest that during the 160,000 years prior to the industrial revolution the atmospheric concentration of carbon dioxide varied from approximately 200 to 300 ppm. The highest level or concentrations of carbon dioxide in the atmosphere other than at present occurred during the major interglacial period about 125,000 years ago.

About 130 years ago, at the beginning of the industrial revolution, the atmospheric concentration of carbon dioxide was approximately 280 ppm, a level apparently constant for the previous 700 years. Beginning in about 1860, the concentration of carbon dioxide in the atmosphere has grown exponentially. Currently, the rate of increase of carbon dioxide in the atmosphere 1s about 0.5% per year; if it continues to grow at this rate, we will see a doubling of the concentration in approximately 140 years (recall the rule of thumb in . Data prior to the mid-twentieth century are from measurements of air trapped in glacial ice. The remaining data are from direct measurement from the monitoring station at Mauna Loa, Hawaii:

MONITORING OF ATMOSPHERIC CARBON DIOXIDE CONCENTRATIONS

Today the concentration of carbon dioxide in the atmosphere is approximately 350 ppm, and it is predicted that the level may raise to approximately 450 ppm by the year 2050-more than 1.5 times the preindustrial level. Compares the global emissions of carbon dioxide to the average concentration of the gas in the atmosphere. These data suggest a direct correlation between the emission of carbon dioxide and its concentration in the atmosphere.

It is interesting to note, however, that the rate of increase of carbon emissions (not carbon dioxide) from the burning of fossil fuels, deforestation, and other anthropogenic processes has been approximately 4.3% per year since the industrial revolution began-more than 8 times the 0.5% per year rate of increase in the concentration of carbon dioxide in the atmosphere.

The high rate of carbon dioxide emissions and the high growth rate of the emissions would seem to suggest that the increase in carbon dioxide in the atmosphere is a direct result of the anthropogenic input of carbon dioxide from sources such as burning fossil fuels and deforestation. Establishing this seemingly simple relationship as a fact has been very difficult, however, because the global carbon cycle is complex; all the linkages and flows of carbon from the various sources to sinks are not yet well understood. What is apparent is that if all the carbon dioxide produced by human activities remained in the atmosphere, the concentration of that gas should be even higher than it is today! Therefore, we must hypothesize that there are sinks for carbon dioxide in the oceans or on the land that are not identified or well understood. In spite of all these cautions and shortcomings it is clear that carbon dioxide concentrations in the atmosphere have increased significantly since the industrial revolution. Furthermore, it is a reasonable hypothesis (something we assume without proof) that these increases will continue to contribute to global warming via the greenhouse effect.

MONITORING OF ATMOSPHERIC CARBON DIOXIDE CONCENTRATIONS

Human activity and other life affect the characteristics of the earth's surface, waters, and atmosphere, even in areas that we believe are far removed from human activity and living things. For example, air pollutants, such as lead, and other artifacts of our urban society are found in glacial ice, and pesticides may be found in lakes far from agricultural areas. Air samples taken near the summit of Mauna Loa, Hawaii (one of the world's largest active volcanoes and the highest mountain in the world based on elevation change from base to top), have helped show another dimension of how life and human activity are affecting the atmosphere. Samples are taken at Mauna Loa because it is far from local, direct effects of human life and other biological activity. Because carbon dioxide is taken up by green plants during photosynthesis and released in the respiration of all oxygen-breathing organisms, a measure of the carbon dioxide in the atmosphere is analogous to a measure of the breathing in and out of all life on Earth.

The Mauna Loa data clearly demonstrate the benefits of long-term collection of information on how the Earth works. Funding for long-term projects is often difficult to maintain because funding agencies may prefer to sponsor new projects rather than long-term monitoring. Nevertheless, understanding global change depends on the collection and maintenance of supportive data. To that extent, the Mauna Loa CO_2 measurement project is unique, and its ef1ectiveness is a tribute to the people who initiated it and have nurtured it for more than 30 years.

Accepting that approximately 50% to 60% of the anthropogenic greenhouse effect is due to carbon dioxide, we can conclude that the remaining greenhouse gases must account for approximately 40% to 50% of the effect.

METHANE: METHANE

(CH_4), until 1991, was increasing in the atmosphere at a rate of approximately 1% per year, and it is thought to contribute approximately 12% to 20% of the anthropogenic greenhouse effect. As with carbon dioxide, there are important uncertainties in our understanding of the sources and sinks of methane in the atmosphere. Natural environments release methane into the atmosphere. Major contributors are termites, which produce methane as they process wood, and freshwater wetlands, where decomposing plants in oxygen-poor environments produce and release methane as a decay product. The several anthropogenic sources of methane include the burning of biomass (organic material such as logs), the production of coal and natural gas, and agricultural activities, such as the cultivation of rice and the raising of cattle. (Methane is released by anaerobic activity in flooded lands where rice is grown, and cattle expel methane gas as part of their digestive processes.) For unknown reasons the increase in atmospheric methane stopped in 1991 and 1992, possibly related to control of leaks in Russian natural gas systems.

CHLOROFLUOROCARBONS (CFCs)

CFCs are highly stable compounds that have been or are being used in spray cans as aerosol propellants and in refrigeration units-the gas that is compressed and expanded in the cooling unit. Although CFCs are no longer used in spray cans in the United States and many other countries, they are not yet banned worldwide. Deliberate release and accidental leaks of CFCs into the atmosphere in recent years have been considerable. The rate of growth of CFCs in the atmosphere in recent years has been about 4% per year . It has been estimated that approximately 15% to 25% of the anthropogenic greenhouse effect may be related to CFCs in the atmosphere. The potential global warming from CFCs is considerable, because they absorb in the atmospheric window (explained earlier), and each CFC molecule may absorb hundreds or even several thousand times more infrared radiation emitted from Eal1h than is absorbed by a molecule of carbon dioxide. Furthermore, because CFCs are highly stable compounds, their residence time in the atmosphere is long. Even if production of these chemicals is drastically reduced or eliminated within the next few years, their concentrations in the atmosphere will remain significant for many years, perhaps for as long as a century.

NITROUS OXIDE

Nitrous oxide (N_2O) is also increasing in the atmosphere and is probably contributing as much as 5% of the anthropogenic greenhouse effect. Anthropogenic sources of nitrous oxide include agricultural activities (application of fertilizers) and the burning of fossil fuels, Reductions in the use of fertilizers and the burning of fossil fuels would reduce emissions of nitrous oxide. However, this gas also has a long residence time; even if emissions were stabilized or reduced, elevated concentrations of nitrous oxide would persist for at least several decades.

In summary, carbon dioxide contributes between 50% and 60% of the anthropogenic greenhouse effect. The rest of the human-made effect comes from trace gases, the most important of which are the CFCs and methane. These trace gases contribute between 27% and 45% of the anthropogenic greenhouse effect and they have accumulated in the atmosphere at much faster rates than carbon dioxide. The Montreal protocol is an international treaty signed in 1987 by 24 countries to reduce and eventually eliminate the production of CFCs and to accelerate the development of alternative chemicals. The treaty calls for production of CFCs to be phased out by the year 2000. Many countries expect to achieve this goal prior to the deadline, because development and production of alternative chemicals has been more rapid than expected. If CFCs had not been regulated by the Montreal protocol, by the early 1990s they would have become the major contributor to the anthropogenic greenhouse effect. The reduced emissions are evidently responsible for the recent decrease in growth rates of atmospheric CFCs commonly used in refrigeration, air-conditioning, and aerosol propellants. It is hypothesized that if the growth continues to decrease atmospheric concentrations of these CFCs will peak before the year 2000 and then decline.

Is global warming occurring?

As stated earlier, there were a number of warm years in the 1980s, and 1990 was the warmest year on record to date. Furthermore, it appears that in the past several decades the mean global temperature has increased approximately 0.5° C (0.9° F). However, these two observations are not sufficient to conclude that global warming is occurring as a result of anthropogenic increases in greenhouse gases. The controversy is not about whether there is a greenhouse effect. The greenhouse effect is not controversial-its existence is one of the best-established principles of atmospheric science. And there is no doubt that anthropogenic processes have resulted in increased emissions of greenhouse gases, such as carbon dioxide, CFCs, methane, and nitrous oxide. Finally, there is good reason to argue that increases in carbon dioxide and other greenhouse gases are likely to be related to an increase in the mean global temperature of the Earth. Over the past 160,000 years there has been a strong correlation between the concentration of atmospheric CO_2 and global temperature. When CO_2 has been high temperature has also been high, and, conversely, low concentrations of CO_2 have correlated with a low global temperature. However, in order to further evaluate the issue of global warming we need to consider both the positive and the negative feedback that occur on the Earth, the sun, and in the atmospheric system.

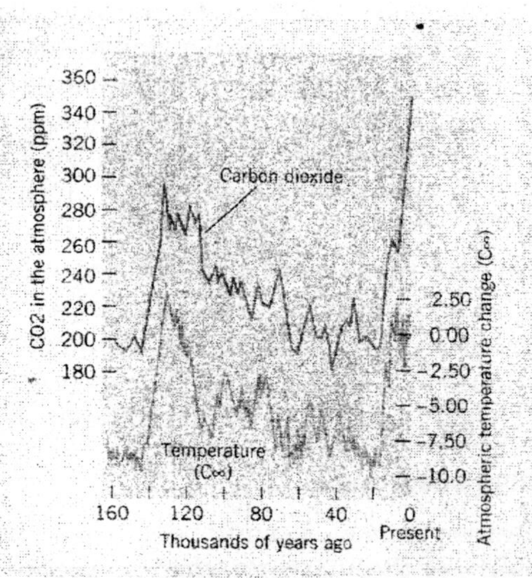

Greenhouse warming is very complex. The warming effect initiates both negative and positive feedback loops that can offset any temperature increase or raise it more. Negative feedback loops are self-regulating and result in global cooling in response to a warming circumstance. Positive feedbacks are self enhancing; thus a perturbation that causes an increase in global temperature leads to further increases in that temperature. We first discussed positive and negative feedback with respect to Earth systems and changes in you may wish to review those concepts.

Several of the potential negative and positive feedbacks concerning global warming are shown. It is important to remember that if the negative feedbacks are strong and persistent, global warming may not occur. On the other hand, if the negative feedback systems are weak relative to positive feedback, warming is likely to occur more readily.

The negative feedback is based on the hypothesis that as global warming occurs there will be an increase in the algae populations in the warming ocean. Algae will absorb more carbon dioxide, reducing the concentration of CO_2 in the atmosphere and causing cooling. Negative feedback is related to terrestrial vegetation. Here it is hypothesized that an increase in carbon dioxide concentration will stimulate plant growth (as it does in laboratory experiments), and the increased amount of vegetation will absorb more carbon dioxide from the atmosphere, facilitating cooling. Finally, negative feedback is related to cloud cover, which is poorly understood but extremely important. The idea is that as the global temperature increases more water will evaporate from the ocean, leading to more water vapour in the atmosphere and thus more clouds. Because clouds tend to reflect incoming solar radiation, the Earth will be cooled by the increased cloud cover.

Positive feedback processes are idealized in the warming Earth causes an increase in the evaporation of water from the oceans, which adds additional water vapour to the atmosphere. But here we look at a different effect of the water vapour-it causes additional warming (water vapour is an important greenhouse gas). The warming Earth causes increased melting of permafrost (areas where the soil, below an active zone that thaws in the summer, remains frozen from year to year) at high latitudes, which may result in additional release of the greenhouse gas methane, a by-product of decomposition of organic material in the melted permafrost layer. Another effect of the warming trend would be a reduction in the summer snow pack, which would reduce the amount of solar energy reflected from the Earth. Collectively these processes would result in additional warming, and thus are part of a positive feedback loop. In cycle the warming of the Earth is felt by people in urban areas, who use additional air-conditioning, thus increasing the burning of fossil fuels, which in turn releases additional carbon dioxide into the environment and results in additional global warming.

Both negative and positive feedback process occur simultaneously in the atmosphere. Which are more important? At present, the answer is not known. A great deal of research is currently being carried out on cloud negative-feedback processes.

Many discussions on the greenhouse effect state that if the Earth's atmosphere did not trap heat, our planet would be approximately 33°C (60°F) cooler at the surface, and as a result all water would be frozen. However, since water vapour is the major greenhouse gas in the atmosphere, no greenhouse effect implies no (or very little) water vapour in the atmosphere. Further, this implies no clouds, which would lead to a substantial reduction in the atmospheric reflection of incoming sunlight-which would result in warmer surface temperatures on Earth. The dual role of atmospheric water vapour as both a negative and a positive feedback with respect to global warming is extremely important to understanding possible climatic modifications created by an anthropogenic greenhouse effect.

There is vigorous debate among scientists as to whether global warming caused by human activities is in fact occurring. Some scientists believe that warming has indeed already started, whereas others suggest that the negative feedback cycles will be sufficient to moderate the effect in the future and that anthropogenic global warming will not be a serious problem. Until data are collected for many more years it may be difficult to prove whether global warming has occurred or is occurring. Nevertheless, all the global modeling experiments suggest that warming as a result of anthropogenic increases in greenhouse gases will in fact occur. Although some model studies suggest that the average global temperature could rise as much as 5° C (9° F) by the middle of the next century, most predict a smaller rise of 2° to 4° C (3.6°-7.2°F). In the most optimistic case, if there are large reductions in emissions of greenhouse gases, the global warming may be less than 1° C. The models on which global climate change is predicted are discussed in Earth System Science and Global Change. Despite the existence of such models, uncertainties related to sunspots, aerosols, nocturnal and daytime temperatures, volcanic eruptions, and El Nino events continue to cloud the issue of the anthropogenic greenhouse effect.

RISE IN SEA LEVEL

A rise in the sea level is a potentially serious problem as it relates to global warming. Although a precise estimate of the potential rise in sea level is not possible at this time, there is a consensus that the level of the sea will in fact rise. The causes for the rise are thought to be twofold: thermal expansion of warming ocean water (the primary cause) and melting of glacial ice (a secondly cause). The various models predict that the rise may be anywhere from 20 cm to approximately 2 m (8-80 in.) in the next century; the most likely rise is probably 20 cm to 40 cm (8-16 in.). Such a change will have significant environmental impacts; it could easily cause increased coastal erosion on open beaches of up to 50 to 100 m 065-230 ft), making buildings and other structures in the coastal zone more vulnerable to damage from waves generated by high-magnitude storms. It could also cause a landward migration of estuaries and salt marshes, putting additional pressure on human structures in the coastal zone. Finally, groundwater supplies for coastal communities may be threatened by saltwater intrusion should sea levels rise.

A rise in the sea level of approximately 1 m (3.3 ft) would have serious consequences. People would have to make significant alterations in the coastal environment to protect investments, and communities would be forced to choose between making very heavy financial investments in controlling coastal erosion and allowing for considerable loss of property.

Considering the amount of coastal defenses present in the world today, it seems inevitable that a rise in sea level will lead to further investment for protecting cities in the coastal zone. Construction of seawalls, dikes, and other erosion-controlling structures will become more common as coastal erosion threatens urban property, In more rural areas, where development is set well back from the coastal zone, the most likely response to a rising sea level will be simply to adjust to the erosion that occurs, coastal erosion is a difficult problem that is very expensive to deal with: it is prudent to allow erosion to naturally take place where feasible rather than to try to control it.

Finally, when considering a rise in the sea level we must be concerned with the hundreds of millions of people who live in low lying areas of developing countries. For example, two cyclones that hit Bangladesh in the past 25 years killed more than 400,000 people and caused over $16 billion in property damage, The double impact of a rising sea level and more frequent and powerful cyclones and other tropical disturbances (owing to warmer oceans, as discussed earlier) would have a devastating effect on people in developing countries.

LIVING WITH GLOBAL CHANGE

Given our present stage of understanding of global warming and trends in energy use and deforestation, it appears that the most likely adjustment will be learning to live with the changes; these include a warmer climate and new variability in weather patterns as well as a higher sea level. If the changes are relatively slow over a period of decades, learning to live with the new conditions may be quite feasible; in fact, in some cases the changes will offer opportunities as well as problems. However, it is emphasized that this may not be the best adjustment, because there may be many unexpected surprises and problems.

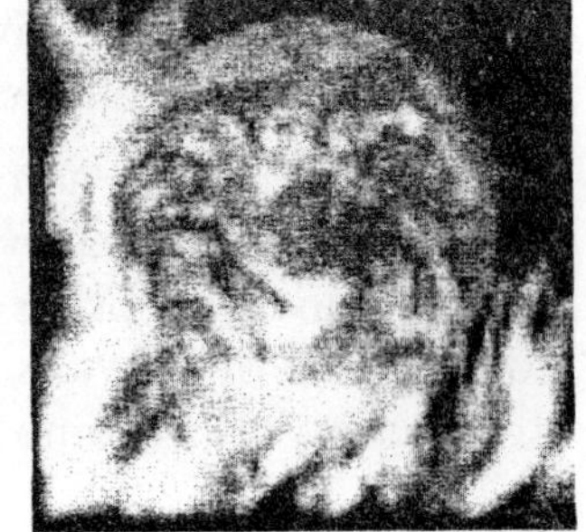

If the hypothesis that global warming is due in part to increases in the emissions of greenhouse gases is accepted, then reduction of these gases is certainly a primary management strategy, It is estimated that reductions of global emissions of carbon dioxide will have to be in the range of 20% to 50% if global warming and its accompanying changes are to be mitigated. Because approximately 70% of anthropogenic carbon dioxide emissions are related to the burning of fossil fuels, energy planning that relies more heavily on energy conservation and efficiency and use of alternative energy sources, such as solar power, wind power, and geothermal power, will reduce emissions, increased use of nuclear power would also reduce emissions of carbon dioxide into the atmosphere. Other ideas or possible policies to reduce emissions of carbon dioxide into the atmosphere include increasing the tax for using fossil fuels; providing economic incentives to increase the use of mass transit and decrease the use of automobiles; providing greater economic incentives to improve the development of energy-efficient technology; requiring higher fuel-economy standards for cars, trucks, and buses; and requiring higher standards of energy efficiency for appliances and buildings. Another important source of carbon dioxide emissions is deforestation. Burning forests to convert lands to agricultural purposes accounts for approximately 20% of the anthropogenic carbon loading into the atmosphere. Management plans that seek to minimize burning and protect the world's forests would help reduce the potential threat of global warming, as would plans to plant additional trees (reforestation).

In summary, if global warming occurs, our most likely adjustment will be to live with it. However, if we are prudent we will plan to reduce the emissions of carbon dioxide and other greenhouse gases into the atmosphere. Doing so will require changes in land management as well as changes in energy use. Of particular importance will be energy conservation, using energy more efficiently, and emphasizing alternative energy sources that don't release greenhouse gases into the atmosphere. These changes will also have other environmental benefits related to the availability of energy and natural resources. Essentially, we should reduce emissions of greenhouse gases into the atmosphere as much as is economically and politically feasible and have contingency plans for greater reductions in emissions should they become necessary. Thus, the recommended strategy is somewhere between full mitigation and learning to adapt to change.

Some people argue that there is consensus among scientists that global warming is now occurring. They might argue that the position taken in this chapter is too conservative, that the problem of global warming should be accepted as something we need to address now before it's too late. They might further argue that steps taken to abate global warming would have tremendous environmental benefits even if global warming doesn't occur. We would respond that the environmental need for energy conservation, reduction in air pollutants, and use of alternative energy sources is clear and need not be tied to the global warming issue.

TRUTH OF GLOBAL WARMING

The average facade temperature of the globe has augmented more than one degree Fahrenheit since 1900 and the speed of warming has been almost three folds the century long average since 1970. This increase in earth's average temperature is called Global warming. More or less all specialists studying the climate record of the earth have the same opinion now that human actions, mainly the discharge of green house gases from smokestacks, vehicles, and burning forests, are perhaps the leading power driving the fashion. The gases append to the

planet's normal greenhouse effect, permitting sunlight in, but stopping some of the ensuing heat from radiating back to space. Based on the study on past climate shifts, notes of current situations, and computer simulations, many climate scientists say that lacking of big curbs in greenhouse gas discharges, the 21st century might see temperatures rise of about 3 to 8 degrees, climate patterns piercingly shift, ice sheets contract and seas rise several feet. With the probable exemption of one more world war, a huge asteroid, or a fatal plague, global warming may be the only most danger to our planet earth.

GLOBAL WARMING CAUSES

As said, the major cause of global warming is the emission of green house gases such as carbon dioxide, methane, nitrous oxide etc into the atmosphere. The major source of carbon dioxide is the power plants. These power plants emit large amounts of carbon dioxide produced from burning of fossil fuels for the purpose of electricity generation. About twenty percent of carbon dioxide emitted in the atmosphere comes from burning of gasoline in the engines of the vehicles. This is true for most of the developed countries. Buildings, both commercial and residential represent a larger source of global warming pollution than cars and trucks.

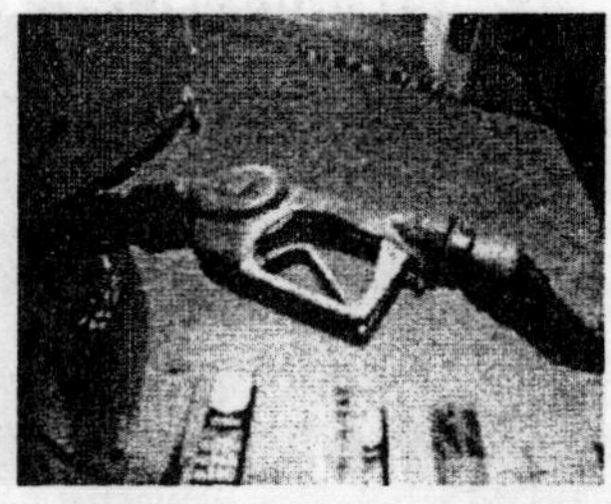

Building of these structures require a lot of fuel to be burnt which emits a large amount of carbon dioxide in the atmosphere. Methane is more than 20 times as effectual as CO_2 at entrapping heat in the atmosphere. Methane is obtained from resources such as rice paddies, bovine flatulence,

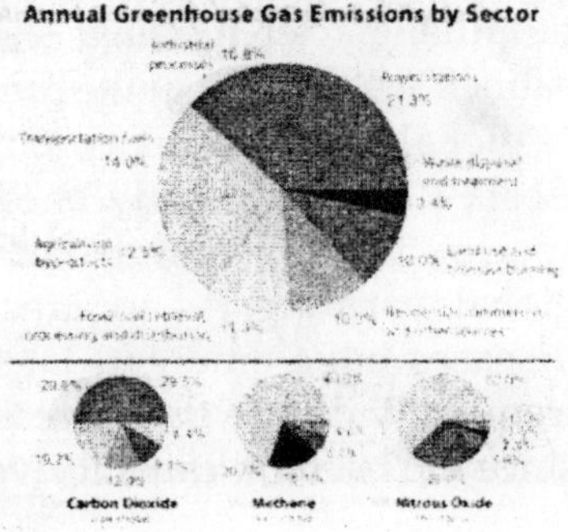

bacteria in bogs and fossil fuel manufacture. When fields are flooded, anaerobic situation build up and the organic matter in the soil decays, releasing methane to the atmosphere. The main sources of nitrous oxide include nylon and nitric acid production, cars with catalytic converters, the use of fertilizers in agriculture and the burning of organic matter. Another cause of global warming is deforestation that is caused by cutting and burning of forests for the purpose of residence and industrialization.

GLOBAL WARMING IS INSPIRING SCIENTISTS TO FIGHT FOR AWARENESS

Scientists all over the world are making predictions about the ill effects of Global warming and connecting some of the events that have taken place in the pat few decades as an alarm of global warming. The effect of global warming is increasing the average temperature of the earth. A rise in earth's temperatures can in turn root to other alterations in the ecology, including an increasing sea level and modifying the quantity and pattern of rainfall. These modifications may boost the occurrence and concentration of severe climate events, such as floods, famines, heat waves, tornados, and twisters. Other consequences may comprise of higher or lower agricultural outputs, glacier melting, lesser summer stream flows, genus extinctions and rise in the ranges of disease vectors. As an effect of global warming species like golden toad, harlequin frog of Costa Rica has already become extinct. There are number of species that have a threat of disappearing soon as an effect of global warming. As an effect of global warming various new diseases have emerged lately. These diseases are occurring frequently due to the increase in earth's average temperature since the bacteria can survive better in elevated tempera-tures

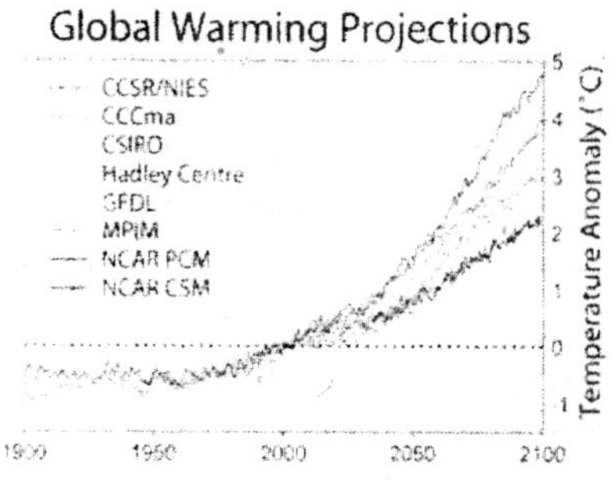

and even multiplies faster when the conditions are favorable. The global warming is extending the distribution of mosquitoes due to the increase in humidity levels and their frequent growth in warmer atmosphere. Various diseases due to ebola, hanta and machupo virus are expected due to warmer climates. The marine life is also very sensitive to the increase in temperatures. The effect of global warming will definitely be seen on some species in the water. A survey was made in which the marine life reacted significantly to the changes in water temperatures. It is expected that many species will die off or become extinct due to the increase in the temperatures of the water, whereas various other species, which prefer warmer waters, will increase tremendously. Perhaps the most disturbing changes are expected in the coral reefs that are expected to die off as an effect of global warming. The global warming is expected to cause irreversible changes in the ecosystem and the behavior of animals.

A group of scientists have recently reported on the surprisingly speedy rise in the discharge of carbon and methane release from frozen tundra in Siberia, now starting to melt because of human cause increases in earth's temperature. The scientists tell us that the tundra is in danger of melting holds an amount of extra global warming pollution that is equivalent to the net amount that is previously in the earth's atmosphere. Likewise, earlier one more team of scientists reported that the in a single year Greenland witnessed 32 glacial earthquakes between 4.6 and 5.1 on the Richter scale. This is a disturbing sign and points that a huge destabilization that may now be in progress deep within the second biggest accretion of ice on the planet. This ice would be enough to raise sea level 20 feet worldwide if it broke up and slipped into the sea. Each day passing brings yet new proof that we are now in front of a global emergency, a climate emergency that needs instant action to piercingly decrease carbon dioxide emissions worldwide in order to turn down the earth's rising temperatures and avoid any catastrophe.

It is not easy to attach any particular events to global warming, but studies prove the fact that human activities are increasing the earth's temperature. Even though most predictions focus on the epoch up to 2100, even if no further greenhouse gases were discharged after this date, global warming and sea level would be likely to go on to rise for more than a millennium, since carbon dioxide has a long average atmospheric life span.

YOU CAN HELP FIGHT GLOBAL WARMING

Many efforts are being made by various nations to cut down the rate of global warming. One such effort is the Kyoto agreement that has been made between various nations to reduce the emissions of various green house gases. Also many non profit organizations are working for the cause. Al Gore was one of the foremost U.S. politicians to heave an alarm about the hazards of global warming. He has produced a significantly acclaimed documentary movie called "An Inconvenient Truth," and written a book that archives his advice that Earth is dashing toward an immensely warmer future. Al Gore, the former vice president of United States has given various speeches to raise an awareness of global warming. He has warned people about the ill effects of Global warming and its remedies.

But an interesting side of the global warming episode is that there are people who do not consider global warming as something that is creating a problem. Skeptics of global warming think that global warming is not an ecological trouble. According to the global warming skeptics, the recent enhancement in the earth's average temperature is no reason for alarm. According to them earth's coastlines and polar ice caps are not at a risk of vanishing. Global warming skeptics consider that the weather models used to establish global warming and to forecast its impacts are distorted. According to the models, if calculations are made the last few decades must have been much worse as compared to actually happened to be. Most of the global warming skeptics believe that the global warming is not actually occurring. They stress on the fact the climatic conditions vary because of volcanism, the obliquity cycle, changes in solar output, and internal variability. Also the warming can be due to the variation in cloud cover, which in turn is responsible for the temperatures on the earth. The variations are also a result of cosmic ray flux that is modulated by the solar magnetic cycles.

GLOBAL WARMING SKEPTICS

The global warming skeptics are of the view that the global warming is a good phenomenon and should not be stopped. There are various benefits of global warming according to them. According to the skeptics, the global warming will increase humidity in tropical deserts. Also the higher levels of carbon dioxide in the atmosphere trigger plant growth. As predicted, due to the global warming the sea levels will rise. But this can be readily adapted. Another argument of global warming skeptics is that earth has been warmer than today as seen in its history. The thought is that global warming is nothing to get afraid of because it just takes us back to a more natural set of environment of the past. Animals and plants appeared to do just fine in those eras of warm climate on the earth. According to few skeptics, the present chilly climate on the earth is an abnormality when judged over the geographical scale. Over geologic time, the earth's mean temperature is 22° C, as compared to today's 15.5° C.

Global Warming: A Fact or Myth?

It is important to know the true facts about global warming. Because it is not a small or localized environmental problem, it is going to require international cooperation as well as personal change from all of us to stop global warming. In fact, it may be the largest challenge humanity faces in the 21st century. Unfortunately, it has also become a highly politicized issue. You need to especially carefully about the information concerning global warming— you can learn which facts are accepted by the scientific community and which are created by ill-informed or politic.

It is a fact, not a theory. Global warming is a measurable process that is already underway. Temperature changes, alterations in rainfall patterns, and an increased frequency of storms are occurring and being measured around the world as we speak. The evidence against global warming is not convincing in light of the effects we are witnessing already.

Warming is destroying ecosystems worldwide that you and other people depend on, according to a highly detailed new study conducted by scientists at the Goddard Space Institute. The study found a trend of change all over planet earth, including the "timing of plant flowering, bird nesting, ice melting, salmon migration and pollen release; declines in populations of polar bears, krill and penguins; and increased growth of Siberian pines and cool-water ocean plankton. This extensive study adds to the already voluminous evidence that global warming is real!

The Real Impact on Humans: *150,000 Dead Every Year*

Global warming has changed precipitation patterns around the world, disrupting traditional agricultural practices that you and the rest of the world depend on to live. The area of land on the Earth suffering from drought conditions has doubled since 1970. Insurance costs in the coastal areas of the United States have escalated dramatically. These are the effects you can see already, and climate change is only beginning to make itself felt. Climate-related deaths will double in 25 years according to a 2005 report from the World Health Organization. Climate change is already tied to 150,000 deaths globally every single year. These deaths are caused by more frequent heat waves and droughts, as well as by floods and more powerful storms linked warming has increased deaths in urban areas as heat waves have exacerbated the effects of smog and related respiratory problems.

WE CAUSE THE PROBLEM

The basic facts are well understood. Human activities are pumping increasing amounts of carbon dioxide, methane, and other heat-trapping greenhouse gases into the atmosphere. The elevated concentration of these gases is raising the temperature of the Earth's atmosphere, thereby warming the surface of the Earth. This process has been repeatedly demonstrated in laboratory experiments and is now being measured on the Earth as a whole.

INTERESTING EFFECTS ON WEATHER

Global warming does not mean a universal and uniform warming of planet Earth, nor does it mean the end of highly unpredictable weather patterns. However, weather patterns are the result of an enormously complex process, and the effects of global warming on this process could be horrific.

There is a lot of uncertainty about how the different "feedbacks" operate, given the complexity of global weather systems. There is concern that global warming could cause changes in massive ocean currents like the Gulf Stream, which is part of a global system referred to as the oceanic "conveyor" because it propels enormous volumes of heat around the world. If this happened, it would cause huge changes in global weather patterns.

The consequences will be enormous no matter which systems are disrupted first. Scientists are unsure about which systems in the world's climate — tropical currents versus polar currents, or events on land versus in the ocean — cause or trigger changes in other systems. Even though you may live in a relatively stable climate, at some point the ecosystem you live in is greatly affected by climates around the world.

Is Uncertainty a Cause for Doubt

Briefly, the answer is no. While we will never comprehend all there is to be known about such a vast and interdependent system, the larger trends are clear. You should use these uncertainties as a springboard for action, not a rationalization for further, unnecessary debate.

We must Act Soon

The most alarming danger is that once warming reaches a certain level, it could cause global climate and weather patterns to shift quickly and dangerously. We now have a fairly detailed understanding of the Earth's climate from the last 600,000 years and more. In the past, the climate has not changed slowly, nor has it changed in a linear, incremental fashion.

Abrupt changes dramatically alter life on Earth. Sudden shifts in temperature or ocean currents result when a certain amount of pressure to change is put in place. Ocean currents like the Gulf Stream that distribute heat and moisture around the world have historically changed course in a matter of a few years, or even a few months. The historical record has shown us the devastation this sort of change can wreak on entire ecosystems.

RUNAWAY GLOBAL WARMING

A Scientific Possibility

There is a chance we may trigger a runaway warming effect that would amplify itself uncontrollably. The most likely source of such runaway warming is the arctic tundra. In the Polar Regions, there are great expanses of tundra that have remained frozen year round for tens of thousands of years. These ice-locked fields contain enormous stores of organic matter. If these areas thaw, the decay of that organic matter will accelerate, releasing stored carbon and methane. That could create a powerful positive feedback loop catalyzing further warming. It could mean and end of life as we know it. Runaway warming could produce an Earth like the one that existed in the age of the dinosaurs: a steamy planet with sea levels hundreds of feet higher than they are now.

SPIKING CARBON DIOXIDE LEVELS

The scary fact is that we are seeing changes faster than any of the climate models had predicted, and that the rate of accumulation of greenhouse gases in the atmosphere is accelerating. Before the industrial revolution started pouring carbon dioxide into our atmosphere, the level of carbon in the air was about 275 parts per million (ppm). The average rate of carbon increase in the atmosphere from 1960 to 2005 was 1.4 ppm per year. But over the decade from 1995 to 2005, the average increase was 1.9 ppm per year, and in 2007 the increase leapt to 2.14 ppm. Carbon is accumulating in our atmosphere ever more quickly.

GROWTH IN METHANE LEVELS

In 2007, levels rose much faster than in previous years. Although there is much less methane than CO_2 in the atmosphere, methane is by far the more potent greenhouse gas per unit volume. Scientists are worried that this spike in methane levels may indicate that global warming is escalating the release of methane from the arctic tundra. This could be part of a positive feedback loop that will lead to further warming, as mentioned earlier. In spite of all the attention global warming has been getting lately, we are headed rather decisively in the wrong direction. That is why you have to act, and act now!

AMPLIFIERS: AEROSOLS

Small particles in the air (aerosols) may have warming or cooling effects, depending on their characteristics. Sulfate (SO_4) aerosol, for example, is light-coloured and reflects sunlight back into space. The cooling effect of volcanic aerosols from the Mt. Tambora eruption of 1815 caused North America's "year without a summer" in 1816. Sulfate aerosol is also produced by fossil fuel burning. Black soot, which is a familiar component of urban smog and smoke from wild fires, has the opposite effect. The dark particles absorb the Sun's energy in much the same way that dark asphalt roads become warm on sunny days.

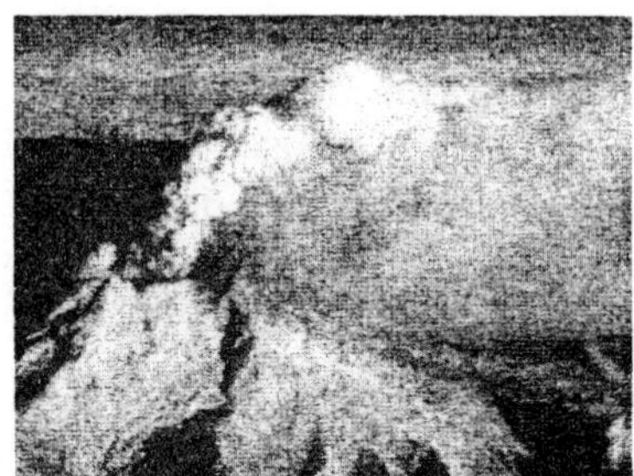

Aerosols can have Different Effects

Different types of small particles can have either warming or cooling effects. Sulfate aerosols released by volcanoes reflect sunlight and cool the Earth. Black soot released by smoke stacks and wild fires absorbs solar radiation and can warm the Earth. (Photo of Redoubt Volcano courtesy of USGS DDS-39).

AMPLIFIERS - CLOUDS

Like aerosols, clouds can either warm or cool the Earth, depending on their density and altitude. Their behavior demonstrates the intricate interactions at work within the climate system. Very small differences in clouds may produce large feedbacks. An increase in high, thin clouds produced by greenhouse warming would further increase the warming. This is because high, thin clouds are relatively effective in trapping infrared radiation (heat) while allowing the Sun's energy to pass through. In contrast, an increase in thick, low clouds could lessen the warming because these clouds reflect sunlight efficiently.

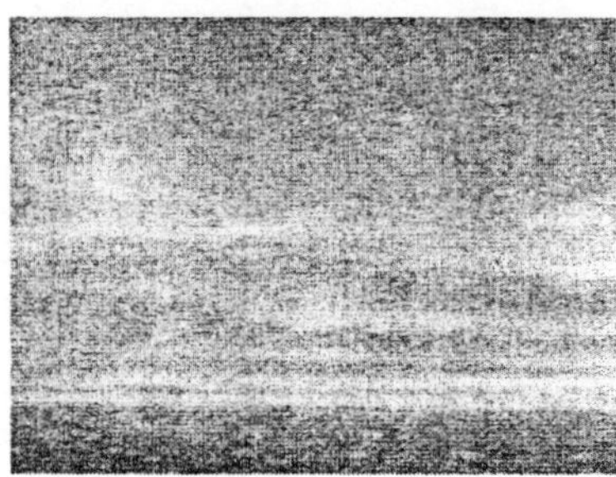

Clouds can have Different Effects

Although not completely understood, differences in clouds may produce large feedbacks in the climate. High thin clouds, such as cirrus clouds (left), may increase warming by trapping infrared radiation, while thick low-level clouds (right) may cool the Earth by reflecting sunlight. Changes in clouds result from changes in the distribution of water vapour, temperature, and winds. The effects of global warming on these factors are complex and not well understood. In addition, aerosols may also play a role in cloud formation. Tiny aerosol particles can "seed" clouds by providing the "nuclei" around which cloud droplets are formed. High concentrations of some aerosol types may affect the character of clouds by causing many tiny droplets to form rather than a few big ones. Clouds with more tiny droplets reflect more solar energy and tend to produce less rainfall.

AMPLIFIERS: WATER VAPOUR

Today, water vapour produces two-thirds of the world's greenhouse effect. All of the other gases – carbon dioxide, methane, nitrous oxide, halocarbons, etc. – contribute the other third. The effect of water vapour is so significant that the global average temperature would be below freezing without it. Warm air can contain more moisture than cold air. This is the basis of the water vapour feedback. As the atmospheric temperature rises and the amount of water vapour increases, the greenhouse effect is enhanced, further increasing temperature. The water vapour feedback is critical for producing the glacial/interglacial cycles. Uncertainty in the magnitude of the water vapour feedback is an important source of uncertainty in projecting future climate warming.

A COMMON SOURCE OF CONFUSION

Does the water vapour added to the atmosphere by cooling towers and smokestacks contribute to global warming?

These sources are tiny compared to natural evaporation from the land and ocean. However, the water vapour feedback is important in increasing water vapour concentration and the greenhouse effect.

AMPLIFIERS: ICE-REFLECTIVITY FEEDBACK

Ice-free surfaces tend to absorb more solar energy than ice-covered surfaces. Therefore, snow and ice cover have a cooling effect on the Earth. If global warming reduces the global snow and ice cover, the warming will be enhanced because more solar energy will be absorbed. This ice-reflectivity feedback does not operate in Polar Regions during the winter, when it is always dark or the Sun is very low in the sky. Ice-covered surfaces reflect more solar energy than ice-free surfaces. If global warming reduces global snow and ice cover, the warming will be enhanced because more solar energy will be absorbed.

CO_2 AND OTHER GREENHOUSE GAS VARIATIONS

Many natural and human-made gases contribute to the greenhouse effect that warms the Earth's surface. Water vapour (H_2O) is the most important, followed by carbon dioxide (CO_2), methane (CH_4), nitrous oxide (N_2O), and the chlorofluorocarbons (CFCs) used in air conditioners and many industrial processes. The increasing atmospheric CO_2 concentration is likely the most significant cause of the current warming. Other greenhouse gases along with other factors discussed in the following sections also contribute.

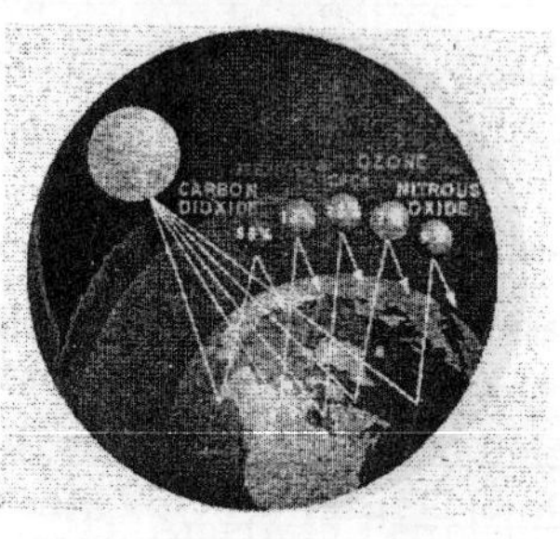

IMPORTANCE OF HUMAN-PRODUCED GREENHOUSE GASES

The above diagram shows the relative importance of the major human-produced greenhouse gases to current warming. CO_2 is the most important followed in descending order by methane, CFCs, ozone and nitrous oxide.

HUMAN ACTIVITY AND GREENHOUSE GASES

The world's economy runs on carbon: the "fuel" in fossil fuels. Coal, oil, and natural gas contribute energy to nearly every human endeavor in industrialized nations, and carbon dioxide

(CO_2) is a by-product of burning these fuels. Immediately eliminating CO_2 emissions would literally stop the industrial world. This graph illustrates how thoroughly fossil fuels and CO_2 emissions are integrated into American life.

In 1997, different sectors of the U.S. economy emitted millions of metric tons of carbon dioxide. Industry was the largest contributor, producing 610 million metric tons. Transportation emitted 470 million metric tons, residential 300 million metric tons, and commercial 280 million metric tons. Agriculture was also a contributor, with 120 million metric tons of carbon dioxide emitted.

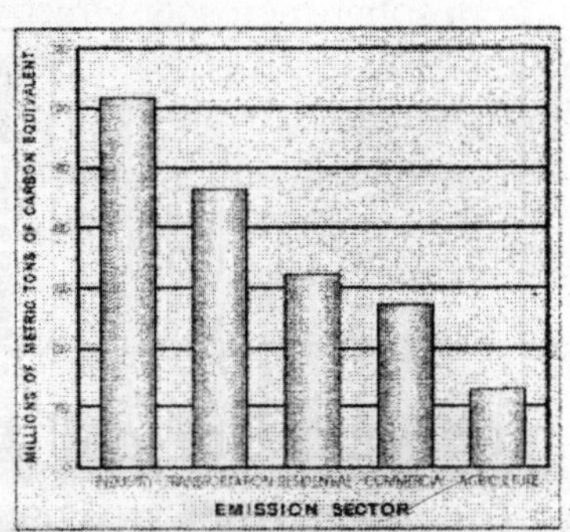

U.S. Greenhouse Gas Emissions by Sector, 1997

The CO_2 contributes more to the recent increase in greenhouse warming than any other gas. CO_2 persists in the atmosphere longer and longer as concentrations continue to rise. Other chemicals such as methane, nitrous oxide, and halocarbons also contribute to the global greenhouse effect. A number of additional chemicals related to urban pollution, such as low-level (tropospheric) ozone and black soot, can have a strong regional and perhaps global warming effect. Sulfate aerosols may have a cooling effect.

CONTRIBUTIONS OF ATMOSPHERIC GASES AND SOLAR RADIATION TO WARMING

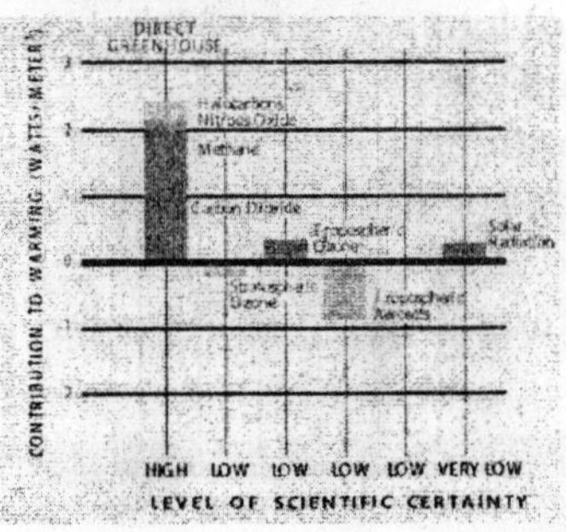

Scientists have esti-mated the contribution to warming made by a range of gases, dust and solar radiation. They have a high level of certainty that greenhouse gases contribute the most to warming, with increases in CO_2 as the greatest contributor with about 1.4 watts/metre^2 and methane, nitrous oxide, and halocarbons making smaller contributions. Scientists have a lower level of certainty about the contributions of reductions in stratospheric ozone and increases in troposphere aerosols, which cool the Earth by 0.3 watts/metre^2 and 0.9 watts/metre^2 respectively. Solar radiation may also contribute to warming but scientists have a very low certainty about the level of this contribution.

OCEAN CIRCULATION

Direct Effect of Oceans on Climate

The atmospheric circulation (winds) and ocean currents carry heat from the tropics toward the poles. Many processes can alter these circulation patterns, changing the climate regionally or even over the whole world. Interactions between the ocean and atmosphere can also produce phenomena such as El Niño, which tends to recur every two to six years. Changes in deep ocean circulation can produce longer-lived climate variations that endure for decades to centuries. The ice age cycles may have been influenced by changes in ocean circulation arising from changes in the Earth's orbit around the Sun.

OCEAN CIRCULATION

Cold water sinks at the poles and travels throughout the world's oceans. It gradually warms, becomes less dense and mixes to the surface. It then moves back towards the poles carrying heat absorbed along the way. Then the cycle continues. Without this cycle the poles would be colder and the equator would be warmer.

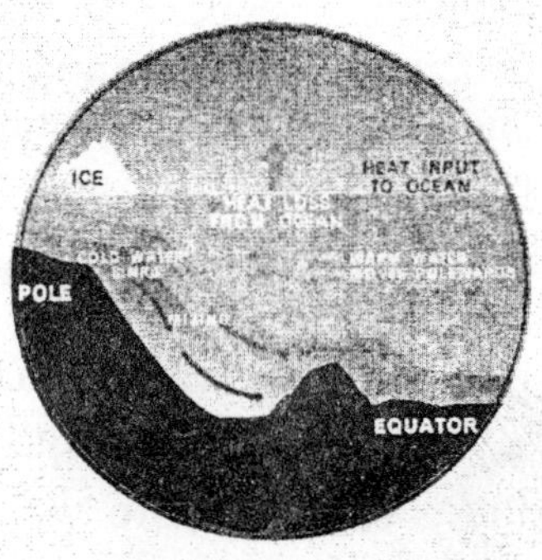

Ocean Circulation

EFFECT OF OCEANS ON GREENHOUSE GASES

The oceans play an important role in determining the atmospheric concentration of CO_2. CO_2 gas in the atmosphere and CO_2 dissolved in the ocean surface reach a balance. Changes in ocean circulation, chemistry, and biology have shifted this balance in the past. Such changes may affect climate by slowly moving CO_2 into or out of the atmosphere. Orbital Variations. Slow changes in the Earth's orbit lead to small but climatically important changes in the strength of the seasons over tens of thousands of years. Climate feedbacks amplify these small changes, thereby producing ice ages.

ECCENTRICITY

Earth's orbit oscillates very slightly between nearly circular and more elongated every 100,000 years. This cycle is evident in the glacial/interglacial cycles of roughly the same period.

ORBITAL ECCENTRICITY

The Earth's orbital path varies in the degree to which it is circular. This change in its "eccentricity" varies between 0.00 and 0.06 on a 100,000 year cycle. When the eccentricity equals 0.00 the orbital path is circular and when it is 0.06 the orbital path is slightly elliptical. The current value is 0.0167.

Orbital Eccentricity

TILT

The Earth spins around an axis that is tilted from perpendicular to the plane in which the Earth orbits the Sun. This tilt causes the seasons. At the height of the Northern Hemisphere winter the North Pole is tilted away from the Sun, while in the summer it is tilted toward the Sun. The angle of the tilt varies between 22° and 24.5° on a cycle of 41,000 years. When the tilt angle is high, the Polar Regions receive less solar radiation than normal in winter and more in summer.

Earth's Tilt

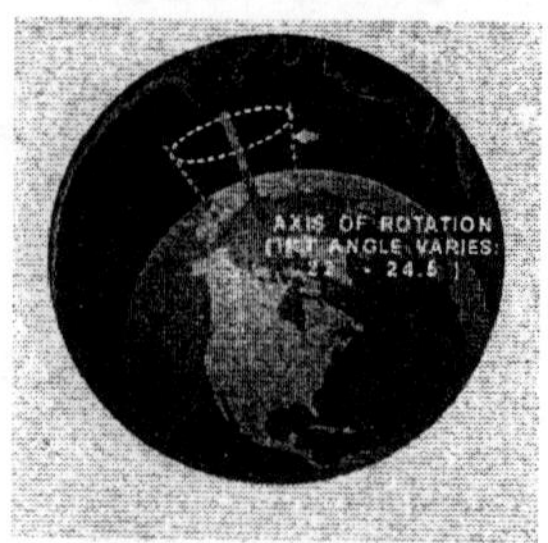

The Earth is tilted from perpendicular in its orientation to the Sun. This tilt varies from 22° to 24.5° on a 41,000 year cycle. The current tilt is 23.3°.

WOBBLE

There is a slow wobble in the Earth's spin axis, which causes the peak of winter to occur at different points along the Earth's elliptical orbital path. This variation in the seasons occurs on an approximately 23,000-year cycle.

Wobble of the Earth's Spin Axis

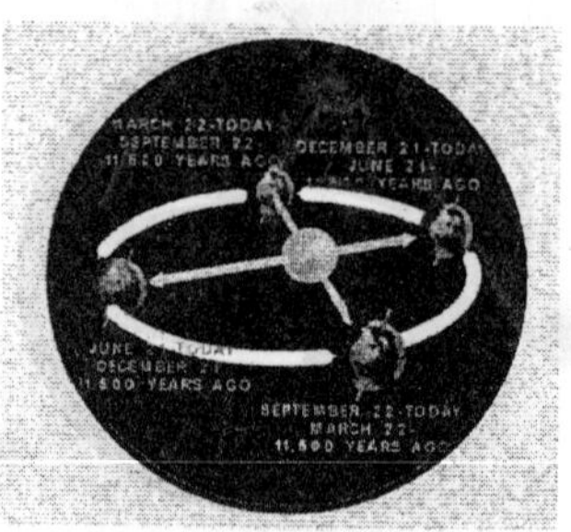

The Earth's axis of rotation wobbles like a top on a 23,000 year cycle. This causes the Earth's seasons to reach their maximum at different distances from the Sun due to the elliptical shape of the Earth's orbit.

REDUCING OTHER GREENHOUSE GASES

Bessy's Stomachs

Methane is the second most significant cause of greenhouse warming, behind carbon dioxide. Bessy, the science cow, and her many brothers and sisters are one of the greatest methane emitters. Bessy's grassy diet and multiple stomachs cause her to produce methane, which she exhales with every breath. The sheer size of her herds makes a significant contribution to global warming.

Bessy the Science Cow

Bessy and her cow friends are one of the world's greatest methane emitters. Cows exhale methane, which is a byproduct of the digestion of their grassy diet.

Livestock lead rice-growing, gas-flaring, and mining in global emissions of this highly potent greenhouse gas. Options for reducing methane emissions go beyond reducing beef and dairy consumption. These mitigation strategies also include reducing methane emissions from mines, gas production facilities, and landfills.

SOLAR VARIATIONS

The Sun is the source of energy for the Earth's climate system. Although the Sun's energy output appears constant from an everyday point of view, small changes over an extended period of time can lead to climate changes. Some scientists suspect that a portion of the warming in the first half of the 20th century was due to an increase in the output of solar energy. Learning how the Sun changed before modern instruments were available is not easy, but it appears that changes in the output of solar energy have been small over the last million years, and probably even longer.

Volcanic Eruptions

A volcanic eruption may send ash and sulfate gas high into the atmosphere. The sulfate may combine with water to produce tiny droplets (aerosols) of sulfuric acid, which reflect sunlight back into space. Large eruptions reach the middle stratosphere (19 miles or 30 kilometers high). At this altitude, the aerosols can spread around the world. A massive volcanic eruption can cool the Earth for one or two years. The 1982 El Chichon eruption and the 1991 Pinatubo eruption caused the globally averaged surface temperature to cool less than 1° F.

Volcanic Eruptions

A volcanic eruption may send ash and sulfuric acid (SO_2) into the atmosphere, which increases planetary reflectivity causing atmospheric cooling. Over time precipitation will remove these aerosols from the atmosphere. Volcanic eruptions can have a worldwide impact.

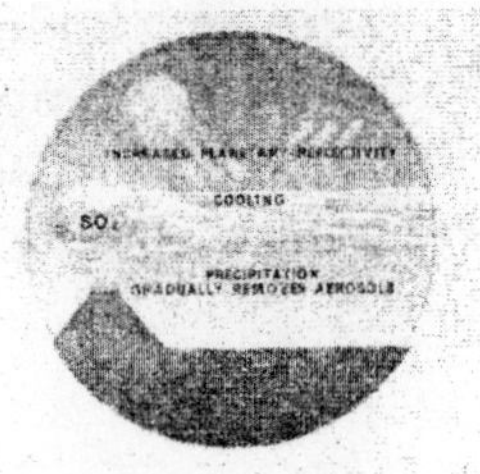

Land-use Changes

Deforestation can significantly increase the amount of atmospheric CO_2, which warms the planet.

Land-use Changes

Urban environments create islands of heat from industry, buildings, automobiles, and the absorption of solar energy by dark-colored surfaces.

Land-use Changes

It's A Global Issue

Climate warming is a global problem but the impacts and potential solutions will affect us locally and in many different ways. The challenge for each of us and for our policy makers is to pursue effective responses that are as fair as possible to all people and nations. In this exhibition the National Academies provide scientific information to help us make informed decisions and to help answer some important questions.

A growing body of evidence indicates that humans now have a significant impact on climate. Nevertheless, it is difficult to identify humans as the only cause of a particular weather event or local climate change.

The general retreat of mountain glaciers during the past century is one example of evidence that the climate is changing.

1928	1979	2003
South Cascade Glacier, Washington	South Cascade Glacier, Washington	South Cascade Glacier, Washington

Will Planting Trees Offset Global Warming?

Some scientists, foresters, environmentalists, and government officials have suggested that planting trees may ease the threat of global warming. Trees take up carbon dioxide during photosynthesis and can store carbon for long periods of time. It is an enticing proposal, since it does not require that we stop doing anything, such as driving large cars, and requires only a simple biological solution, which would have other advantages, such as shading buildings, improving the aesthetics of urban areas, and providing more wood, a renewable resource.

Who could argue against planting a tree? Or even millions or billions of tree? But if we are to ask millions of people to plant billions of trees we should do so only if we are confident that they will have a substantial effect on reducing carbon dioxide in the atmosphere. According to current estimates, humans are adding 5 gigatons (1 gigaton equals 1 billion metric tons, or 1.1 billion U.S. tons) of carbon, as carbon dioxide, to the environment each year, almost entirely a result of burning fossil fuels. About 60% of that, or 3 gigatons, goes into the atmosphere. What happens to the remaining 2 gigatons is controversial; some scientists think it is absorbed by the oceans; others think it is absorbed by the forests; still others think that both the oceans and the forests are involved.

Living trees contain on the order of 500 gigatons of carbon, the atmosphere 700 gigatons as carbon dioxide, and soils an estimated 2000 to 4000 gigatons of carbon. Each year, the trees of the world remove about 5 gigatons of carbon through photosynthesis and return an equal amount to the atmosphere through respiration and decay. The forests of the world occupy an area of 4 Gha (1 Gha, a gigahectare. equals 1 billion ha, or 2.5 billion acres). Annual rates of deforestation are estimated at 0.2% (0.008 Gha, or 8 million ha, or 19.8 billion acres), a rate of 1 ha every 4 seconds.

FUTURE STRATEGIES

Future greenhouse gas emissions depend on the development pathways driven by economic, demographic, land use, agricultural and energy drivers. The interactions among these key driving forces are very complex, and have profound regional specificity. The galloping population growth of many countries in the Afro-Asian region acts as an important catalyst to the emission of GHGs. India, which has only 2.5% of the total global land area, supports population of about 1.1 billion. There is tremendous population pressure on the limited resources within the country, be it the land availability for agriculture, water resources, or energy for consumption. Developing countries must make genuine efforts to contain the unbridled population growth to ensure sustained development of the society.

There is a need for greater promotion of use of renewal sources of energy such as wind, water, and solar energy. India is the fourth largest producer of wind energy with total wind power potential of over 45000 MW. There are at present large number of wind mills operating in Tamil Nadu that generate electricity to cater to the power needs of the local industries. Simple measures such as switching over to compact fluorescent lamp (CFL) from the conventional light bulb, and larger use of solar energy for household consumption will go a long way in creating awareness about the need for conserving energy and thereby cutting down the GHG emission.

Pollution curbing measures such as compliance of Euro/ Bharat emission norms for the different categories of vehicles, banning use of leaded petrol, reduction of sulphur in diesel vehicles, and court mandated conversion of all commercial passenger vehicles - buses, three wheelers and taxis to CNG (compressed natural gas) in Delhi and elsewhere in the country have brought about significant improvements in vehicular emissions in many urban centers in India. There is exigency to ensure strict compliance of the emission norms for different categories of vehicles to curb the vehicular pollution in towns/ cities across the country.

Notwithstanding the skepticism over the prevailing notion of global warming, if humanity along with the other flora and fauna has to survive on this planet, all nations - developed and developing must make sincere endeavor to strike balance between the two or else we are heading for major breakdown of the ecosystems of our mother planet in the coming years.

CLIMATE CHANGE WILL WREAK HAVOC ON HEALTH

(Elderly and the young will be the most affected)

It is high time we take note of the changing climate and do something before it takes a toll on our health. The World Health Organization (WHO) is placing health at the centre of global dialogue by making it the theme of the World Health Day, April 7. This follows an overwhelming scientific consensus that climate change is happening and is human induced, making it one of the most critical challenges of our time. If the increase in greenhouse emissions continues at the current pace, air quality will suffer greatly and respiratory illnesses will worsen. Lack of safe water will most probably trigger outbreaks of diarrhea and other food and water-borne diseases.

The objective of World Health Day 2008 is to catalyze public participation in the global campaign to protect health from the adverse effects of climate change. This is an opportunity for the international agencies, non-governmental organizations, and governments as well as WHO to: Establish links between climate change and health and other development areas such as environment, food, energy, transport; Hold events/activities in countries to publicize issues related to the impact of climate change on health; Involve as wide a spectrum of the world population as possible in efforts to stabilize climate change; Create advocacy campaigns for generating momentum that compels governments, the international community, civil society and individuals to take action; Protect poor and vulnerable populations from the effect of climate change.

HEALTH HAZARDS

Health hazards from climate change are diverse and global in nature. The hazards range from higher risks of extreme weather events to changes in the dynamics of infectious diseases. Many of the leading killer diseases are sensitive to climatic conditions; their incidence and spread are likely to be affected by changing weather patterns.

The health impacts of climate change are already evident in different ways: more people are dying from excessive heat than before, changes are occurring in the incidence of vector-borne diseases, and the pattern of natural disasters is altering.

These impacts will be disproportionately greater in vulnerable populations, which include the very young, elderly, medically infirm, poor and isolated populations. Vulnerability is also high in:

Areas with a high endemic of climate-sensitive diseases, severe water scarcity, and low food production.

FUNDAMENTAL RIGHT TO LIVE IN A HEALTHY AND LEGISLATION ENVIRONMENT

Legislative Framework

In India, none of the existing environmental laws have any direct reference to electronic waste or refer to its handling as hazardous in nature. However, several provisions of these laws may apply to various aspects of electronic waste. Since e-waste or its constituents fall under the category of 'hazardous' and 'non-hazardous waste', they shall be covered under the purview of The Hazardous Waste Management Rules, 2003. India is also a signatory to the Basel Convention on the Control of Tran boundary Movements of Hazardous Wastes and their disposal. It covers all discarded/disposed materials that possess hazardous characteristics as well as all wastes considered hazardous on a national basis.

In April 2008 Ministry of Environment and Forests has issued 'Guidelines for environmentally sound management of e-waste'. The spirit behind these guidelines is to address sustainable development concerns in accordance with the National Environment Policy (NEP), 2006. It focuses on need to facilitate the recovery and/or reuse of useful materials from waste generated from a process and/or from the use of any material thereby, reducing the wastes destined for final disposal and to ensure environmentally sound management of all materials.

It also lays down that under Rule 3, "Definitions", of "The Hazardous Waste Management Rules, 2003, e-waste in Indian context can be defined as "Waste Electrical and Electronic Equipment including all components, sub-assemblies and their fractions except batteries, falling under Schedule 1, Schedule 2 and Schedule 3 of these rules. The objective of these Guidelines is to provide guidance for identification of various sources of waste electrical and electronic equipments (e-waste) and prescribed procedures for handling e-waste in an environmentally sound manner. These guidelines are reference document for the management, handling and disposal of e-waste. They provide the minimum practice required to be followed in the management of e-waste.

HISTORY OF ENVIRONMENTAL PROTECTION IN ANCIENT INDIA

An appraisal of the historical background to environmental protection in India would indicate that forests and wildlife were considered as vital ingredients of the global system. Here, the entire scheme of environmental preservation was essentially duty-based. In this sense, the ancient Indian society accepted the protection of the environment as its duty to do so.

HINDU ERA

Opening up the Hindu mythology, the *Vedas, Puranas, Upanishads* and other ancient scriptures of the Hindu religion have given a detailed description of trees, plants, wildlife and their importance to people. *Yajnavalkya Smriti* prohibited the cutting of trees by prescribing punishment for such acts. Kautalya's *Arthashastra,* written in the Mauryan period, realized the necessity of forest administration and Ashoka's 5th Pillar Edict expressed his view about the welfare of creatures in the State. Evidence from civilizations of Mohenjadaro and Harappa has further proved that the small population lived in consonance with the ecosystem and their needs maintained harmony with the environment. Thus, the Hindu society was conscious of the adverse environmental effects caused by deforestation and extinction of animal species.

MUGHAL ERA

In Islam, there is close harmony between man and nature. However, during the medieval period, the only contribution of Mughal emperors has been the establishment of magnificent gardens, fruit orchards and green parks, which were used as holiday resorts, palaces of retreat or temporary headquarters during the summer season. The common opinion of environmentalists has been that the Mughal emperors though were great lovers of nature and took delight in spending their spare time in the lap of natural environment, made no attempts on forest conservation.

BRITISH ERA

The British conquest in India brought about a plunder of natural resources coupled with a complete indifference towards environmental protection. A general survey of early environmental legislation reveals that apart from the forest laws, nineteenth century legislation also partially regulated two other aspects of Indian environment, water pollution and wildlife. These laws, however, had a narrow purpose and limited territorial reach.

Some of the early efforts include the enactment of the Shore Nuisance (Bombay and Kolaba) Act of 1853 and the Oriental Gas Company Act of 1857. The Indian Penal Code, enacted in 1860, imposed a fine on a person who voluntarily fouls the water of any public spring or reservoir. In addition, the Code penalized negligent acts with poisonous substances that endangered life or caused injury and proscribed public nuisances. Laws aimed at controlling air pollution were the Bengal Smoke Nuisance Act of 1905 and the Bombay Smoke Nuisance Act of 1912. In the field of wildlife protection, early legislation was limited to specific areas and particular species, thereby aiming at the conservation of biodiversity.

It is clear that legislative measures were taken by the British Government for prevention of pollution and for conservation of natural resources. Although critics point out that the British enacted these legislations, not with the object of protecting the environment but with the aim of earning revenue for themselves, it should be regarded as the first step towards the scientific conservation of natural resources. Despite the fact that these measures were made with ulterior motives, British-enacted legislations have contributed significantly to the growth of environmental jurisprudence in India.

WORLD SUMMIT ON SUSTAINABLE DEVELOPMENT

The World Summit on Sustainable Development was held at Johannesburg, where after 10 years of the Rio Conference, the

Summit reaffirmed sustainable development as a central element of the international agenda and gave new impetus to global action to fight poverty and protect environment. The Summit's plan of implementation is a seventy-one page document that is intended to set the world's environmental agenda for the next ten years and is expected to be a model for future international agreements. The plan of implementation aims at building further on the achievements made at UNCED and make commitment to undertake actions and measures at all levels to implement Rio principles and Agenda 21.

IMPACT IN INDIA

In the early years of Indian independence, there was no precise environmental policy. Government tried to make attempts only from time to time as per the growing needs of the society. The period of 1970s witnessed a lot of changes in policies and attitudes of the Indian Government when its attitude changed from environmental indifference to greater and subsequently, manifold steps were taken to improve environmental conditions.

NATIONAL COMMITTEE ON ENVIRONMENTAL PLANNING AND COORDINATION

The year 1972 marks a watershed in the history of environmental management in India. This is because prior to 1972, environmental concerns such as sewage disposal, sanitation and public health were dealt with by different federal ministries and each pursued these objectives in the absence of a proper coordination system at the federal or the intergovernmental level. When the 24 UN General Assembly decided to convene a conference on the human environment in 1972, and requested a report from each member country on the state of environment, a Committee on Human Environment under the chairmanship of Pitambar Pant, member of the Planning Commission, was set up to prepare India's report. With the help of the reports, the impact of the population explosion on the natural environment and the existing state of environmental problems were examined.

By early 1972, it had been realized that unless a national body was established to bring about greater coherence and coordination in environmental policies and programmers and to integrate environmental concerns, an important lacuna would remain in India's planning process. Consequently, as a result of the major issues highlighted by the reports, a National Committee on Environmental Planning and Coordination (NCEPC) was established in the Department of Science and Technology.

The NCEPC is an apex advisory body in all matters relating to environmental protection and improvement. At its inception, the Committee consisted of 14 members drawn from various disciplines concerning environmental management. Most of the non-official members were specialists. The Committee was to plan and coordinate, but the responsibility for execution remained with various ministries and government agencies.

ENVIRONMENTAL LEGISLATIONS

As part of its campaign on green environment, Indian Parliament has enacted nation wide comprehensive laws. One of the major environmental enactments came just two years after the Stockholm Conference in 1974. The Water (Prevention and Control of Pollution) Act was passed for the purpose of prevention and control of water pollution and for maintaining and restoring the wholesomeness of water. The Water Act represented India's first attempt to deal with an environmental issue from a legal perspective.

From this period onwards, the Central Government has been considered as highly environmentally active. In 1976, the Constitution of India was amended to insert a separate fundamental duties chapter. The 1980s witnessed the creation of many eco-specific organizations. In the year 1980, the Forest (Conservation) Act was passed for the conservation of forests and to check on further deforestation. The Air (Prevention and Control of Pollution) Act of 1981 was enacted by invoking the Central Government's power under Article 253. The Air Act contained several distinguishing features. The preamble of the

Air Act explicitly reveals that the Act represents an implementation of the decisions made at the Stockholm Conference. Also, a notification relating to Noise Pollution (Regulation and Control) Rules was made in the year 2000 with the objective of maintaining Ambient Air Quality Standards in respect of noise.

In the wake of the Bhopal gas tragedy, the Government of India enacted the Environment Protection Act, 1986 (EPA). The laws that existed prior to the enactment of EPA essentially focused on specific pollution (such as air and water). The need for a single authority which could assume the lead role for environmental protection was answered through the enactment of EPA. It is in the form of an umbrella legislation designed to provide a framework for Central Government to coordinate the activities of various central and state authorities established under previous laws. It is also in the form of an enabling law, which delegates wide powers to the executive to enable bureaucrats to frame necessary rules and regulations.

Apart from this, several notifications and rules have also been made, some of which include the Hazardous Wastes (Management and Handling) Rules in 1989, the Biomedical Wastes (Management and Handling) Rules in 1998, Recycled Plastics (Manufacture and Usage) Rules 1999, Environment (Silting for Industrial Projects) Rules 1999 and the Municipal Solid Wastes (Management and Handling) Rules in 2000.In addition to these eco-specific legislations, realizing that there is no comprehensive legislation dealing with biodiversity in India, and to fulfill its international obligation under the Convention on Bio-Diversity, the Government of India has enacted the Biological Diversity Act, 2002.

It is a paradox that despite the presence of such diverse laws, the pollution rate has crossed the dead line. This is probably because of the reason that the law is so complicated and vague that even the expert may not know the intricacies of it.

CONSTITUTIONAL MANDATE ON ENVIRONMENTAL PROTECTION

The Constitution of India originally adopted, did not contain any direct and specific provision regarding the protection of natural environment. Perhaps, the framers of the Indian Constitution, at that time, considered it as a negligible problem. That is probably why it did not even contain the expression environment. However, in fact it contained only a few Directives to the State on some aspects relating to public health, agriculture and animal husbandry. These Directives were and are still not judicially enforceable.

Nevertheless, on a careful analysis of various provisions prior to the 42nd Constitutional Amendment, reveals that some of the Directive Principles of State Policy showed a slight inclination towards environmental protection. It can be inferred from Art 39(b), Art 47, Art 48 and Art 49. These directive principles individually and collectively impose a duty on the State to create conditions to improve the general health level in the country and to protect and improve the natural environment.

Regarding the expression material resources of the community present in Art 39(b) it was held in *Assam Sillimanite Ltd. v. Union of India* that material resources embraces all things, which are capable of producing wealth for the community. It has been held to include such resources in the hands of the private persons and not only those, which have already vested in the State.

The Supreme Court in Municipal Council, Ratlam v. Vardhichand observed that:

> The State will realize that Art 47 makes it a paramount principle of governance that is steps taken for the improvement of public health as amongst its primary duties.

From these Articles, one can understand that the Constitution of India was not as environmentally blind as suggested by some eminent jurists. Though the word environment was not expressly used in the Constitution, the object of the above Articles was to conserve the natural resources, thereby protecting the environment. However, it must be accepted that only with the strengthening of public interest litigations and an enhanced commitment from the Central Government during the late 1970s, did an expansion of constitutional provisions to include aspects relating to the environment take place.

ROLE OF JUDICIARY

The judiciary, to fulfil its constitutional obligations was and is always prepared to issue appropriate orders, directions and writs against those persons who cause environmental pollution and ecological imbalance. This is evident from a plethora of cases decided by starting from the *Ratlam Municipality Case*. This case provoked the consciousness of the judiciary to a problem which had not attracted much attention earlier. The Supreme Court responded with equal anxiety and raised the issue to come within the mandate of the Constitution.

FUNDAMENTAL RIGHT TO LIVE IN A HEALTHY ENVIRONMENT

Man's paradise is on earth; this living world is the beloved place of all; it has the blessings of Nature's bounties: Live in a lovely spirit. - *Atharva Veda* (5.30.6)

The right to live in a clean and healthy environment is not a recent invention of the higher judiciary in India. The right has been recognized by the legal system and the judiciary in particular for over a century or so. The only difference in the enjoyment of the right to live in a clean and healthy environment today is that it has attained the status of a fundamental right the violation of which, the Constitution of India will not permit.

It was only from the late eighties and thereafter, various High Courts and the Supreme Court of India have designated this right as a fundamental right. Prior to this period, as pointed out earlier, people had enjoyed this right not as a constitutionally guaranteed fundamental right but as a right recognized and enforced by the courts under different laws like Law of Torts, Indian Penal Code, Civil Procedure Code, Criminal Procedure Code etc. In today's emerging jurisprudence, environmental rights which encompass a group of collective rights are described as third generation rights.

Right to Environment – Derived from the Right to Life Right to life, implies the right to live without the deleterious invasion of pollution, environmental pollution, environmental degradation and ecological imbalances. Everyone has the right to life and a right standard of living adequate for health and well-being of himself and of his family. States should recognize everybody's right to an adequate standard and to continuous improvement of living conditions. Thus, inherent right to life shall be protected by law.

Principle 1 of the declaration of UN Conference on Human Environment, 1972 proclaimed that man has the fundamental right to freedom, equality and adequate conditions of life in an environment of a quality that permits a life of dignity and well being. After this Stockholm Declaration, references to a right to decent, healthy and viable environment was incorporated in several Global and Regional Human Rights Treaties and in resolutions of International Organisations.

Right to Environment - As a Fundamental Right guaranteed in Indian Constitution. Environmental values or rights may be constitutionalised either explicitly by amending the constitution or implicitly by interpreting the existing constitutional language to include environmental protection. Immediately after the Stockholm Declaration, there was a growing trend in national legal systems to give constitutional status to environmental protection. India followed in the pursuit by amending the Constitution to include environment specific provisions in 1976. The birth of right to environment was the direct result of an inclusion these additional provisions.

The Indian Supreme Court, being one of the most active judiciaries in the world, also created a landmark in the quest of international judicial activism by developing the concept of right to healthy environment as a part of right to life under Art 21 of our Constitution. Article 21 reads as follows:

> No person can be deprived of his life and personal liberty except according to the procedure established by law.

Thus, in India, the higher judiciary has interpreted Article 21 to give it an expanded meaning of including the right to a clean, safe and healthy environment. Class actions have been entertained by the Supreme Court under Article 32 of the Constitution as being part of public interest litigation actions. The High Courts, also being granted this jurisdiction under Article 226 have intervened by passing writs, orders and directions in appropriate cases, thereby giving birth to an incomparable environmental jurisprudence in the form of the constitutional right to healthy environment. A chronological analysis of the environmental mission of the courts has been undertaken in order to explicate the development of the ideology of right to environment as being part of the right to life in the Indian context.

THE "POLLUTER PAYS PRINCIPLE"

This Principle makes the polluter liable to pay compensation and the costs to remedy the environmental harm caused. This Principle is considered to be the most efficient way of allocating costs of pollution prevention and control measures introduced by the Public Authorities to encourage rationale use of scarce environmental resources.

Principle 16 of the Rio Declaration states that:

> "National Authorities should endeavor to promote the internalization of environmental cost and the use of economic instruments, taking into account the approach that the polluter should, in principle, bear the cost of pollution, with regard to the public interest and without distorting international trade and investment".

According to Article 2(2)(b) of the 1992 Convention for the Protection of Marine Environment in the North East Atlantic, the Polluter Pays Principle means that:

> "the costs of pollution prevention, control and reduction measures are to be borne by the polluter".

According to this Principle the polluters should pay for the expenditure of pollution control measures such as, the cost of running anti-pollution installations, the investment in anti-pollution installations and equipment and introduction of new processes, so that a necessary environmental quality objective is achieved.

INTERGENERATIONAL EQUITY AND RESPONSIBILITY

Sustainable Development as defined in "Our Common Future" is closely associated with the goal of Intergenerational Equity. Sustainable development recognizes each generation's responsibility to be fair to the next generation, by leaving an inheritance of wealth no less than they themselves had inherited. At a minimum, meeting this goal will require emphasizing the sustainable use of natural resources for subsequent generations and avoiding any irreversible environmental damage.

The concept in intergenerational responsibility has been important since the 1972 Stockholm Conference on the human environment.

Principle 1 of the Stockholm Declaration proclaims that "man bears a solemn responsibility to protect and improve the environment for present and future generations". After being repeated in many difference contexts intergenerational responsibility was reaffirmed at the UN Conference on Environment and Development held at Rio as a Central component of the shift to sustainable development.

Principle 3 of the Rio Declaration states that:

> "the right to development must be fulfilled so as to equitably meet development and environmental needs of present and future generations".

ENVIRONMENTAL HAVOC AND ITS LEGISLATIONS

EIA: Water (Prevention and Control of Pollution) Act, 1974

The concept of environmental impact study still remains alien to the India Law. Water Act of 1974 does not envisage such a study before the Board decides to grant or not to grant consent. The Board has no statutory obligation to examine the environmental impact either of proposed or of an existing industrial activity causing pollution.

The State Board can impose binding conditions on the nature and composition, temperature, volume, rate of discharge of effluent when it grants consent. The people are not involved in inquiry prior to the granting of consent or imposing of conditions. Even afterwards people were not permitted to know the nature of conditions. They are not given an opportunity to have any say on the conditions imposed which granting consent. Access to registers of conditions maintains by the Board is also restricted. This register can be inspected only by a person interested in, or, affected by the outlet or effluent in the land or premises, or by another person authorized by such person.

Declaration of Control Zone: No provision is made to consult the people before a control zone is declared by the State Government which excluding any area from the application of the Act. True that the State Board is consulted or the declaration made on the recommendation of the Board. Only for altering any such area where notification in the official Gazette is necessary, this signifies a limited public participation.

Prosecution by a Member of Public: Control of pollution being a matter of interest not only to the Board but also the public in general, a member of public should have the right to see that the provisions of the Act are implemented properly. The Water Act confers their right on a member of public only to a limited extent. He can prosecute the polluter only after giving a 60 days notice perhaps this may be to give Board an opportunity take appropriate action within the period.

Appeals by a member of the Public: The Act does not confer on a member of public the right of appeal against an order of the Board. Only a person aggrieved by an order of the State Board can file an appeal within 30 days from the date on which the order is communicated to him.

EIA: THE ENVIRONMENT (PROTECTION) ACT, 1986

The Environment (Protection) Act, 1986 although a step ahead in adoption a comprehensive policy of environmental protection lacks in build in mechanism of preventing and controlling repetition of similar pollution tragedies. It is true that this Act contain significant provisions. The power to issue binding direction for regulation. Closure, prohibition of industry, to operation or process and for the stoppage or regulation of supply of electricity or water or any other service to the industry is a potent weapon of control of environmental pollution. But the law does not provide for any mechanism making it compulsory to make an Environment Impact study before a measure affecting the environment is given permission. In other words we do not have an environmental policy which strikes at the source and thus prevents evil but do still follow a policy of trying to cushion the impact of environmental change already taking place.

The late eighties and early nineties have witnessed a few attempts in India towards evolving mandatory model and a better regime of environmental protection. In 1987, by an amendment of factories legislation the states were empowered to appoint site appraisal committee, to examine proposals of initial location or expansion of factories involving hazardous process and to advise the Governments.

Hazardous Waste (Management and Handling) Rules, 1989 framed under the Environment Act, provided for an environmental impact study before identifying a site for waste disposal in a state but this responsibility of making the study to the State government person authorized by it. In the beginning of the year 1992, the ministry of Environment and Forests issued a significant draft notification. It had provisions for industrialization of EIA and preparation of Environment Management Draft plan for the prevention, elimination or mitigation of the adverse impact right from the inception of a project. Under the notification a new development project or expansion or modernization of existing industry shall not be undertaken unless it has been accorded an environmental clearance in accordance with the procedure specified in the notification.

Preliminary site clearance from Central Government is also necessary for four kinds of Industries, namely mining, pithead thermal power stations, hydro-electric power projects and multipurpose river valley projects before initiating any instigation involving cutting of trees, drilling digging or construction of any sort temporary or permanent. The project report should include EIA report and EIA plan prepared in accordance with the guidelines of Ministry of Environment and Forest. Consisting of experts including ecologists, social, scientists and representatives of Non-government organization (NGOs), the impact assessment agencies for Central and State Governments, envisaged under the notification shall make recommendations based on technical assessment of documents and date collected during their visits to site or factory and inter-action with affected population and environmental groups.

EIA: "BHOPAL": A VICTIM OF DISCRETIONARY MODEL

The Bhopal gas tragedy, a typical example of mishap born out of legal vacuum, points to the grave consequences of the lacuna in the legal system following on administrative discretionary model and high-lights the need for a mandatory model of an open Environmental Impact Assessment.

The licensing mechanism existing in India are too weak and ill-equipped to consider an environmental impact study as a sine qua non for granting a license. No law makes it compulsory for the license granting authority to have environmental impact assessments before license is granted. No rules framed in pursuance of law lay down a mandate for the government or other agencies to have a prior study of the impact of a proposed action affecting environment. Bhopal catastrophe discloses tragedy - the tragedy of a legal regime which did not provide for a mandatory EIA. It does not strike at the source and prevent the evil but instead. Make an attempt to cushion the impact of environmental assaults after damage was already done. EIA rooted on the principle of prevention rather than cure should not remain alien to Indian Law.

The mystery attached to the procedure and resultant absence of public scrutiny, the preclusion of judicial review the influence of political consideration in decision-making the lack of sufficient help from trained experts and the belated assessment after relating location are pointed out to be conspicuous drawbacks of the model followed in India. Nobody knows whether at any of the stages was there an impact assessment on the location of the factory, on control mechanism in case of an accident, or on the secondary effects on the environment such as possibility of squatting of migrant labor (who in large number turned to be the unfortunate victims of the tragedy). On the other hand approval was given to a plant whose design was defective from the stand point of safety aid which had reportedly been rejected by Canada on this regard.

The important lesson of Bhopal catastrophe is to enforce the people's right to know and participate in various stages of environmental decision-making. The cause of these woes can very well be traced to the fact that our legal system does not recognize the compulsory statutory need to have an impact statement before any project is designed or approved.

EIA - JUDICIAL ACTIVISM

In the countries where the mandatory model of EIA exists it is found that judicial review makes a significant contribution in evolving procedural standards and developing EIA as a strong weapon in maintaining the balance between development and environment. In countries following discretionary model also courts can play a significant role in filling the gaps in law. The recent history of judicial pronouncement on environmental question in India is an illustration. The judicial activism fostered through public Interest litigation and supported by the liberalization of rule of locus stand, generated immense judicial concern and discourse on the environmental consequences of action taken up or approved by the Government.

The Right to clean and healthy environment the new dimensions to the Right-to-life concept in Article 21 of the Constitution compelled the courts to have a hard look at the environmental processes. In few cases the Supreme Court appointed commissions to study environmental impact of mining activities for which licence were already granted. In *Tarun Bharat Singh v. Union of India,* the Court directed stoppage of mining activities till a decision was taken on the report of the expert committee appointed by the Court. In *Rural Litigation and Environment Kendra State of UP.,* the Court appointed commission to assess the impact of mining activities. The commission found that some of the activities caused ecological imbalance. The Court ordered the permanent stoppage of those activities.

NEED FOR MANDATORY MODEL

The World Commission on Environment and Development recognizes the need to tailor environmental values in development process and aim at sustainable development the economic growth without disturbing the existing source base but meeting the aspirations of the present without compromising the ability to meet those of the future.

ENVIRONMENTAL COURTS – NEED OF THE HOUR

The proposed Environment Court Bill should also make provision for the constitution of a special cell, with power to make periodical inspection of the plants and industrial areas and to bring the cases which involve the environmental degradation *suo moto* to the notice of the Environment Courts.

Similarly, provision should also be made for the grant of injunctive relief, rather than damages. In the absence of a provision for injunctive relief, a polluter may prefer to pay the damage award imposed by the Court and continue to pollute rather than stop production; such a situation would demand that a provision be made in the bill for injunction relief.

Further, the proposed Environmental Experts Pool should, before hand, lay down a set of effluent treatment standards and rules relating to the Constitution of the primary treatment plants, in order to minimize the effect of the effluent. They should set precise standards tailored to the technological aspects of each type of pollution and implement a plan which will ensure compliance with such standards within a certain time limit. If prior standards are fixed on these lines, it will reduce litigation to a certain extent.

It should be realized that environmental damage is irrevocable; our country can't afford to bear the environmental costs of grandiose schemes such as the Narmada and the Tehri dams. As aptly remarked by an author "If our country can't afford to set up environmental courts, we can not afford projects like these either".

To conclude, in the words of Aparna Vishwarathnam:

> "failure to create in effective regulatory agency will only lead India' further down the concrete path to self-destruction the ultimate irony in an ancient land where man once knew how to live in harmony with nature".

Protection of Environment is a *sine quo non* in this age of ever increasing use of Science and Technology, deforestation and conquest of space. The proposed Environment Court will be an effective instrument to halt the indiscriminate interference with Nature. The Bill now in cold storage needs to be redeemed and processed through the required legislation.

Healthy surroundings, ecological balance and environmental purity are the greatest gifts of Nature to man.

Tampering with them can be at his own perli. The proposed Environmental Court, we may hope will serve as watch dogs to safeguard the relationships between man and nature.

CONCLUSION

We are concluded that the convincing evidence is available now on the warming of the earth's atmosphere due to higher carbon emissions from human activity. The discussion on climate change, therefore, touches upon some emerging areas of concern. The perspectives could be economic or environmental but they converge on the consensus that they are interdependent. Environmental losses linked to climate change have enormous economic costs. On the primary question of climate change sharpened its forecasts during the year. The stern Review on the Economics of Climate Change published prior to the IPCC report argues in favour of affordable action today in order to sustain future economic growth. This section of the survey looks at adaptation to sustain future economic growth. This section of the Survey looks at adaptation to climate change, the impact of warmer seas on coral reefs, aerosols as complex agents influencing atmospheric conditions, and the option of solar power for rapidly growing India.

There has been a paradigm shift over the concept of right to environment since the past three decades, primarily after a series of global cooperative initiatives. Among these, the Stockholm Conference played a significant role in throwing light on environmental degradation that has been caused worldwide. As a result, the international stature of environmental and ecological balance has been enhanced to such a level which the countries of the world had never imagined in history. The courts in India have played a distinguishing role in gradually enlarging the scope of a qualitative living by applying various issues of environmental protection. Consequently, activities posing a major threat to the environment were curtailed so as to protect the individual's inherent right to wholesome environment. Article 21 has been relied in the plethora of cases, although certain cases have incorporated a wider perspective of the Constitution. Hence, the Supreme Court of India, apart from being environmental friendly, has given birth to a wide range of doctrines and principles have in turn been adopted and implemented throughout the country. Environmental Impact Assessment process is a means not only of identifying potential impact but also of enabling the integration of environment and development. In achieving this object an effective EIA within a legal framework has a major contribution to make the legislative mandatory model is not panacea for all these ills nor is it a substitute for other essential requirements such as obtaining baseline data, strengthening the hands of enforcing agencies, making the people aware of environmental issues providing incentives for making natural resources, enforcing or changing existing laws and monitoring actual impact as and when they occur. National Environmental Policy Act of 1969 called NEPA is a remarkable legislation in United States representing best example for statutory mandatory model of environmental impact assessment. In England the concerned regulations list out certain projects which are subject to mandatory assessment and certain other which are likely to give rise to significant environmental effect which requires the threshold enquiry to find out whether or not it will impose significant effect upon the environment. In countries viz. New Zealand, Australia and Canada effective discretionary models of EIA exist as a viable means without sacrificing known benefits. But that does not rule out the need for giving EIA the legislative basis and for doing away with the maladies plaguing the discretionary process. In a potential area where the members of public could have been actively involved on large scale, Indian Law totally fails to keep abreast of modern trends in other countries. The new Environment (Protection) Act, 1986 does not provide for an environmental impact study before a proposed action impacting on the environment is taken, nor it lays emphasis on meaningful and active public involvement in environmental decision-making.

The trends of judicial interference signify a remarkable development at, the time when the laws of country are silent and mandatory EIA before a license is issued or project is approved. We urgently require a national planning body to define national policy on environmental education which can be implemented successfully by listing environmental problems. This will help not only for this generation but also for the future generations to live and enjoy the freedom of this planet and beyond. Environment education should be made compulsory in becoming an essential component of non-formal literacy programmes. Radio and TV can make people aware of the problems. It is a problem of restructuring the economic policies of the Government so that the disparity of Income among groups of people is reduced. It is a problem of incurlating among the people a sense of duty and responsibility towards Mother Nature. Indeed legislations can help. But, the first thing to do is to launch a programme through the length and breadth of the country to Impart environmental education among people. But It is only this way that the problem of pollution can be checked and a better environment be created. Automobiles contribute to more than 60% in cities like Mumbai and Bangalore. Air pollution due to other activities by Public sector and Government agencies such as transport, power generation mining and ONGC operations is far greater than that contributed by Industry. Industry has urged for a comprehensive action plan towards setting up new projects. AI so improving air quality in cities and industrial zones must be given top priority.

SUGGESTIONS

We suggest that India should adopt Environmental Impact Process, carried out in the open field in which public get a fair and effective opportunity of contributing significantly a sound and objective decision-making. More emphasis should be given to the open public enquiry at the time of granting license or consent to any project. The right of people to participate in various stages of decision-making should be guaranteed and enforced. Their right to know should be recognized. The registers of conditions under pollution control Jaws should be kept open to public and they should have a right to lodge prosecution in a court of Law without requirement of any notice to environmental control agency. Either the Environment (Protection) Act, 1986 should be amended or a new legislation is to be enacted to enable for incorporating mandatory assessment and laying down the manner and circumstances under which the assessment is to be carried out. It is necessary that the 1992 draft notification issued by the ministry of Environment and Forests needs to be modified or to be substituted with an Impact Legislation . In a country like India with an enlightened judicial activism' and environmentally not well conscious people, Environmental impact Assessment Legislation will be a leap forward in evolving substantive and procedural norms to do environmental justice. It is high time that in addition to impact assessment legislation, the voluntary organizations should take up an active role in assessment of Environmental Impact.

REFERENCES

Kurukhetra – Vol. 56, No. 8, June 2008.

Yojana – June 2008.

Survey of the Environment – *The Hindu* – 2008.

Supreme Court Journal – 1995 – Vol. 2 (May-August).

Supreme Court Journal – 1994 Vol. 2 (May-August).

Supreme Court Journal – 1994 Vol. 3 (Sept.-Dec.).

Supreme Court Journal – 1991 Vol. 1 (Jan.-April).

Supreme Court Journal – 1998 Vol. 3 - (Sept.-Dec.).

Supreme Court Journal – 1990 Vol. 2 - (May-Aug.).

Supreme Court Journal – 1990 – Vol. 3 – (Sept.-Dec.)

Osho World – June 2008.

Osho Times – June 2008.

De., A.K., *Environment Chemistry*, Third Edition.

Jaswal, P.S., *Environmental Law*.

International Conference on Environment.

Murthy., D.B.N., *Environmental Awareness and Protection*.

Kumar., S. Shantha, *Introduction to Environmental Law – 2nd Edition-2007*.

Purohit/Agarwal, *Ecology and Environmental Biology*.

Botkin Daniel & Edward, *Earth as a Living Planet*.

http://sdnp.delhi.nic.in.

http: //envfro.nic.in.

http://www.india.ford.com

http://sdnp.delhi.nic.in/funding/moef/funding/funding.html.

http://effects of global warming causes of global warming.mht.

http://Facts About Global Warming Do You Know the Truth.mht.

http://Global Warming Basics□□Climate Change□□Allianz Knowledge.mht.

http://Global Warming Facts and Our Future - Causes of Change - Ocean Circulation.mht

http:// NASA - Global Warming.mht.

http:// Reconstructing Climatic and Environmental Changes of the Past 1000 Years A Reappraisal - by Dr_ Willie Soon, Dr_ Sallie Baliunas, Craig Idso, Sherwood Idso and David R_ Legates.mht

Soon, Dr. Willie, Dr. Sallie Baliunas, Craig Idso, Sherwood Idso and David R. Legates. In: *Energy & Environment*, Vol. 14, Issue 2 & 3, pp. 233-296, Publication date: 04/11/2003, American Petroleum Institute.

7

Land-use Mapping – A Tool for Analyzing Wetland Reclamation Process

A Case Study of Cochin City, Kerala

Dr. Lancelet T.S.[1]

INTRODUCTION

Accurate spatial data about the rate and changes in land degradation in any region are essential for proper planning and management. Spatio-temporal land-use mapping with the help of remote sensing and GIS technique are so popular and rapidly developing technology. Wetland reclamation through urbanization in newly developed urban spaces is one of the interesting fields of researchers. Land-use mapping is a tool for analyzing land cover change of an area and helps to find out the spatio-temporal change systematically. The spatio-temporal variation in the reduction of wetlands, cultivated areas, restricted area, open space, water body in the immense rate of reclamation and how the land changes into industrial,

1. **HOD, Department of Geography, Sree Sankaracharya University of Sanskrit, Kalady - 683 574.**

commercial and residential zone from 1914 to 2004 will be mainly forwarded through this study.

STUDY AREA

The study area consists of the main land of Ernakulam and the adjoining islands. Cochin is an emerged land from sea called as *'puthuvaippu'* means 'new island'. The central city of Cochin extends between 9°53'N to 10°05'N latitude and $76^{6}12'$E to 76°23"E.The study region has an area of 275.85 sq.km and it consists of Cochin Corporation, Municipal towns of Kalamassery and Trippunithura and adjoining Census towns and two Panchayats.

MAJOR OBJECTIVES

(a) To find out the spatio-temporal change of landuse pattern from 1914-2004.

(b) To assess the influencing factors of wetland reclamation in Cochin city.

METHODOLOGY

The existing land-use data and data regarding urban infrastructure are collected from the office of Kerala State Land-use Board, Greater Cochin Development Authority Office, Cochin Corporation Office etc. The coastal land-use data of the study area is obtained from Centre for Earth Science Studies, Thiruvananthapuram.

Survey of India toposheet of 1: 63360(1914), 1: 50,000(1968) and 1:25000(1985) is collected from SOI Regional Office, Thiruvananthapuram. With the help of the satellite imagery of IRS, IC, LISS-III, FCC 1:10,000 (February 2000) from NRSA, is used to study microlevel land-use change. The rate of change in wetland reclamation is investigated with the help of people's participation resource map of Cochin 1:3960 (2004).

The collection of ground data through intensive field check up is carried to understand existing landuse and their socio-economic dynamics.

ANALYSIS

The maps regarding spatio-temporal change in land-use pattern are prepared by the use of GIS arc view software. Changes in land-use pattern with physiographic zone are calculated in percentage and necessary cartographic techniques are applied. The detailed analysis has been made regarding the changes in land-use especially the reclamation of wetlands during the past 100 years (1914, 1968, 1985 and 2000).

SOME REVIEWS REGARDING LAND DEGRADATION AND LANDUSE CHANGE

The spatio-temporal landuse change of cities can be seen in the book of Peter Hagget and Andrew D Chiff (1977). The major part of the book by David Rhint (1980) is devoted to the description of land-use change in Eruopean-Economic Community. Among the Indian authors, the empirical work by Dr. Athahullah (1985) strongly emphasized on Urban landuse and misuse of Mysore city. Another study conducted by Prof. P.R. Trivedi (1992) is about the purpose of Environmental Assessment Methods and its landuse relationship.

The studies conducted by Gautam N.C. (1998) is about landuse/land cover spatial analysis in India by using remote sensing data and he evaluated wetland reclamation through land cover change. S.K. Soha (2004) has made a wetland degradation and environmental assessment of India using remote sensing data. He covered about 173 million hectares of land and reported that half of our country is threatened by various degradation like water erosion, wind erosion, salinity, alkalinity, water logging and desertification.

DISCUSSION AND RESULTS

The major factors influencing wetland reclamation in Cochin City are the following.

Physiography

Cochin region lies in the lowland about 0-10 metres above sea level. About 1/3 of the area is located in the coastal region

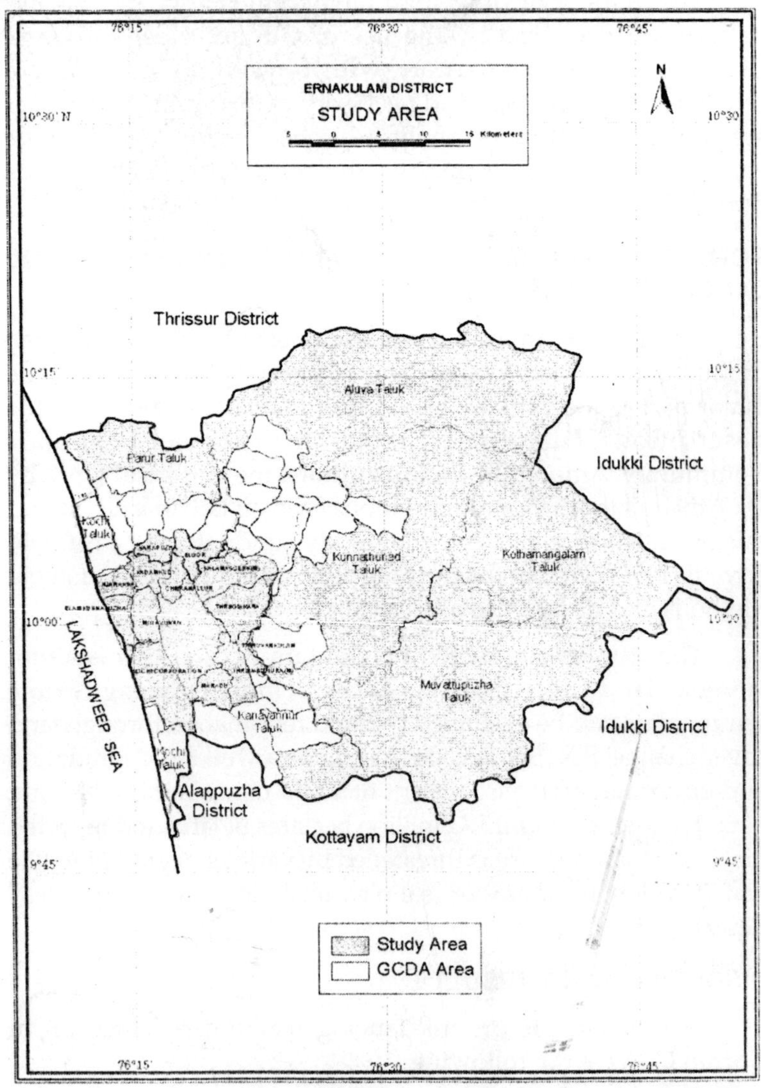

Fig. 7.1: **Ernakulam District**

and the rest in mid-lands. Among the 13 administrative units of the study area 11 units became urbanized and two units continued as rural village panchayats. They are Elamkunnuppuzha and Njarakkal panchayats (Fig. 7.1). The dissected landforms consisting of backwaters, canals, lagoons and a number of small and big islands acted as natural barrier for further growth and development in these panchayats. These physical restrictions promoted the growth of tourism industry and related infrastructure towards North Eastern direction of the study area.

Urban Sprawl

It is found that the direction of urban sprawl in Cochin region is towards the North-East due to the location of Cochin International Airport, Alwaye Industrial town, and Angamaly Commercial town. A large amount of wet lands including paddy fields were reclaimed for various construction activities.

Expansion of Roadways

A radical change was brought about in the reclamation of wetlands for construction of more roadways directly connected Cochin City to other urban centres through Highways and district roads. The important roads in the group are Ekm-Vaikom, Ekm-Moovattupuzha, Ekm-Kadavanthura, Vypeen- Parurand Kaloor-Peruumbavoor etc., connects the places of North and North-Eastern parts of the districts. The following table reveals the expansion rate (1961-2001).

Extinction of Wetland Ecosystem

Wetland ecosystem including marshylands, mangrove forests, rivers, canals, backwaters, swampy lands and permanent waterlogged areas in Cochin City is reducing at a rapid rate from 1914 to 2004. The Total area under wetland in 1914 was 62.25 sq; kms, which shows 23.3 percentage of the total wetland in Cochin City. But in 1968 it reduced to 57.50 sq; km that shows 21.3 percentage of loss in wetland ecosystem. During the period of 1985 it again reduced to 44.5sq; kms, i.e.,16.2 percentage of reduction in the area under wetland. In 2004 it again reduced to 38.99sq km, i.e. 14.2 percentage of total area. Almost 40 percentage of reduction can be seen in 2004.

Table 7.1: Expansion of Road Length in Ernakulam District (in km)

Sl. No.	*Type of Road*	*In 1961*	*In 1981*	*In 2001*	*Direction*
1.	National Highway	45.61	51.20	100.54	NE
2.	State Highway	200.46	185.495	62.80	NE
3.	Major district road	878.33	810.49	1295.46	NE
4.	Other district Road	326.42	758.861	1049.27	NE
	Total	**1450.82**	**1806.046**	**2408.03**	

Source: Executive Engineer, Buildings and Roads, Ernakulam [2004].

The above table clearly shows that due to the process of urbanization, large tracts of virgin lands are converted for the construction of roads, which also paved the way for land cover change and its bio-diversity in the study area.

Degradation of Wet Lands to the Level of Zero

In order to examine thee micro-level changes of wetlands in the study area, mainly depend upon LISS-III-IC, FCC Satellite data, 2000, February. The micro-level analysis of Erur region in the study area which is one of the major industrial areas clearly showed the temporal change of wetlands, mixed cropped areas and of which the wetland area was completely reclaimed for various urban activities especially for industrialization.

Figure 7.3 shows the reduction of wetlands in Erur region from 1914-2000 is getting decreased to zero level. The spatio-temporal landuse analysis clearly reveals that the reduction of natural ecosystem of Cochin with resident-cum- mixed cropped area and area under wetlands are getting diminished with the increasing rate of built-up-land with high population density.

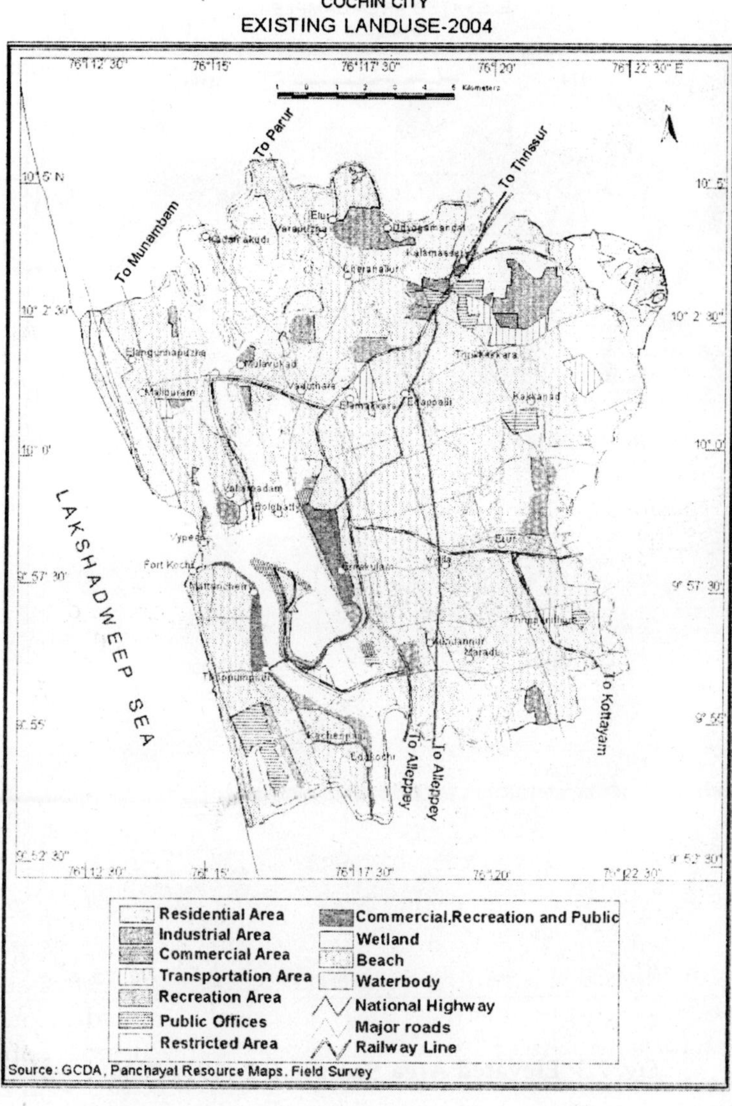

Fig. 7.2: Cochin City Existing Land-use-2004

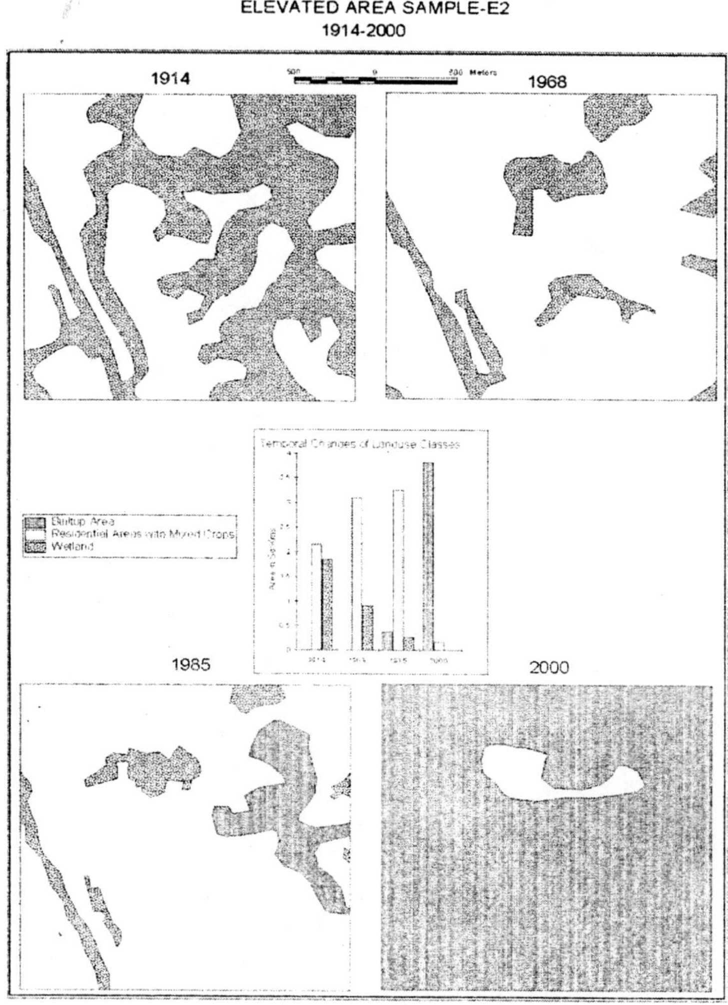

Fig. 7.3: **Elevated Area Sample E-2 (1914-2000)**

Table 7.2: Population and Land-use pattern

Year	*Total Population*	*Population Density person per sq. km*	*Built-up Area (in sq. km)*	*Residential Area with mixed crops (sq. Km)*	*Area under Reclamation (in sq. km)*	*Total Wetlands (in sq. km)*
1914	277723	131	0.75	144	-	62.25
1968	636384	750	32.05	126	9.75	57.50
1985	864831	1250	90.51	91.50	18.75	44.50
2004	1017002	2150	141.98	39.27	28.92	38.99

Source: Computed by the investigator using field data and Census data.

RESULTS

1. Physiography of Cochin especially landforms had decided the reclamation activities through urbanization.
2. The factors influencing the direction of urban sprawl towards North-East changed large tracts of virgin land under mixed crops into urban land.
3. There is an inverse relationship between increasing built-up-area and decreasing wetland ecosystem in the study area.
4. Spatio-temporal landuse changes are occurring as a result of urbanization and pressure of population on urban land.
5. The spatio-temporal landcover change in the study area is a result of reclamation activities by Governmental measures and real estate agents in Cochin.
6. Creation of new dry land for various urban uses is making compulsion for reclamation activity day by day.

MAJOR RECOMMENDATIONS

1. To preserve existing wetlands in the study area.
2. To prevent further reclamation activities through Governmental policies and regulations.
3. To encourage mangroves in the Coastal areas.
4. To organize campaigns to discourage land degradation activities. The medias and Local Action Committees have a major role to play in this regard.

8

Clean Water and Sanitation

People's Responsibility Lessons from the Experience of 'Gram Vikas'

Aditya Kumar Patra[1]

Environment refers to all those conditions and their effects which influence the life of a human being at any place and at any time. The environment may be defined as "the natural world in which people, animals and plants live" to survive and reproduce. The environmental factors that influence the life on earth may be broadly classified as 'abiotic' and 'biotic' elements. The former includes climatic factors related to aerial environment, soil condition, topographic factors etc., while the latter includes the living organisms. Nature has maintained a fine balance among the various entities of environment to enable the plants, animals and human beings to survive. But in the name of economic development and progress of civilization this balance is disturbed by the human beings and the net result is

1. **Lecturer in Economics, Kalinga Mahavidyalaya, G.Udayagiri, Kandhamal, Orissa, 762100, *E-mail*: adityapatra@rediffmail.com**

environmental crisis. This crisis is manifested in the form of pollution. Pollution of environment refers to the presence of pollutants in the environment. Pollutants are of solid, liquid or gaseous matters. Too much presence of these matters in the environment leads to a harmful impact on health and efficiency of the people in the society. Pollution can be classified as: water, air and noise pollution. The objective of this article is to examine the issue of water pollution and related sanitation problem.

OBJECTIVE AND SCHEME

The objective of the article is two fold:

(i) To examine the policy of the Government with regard to the supply of safe drinking water in rural area;

(ii) To highlight the innovative experiment of 'Gram Vikas' in the field of provision of water supply in rural area round the clock with sanitation facility on a sustainable basis.

ROLE OF WATER AND SANITATION

Water is life. It is the basic ingredient of the life cycle. Human being requires at least 2 to 3 litres of drinking water per day just to maintain the crucial liquid balance within the body. Water is a predominant component of all life forms – plants and animals, human and non-human beings. Everything is originated from water and everything is sustained by it.

Drinking water and sanitation are not only the basic necessities of life but they are also pivotal for achieving the goal of 'Health for All'. The sanitation facilities in rural India have been very poor for ages now. By the end of Ninth Five-year plan, i.e., 2002, it is estimated that 20 per cent of the rural households may have sanitary facilities through the Central Rural Sanitation Programme (CRSP). So, in 1999 CRSP was restructured and a new programme namely 'Total Sanitation Campaign' was launched to link sanitation, health, hygiene awareness and environmental issues for addressing the needs of rural community.

The sanitation and health are two sides of the same coin. World Health Organisation (WHO) statistics shows that most of the diseases in developing countries are related to unsafe water supply. The quality of water is as important as the provision of adequate water supply – the latter satisfies the quantity, while the former ensures its potability. In India drinking water gets contaminated due to a variety of reasons. In rural area improper maintenance of hand pump sites and open-air defecation causes havoc on water.

Lack of access to safe drinking water is a major cause of ill health and loss of productivity. It is perhaps the principal cause of life-threatening diseases among infants and children. A majority of the causes of morbidity and mortality could be traced to poor quality of drinking water. The incidence of skin diseases, gynecological and reproductive health problems among women are the result of sharing of ponds for common bathing. The habit of defecating in the open resulted in large-scale spreading of water-borne diseases. Altogether, unclean habits of sanitation and absence of protected drinking water were affecting not just the health of people, but each and every aspect of their life. Fetching of water is traditionally a major chore for women and girl children. Disease, drudgery, loss of human dignity and millions of deaths every year are directly attributed to the lack of these basic services.

Hence, providing adequate safe drinking water to all sections of the rural population on a continuous basis is of paramount importance, and it is necessary that the facilities provided are not short lived for lack of proper maintenance and upkeep.

POLICY ASPECT

Government of India along with the State Governments has been trying to provide safe drinking water to rural population since the implementation of First Five-year Plan. However, a serious effort was made in 1972-73 through the introduction of Accelerated Rural Water Supply Programme (ARWSP) to address the problem of Rural Water Supply. The focus was physical coverage of all rural habitations with the facility of drinking water. The scheme is a Centrally-sponsored scheme. Government of India provides 50 per cent of the cost and rest 50 per cent matching share is borne by the State Governments/ UTs. The ARWSP, however, was withdrawn with the introduction of Minimum Needs Programme (MNP) during Fifth Five-year Plan (1974-75). Despite the huge investment, the progress under the scheme was found to be unsatisfactory. As a result ARWSP was reintroduced in 1977-78.

The strategy adopted by ARWSP revolves around the following three inter-related elements:

1. To accelerate the coverage of 'Not Covered and Partially Covered' habitations with safe drinking water system.
2. To tackle the problem of water quality in affected habitations and to institutionalize water quality monitoring and surveillance system.
3. To promote sustainability of safe drinking water facility in the covered area.

The supply of safe drinking water in rural area is based on the following norms:

- Forty litres of safe drinking water per capita per day (lpcd) for human beings.
- Thirty lpcd additional for cattle in the Desert Development Programme Area.
- One hand pump/stand post for every 250 persons.
- The water source should exist within the habitations/ within 1.6 km in the plains and within 100 metres elevations in the hilly area.

Recognizing the enormity and urgency of providing safe drinking water to rural areas, the ARWSP was given the shape of the National Drinking Water Mission (NDWM) in 1986, which was renamed as Rajiv Gandhi National Drinking Water Mission (RGNDWM) in 1991. Under this mission some major reforms have been introduced to bring about sustainability in the water sector in rural India. The programme of RGNDWM may be classified into two categories: Main Programme and Supportive Activities.

The main programmes include: ARWSP and Sector Reform Programmes. Based on the norms mentioned earlier ARWSP continues with the aim of providing drinking water to all habitations. For the sustainability of the system the Government of India under the Sector Reforms Programme adopts a new strategy. Here the policy signifies a paradigm shift from a centralized, government oriented and supply-driven programme to decentralized, people centered and demand responsive programme. The reform envisaged encompasses the following elements:

- Ensure the full participation of villagers in the project through a decision making role in the choice of schemes, their design and management.
- Focusing on capacity building at the village level by constituting village water and sanitation committee (VWSC).
- Ensuring an integrated service delivery mechanism by streamlining the functions of the agencies involved in project implementation.
- Sharing at least 10% of the capital cost and 100% of O & M cost by the users.
- Taking up of water conservation measures like rainwater harvesting and ground water recharge structures.

Supportive Activities under RGNDWN includes the following:

- Set up of Human Resource Development Cell at State level for planning, designing, implementing and monitoring the scheme.

- Information, Education and Communication (IEC) programme aims to disseminate information about the programme.
- Set up of Management Information System (MIS) for effective planning, monitoring and implementation of various schemes.
- Monitoring and Investigation units have been set up at the state headquarters to carryout investigation and feasibility studies of the planned schemes.
- Provision has been made for taking up monitoring and evaluation studies about the implementation of RWS through reputed organizations/institutions.
- Research and Development (RD) cells have been established by the State Governments.
- Provision has been made for drinking water and sanitation in rural schools.

To achieve the objective of supply of safe drinking water and sanitation in a sustainable manner most states have taken steps to institutionalize community participation through various pilot projects. The 'Swajaladhara' was a pilot project introduced in different States as a community and demand driven water and sanitation scheme in the year 1992. The main objectives of the project were to:

- Provide sustainable health and hygiene benefit to the rural masses through improvements in water supply and environmental sanitation services.
- Examine an alternative mechanism in place of the current supply-led approach.
- Promote sanitary awareness in relation to gender.
- Raise the rural income through time saving and income opportunities for women.

To accomplish the above stated objectives the 'Swajaladhara' scheme is based on demand-responsive and decentralized management. A democratically elected VWSC (a sub-committee of GP) choose the appropriate technology and are responsible for planning and implementation of all project activities at the village level. These committees assume the responsibility of funding 10% capital cost and 100% operation and maintenance (O & M) cost of the project. The community contribution could be in the form of cash/kind/labour or a combination of these subject to the condition that 50% shall be in cash. Since the entire fund may not be made available in one financial year, community contribution could be proportionate to the size of fund available for the scheme during a financial year. MLA/MP LAD funds, contributions from GP, NGO and such other organizations could be used to bridge the shortfall in community contribution. However, the assistance received from all such sources should not exceed 50% of the total contribution payable by the community.

IMPLEMENTATION BY THE GOVERNMENT OF ORISSA

In Orissa the Sector Reforms Pilot projects were implemented in Sundargarh, Ganjam and Balasore districts. The project activities were designed to ensure community participation in drinking water supply projects. In order to promote community participation the State Government has taken the following decisions:

- In order to promote community ownership of the projects for sustainability government have further decided that for sanction and implementation of projects outside sector reform districts from normal budgetary allocation, preference will be given to the projects where the potential beneficiaries, user committee or concerned GP agree to contribute at least 10% of Project cost as labour/cash and also agree to take over operation and maintenance of the projects after implementation.
- In sector reform districts the village water and sanitation committees or PRIs are required to take over O & M of Piped Water Supply (PWC) projects. Accordingly, it is

decided that GPs/User Committees/Village or District WATSAN Missions, wherever they agree, may take over the O & M of rural water supply projects be it in sector reform districts or in any other districts.

The aforesaid principle has not been strictly adhered to and the intended transfer of O & M of the commissioned PWS projects has not evoked the desired response from the GP/VWSC. In the mean time the reform initiatives have been scaled up and are being operationalised State Wide as 'Swajaladhara'.

Recently the 12th Finance Commission has recommended Rs. 803 crore (@ Rs. 160.60 crore per annum) for the years 2005-06 to 2009-10 for the Rural Local Bodies of Orissa, which is to be utilized for the following purposes:

- To improve the services delivery by the panchayatas in respect of water supply and sanitation.
- To take over the assets of 'Swajaladhara' schemes and utilize these grants for repair/rejuvenation and maintenance of these projects to make them fully operational and to bear the entire cost of O & M of water supply for an initial period of five years.
- For disposal of solid waste, cleaning of drains etc. to maintain the environmental sanitation.
- For creation of database and maintenance of accounts through the use of modern technology and management systems.

At the State Government level an amount of Rs. 370 crore out of Rs. 803 crore has been earmarked for water supply and sanitation related activities. In order to improve the quality of governance of water supply and sanitation services in rural areas, the GPs have taken over the rural drinking water supply assets (w.e.f. 20-10-06) and manage the drinking water supply programme in their respective GPs. The GPs will utilize the grants made available under 12th Finance Commission Award for repair/rejuvenation and also the O & M cost. The RWS&S

organization will continue to provide technical support for restoration/rejuvenation/upgradation of drinking water supply systems.

THE EXPERIMENT OF 'GRAM VIKAS'

Orissa is one of the poorest States in India. The average per capita income is 73 per cent of the national average, with 47 per cent of its population living below the poverty line. Almost 85 per cent of the poor live in rural areas. 'Gram Vikas' is a NGO working with poor and marginalized communities of Orissa since 1979. Gram Vikas efforts are geared towards reducing the vulnerability of poor communities and through systematic process improving the living conditions and livelihood options in village, helping communities to gradually emerge from the orbit of poverty to a spiral of sustained growth, where they have the confidence to take the responsibility of their own development. Movement and Action Network for Transformation of Rural Areas (MANTRA) is 'Gram Vikas' tool for fostering social inclusion among the poor and marginalized communities (such as *dalits, adivasis,* lower castes, widows and women) and establishing sustainable system in rural areas. Water and sanitation forms the entry point activity.

The Rural Health and Environment Programme (RHEP) is an integrated rural development intervention being implemented by Gram Vikas since 1992. The programme was initiated with 336 families in five villages in Ganjam and Bolangir districts. It spread to 3000 families in 40 villages by the end of 1998. Currently (up to March 2003) the coverage extends to 8114 families (about 46000 people) in 105 villages across 12 districts of Orissa. In every village covered by the project more than 80 per cent of the families are below the poverty line.

In the long run, "RHEP aims to enable convergent community action through the provision of services and resources to overcome the inertia that has been caused by the long spells of marginalization and deprivation suffered by rural communities. RHEP also aims to transform the momentum created through such community action into sustainable community owned and managed development systems.

The sanitation infrastructure (i.e., a separate toilet and bathing room for each family) and supply of piped drinking water for 24 hours, all through the year to all houses is only the entry point and the core rallying element to bring the people together cutting across the barriers of patriarchal system, caste, politics and economic differences. For ensuring effective protection of water and environment sanitation in any habitat, 100 per cent coverage is essential. Even one family left out would result in continued pollution of the environment. RHEP goes against the prevalent paradigm of subsidy linked programme. The intervention is time bound and has clear mechanism of withdrawal of 'Gram Vikas' in a phased manner. As a development intervention RHEP has distinctive features, based primarily on 'All or none', 'pay for use', 'taking responsibility', 'participatory management' and 'in-built financial sustainability'.

To implement the RHEP in a village the Gram Vikas staff members establish contact in the village, identify key opinion leaders and work through them to initiate discussions among all the households. The time taken for motivating the communities is quite long, often 2-3 years. There are certain conditions that the community needs to agree to at the beginning of the process, these are:

- 100 per cent participation of households in the village.
- Creation of 'Corpus Fund' with contribution from all families.
- Development of monitoring systems to ensure full usage of facilities.

The RHEP firmly believes that unless all families in a village agree to be the part of the programme it should not be implemented. This is because of the reason that the sanitation aspect can be addressed only if everybody adopts safe sanitation practices. Without 100 per cent participation environmental pollution and resultant health hazards cannot be prevented. All families in the village establish a minimum standard of facilities, including toilets and bathing rooms for each family and individual connections for piped water supply to all houses. It is in the best interest of all, to ensure that even the poorest have access to the minimum level of services. This approach of complete participation is considered critical to the programme.

Creation of the 'Corpus Fund' is a prerequisite for Gram Vikas to start contributing to the activities under RHEP. At the initiation of the programme a family-wise plan is made to raise on an average Rs 1000 per family towards a village corpus fund, where the rich subsidizes the poor, but even the poorest widow has to contribute Rs 100. This corpus fund placed in a term deposit earns interest, which can be used only to support 'new families' that may come up in future as the village grows, ensuring cent per cent coverage at all times. This support will subsidize the cost of external materials required for construction. Creation of the corpus with the involvement of each family in the village is the acid test of the eagerness and motivation in the village to undertake the programme.

Implementation of RHEP in a village begins with the execution of an agreement between the villagers and Gram Vikas with the norms clearly spelt out. This is followed by orgasnisation of the Village General Body. There are separate general bodies of men and women, consisting of all male and female heads of households in the village. The separate General Body of women serves as the first step in their integration with the larger community. Interaction in this forum provides women with the necessary confidence and skills to enlarge their scope of interactions.

The two General Bodies nominate/selects four men and four women from amongst them to form the Village Executive Committee (VEC). In all villages, the VEC is registered under law, as societies. This enables the committee to become a legally recognized entity and this helps in dealing with external agencies, especially Government agencies.

The VEC assumes all decisions-making powers with respect to the programme in the village. The committee lays down the modalities of collecting the corpus fund and oversees the collection. It constitutes various sub-committees to monitor the implementations of different components of the programme. The various sub-committees formed in the village and their functions are the following:

1. *Sanitation Sub-Committee:* To ensure timely and proper completion of construction of facilities, monitor proper use of sanitations facilities, detect and punish persons who violate rules set by the General Body regarding the use of toilets and bathing rooms, ensure cleanliness of the village surroundings.
2. *Water Sub-Committee:* To ensure proper and timely completion of water supply mechanism, monitor proper use of water and maintenance of the system.
3. *Pisciculture/Social Forestry Sub-Committee:* To plan and monitor the utilization of village common property resources as the case may be. To ensure proper utilization of the resources and monitor income flows.

Before constructions of toilets and bathing rooms, Gram Vikas imparts training to young unskilled men and women in masonry trade. On completion of training, they construct the toilet, bathing room and overhead tank under the supervision of master mason and an engineer. Similarly the plumbing assistance is provided by Gram Vikas - pipes, pans, fittings. Local youths are also trained in this process. Through these efforts, all repair maintenance and future construction can be taken care of with skills available within the village.

Gram Vikas takes special effort to involve women, empowering them socially and economically. This results in the formation of women Self-help Groups (SHG). Since educating a woman is rightly referred to being the equivalent of educating an entire family. So Gram Vikas embarks on women SHGs to inculcate the sense of personal hygiene among the family members.

A typical sequence of events that unfolds after villagers reach a consensus to join the RHEP as follows:

- Formation of Village Committee/Sub-Committees.
- Creation of 'Village Corpus Fund'.
- Construction of individual toilets and bathing rooms.
- Construction of the water tank and water distribution system.
- Linkage with governance structures.

Each village prepares a budget on how finances will be raised, including their own contribution of labour and materials support from government schemes and from Gram Vikas. Villages undertaking construction of water supply and sanitation infrastructure needs an initial investment of around Rs 20,000 per family of which 27 per cent is towards capacity building and strengthening village institutions. seventy per cent is for construction of toilets-bathing rooms and water supply systems with the community contributing 32 per cent and the rest 41 per cent as a one-time subsidy from external donor agencies as 'seed capital'. Government programmes including Swajaladhara under RGNDWM provide funds for water and sanitation. In some areas ITDA & ZPs have also contributed resources. In recent years there has been interest from elected representatives to contribute towards this programme from their discretionary funds viz. MLA/MP LAD fund. Table 8.1 gives an indication of the contributions towards RHEP.

Operation and maintenance (O&M) has assumed importance to sustain water supply systems already created. The responsibility for maintaining all facilities created by the RHEP rest with the villagers themselves. In order to do this systems are built into the project from the very beginning through creation of maintenance fund. Villages are encouraged to undertake and develop community income generation activities like pisciculture, horticulture plantations, consisting of a mixed variety of timber, fuel, fodder and fruit trees are raised on village

Table 8.1: Contributions to RHEP

Gram Vikas Contribution	*People's Contribution*
Construction of Toilets & Bathing Rooms	
Required quantity of cement, bricks, aggregate, sand, steel, materials of roof, ceramic pan, water seal, foot rests, door for toilet, skilled labour up to a maximum of Rs 2500 per family.	Required quantity of stone for up to the plinth level, mud for joining bricks, centring materials and all unskilled labour, door for bathing room, construction of two soak pits with covers and whitewashing.
Construction of Water Tank and Piped Water Supply	
Required quantity of cement, brick, aggregate and steel for the overhead tank.Pipe for the main pipeline and motor. pump. Partial cost of digging well. Skilled labour for laying main pipeline and all construction.	Required quantity of stone for the foundation.Unskilled labour for the foundation, construction of overhead tank, laying of water distribution system, cost of water pipes from the main pipeline to individual houses, toilets and bathing rooms.
Drainage systems	
Required quantity of bricks and cement. Skilled labour	Required quantity of stone, aggregate and sand. All unskilled labour.

common lands and wastelands. Income from these sources is used for paying electricity bills, repair and maintenance of pumps and salaries of the pump operator etc. to keep the water supply systems functional at all times to come.

The first phase of RHEP (1992-98) was characterized by the 'push' factor. However, in the second phase, since 1999, the 'pull' factor is gradually emerging. Earlier, convincing villagers to join in this programme took at least 2-3 years but now quite a few villages have been shown their own interest to work with Gram Vikas. The demonstration effect is clear as neighbouring villages are tempted to undertake the programme. Old villages often play a lead/key role in motivating new villages. Total inclusion of all communities and every one being treated on par are striking symbols of the progress that these villages have made under RHEP. Piped water supply and sanitation infrastructure contributes to improvements in the quality of life of the people in the village. There are no losers here. The reduction in the drudging of women and the comfort of privacy they now enjoy are also powerful motivating factors for adjoining villages. The improvement in the general cleanliness levels of the village and the confidence emanating from the ownership of good quality service infrastructure draws the attention of the adjoining villages to becoming a part of this programme.

In addition to these, the people's organizations in the villages are becoming active advocates in the spread of the programme. The Panchayati Raj Institutions (PRIs) play an active and effective role for the replication of the programme.

Communities, with whom Gram Vikas works for a period of 3-5 years, demonstrate governance mechanism with high degree of accountability and transparency. These along with the character of social inclusion are built in to the social fabric of the village. The first experience in managing their own village institution and financial resources builds the capacities of the community and instill in people, a high level of confidence, especially among the erstwhile excluded sections of the community. Several villages have leveraged the community bonding to improve management of other common services and resources in the village including the village school, health center, common ponds, wastelands etc. Villagers learn how to deal with conflicts and act as pressure group against vested interests within their village and outside. They learn to question and hold accountable the village committee that is elected by them, thus exerting a social pressure on the governance mechanism that are established.

Water and sanitation as an activity has the potential to bring a village community together. It works as an energizing activity which raises the enthusiasm of the villagers and in the long term enables convergent community action in establishing sustainable systems through mobilizing community's own resources to break the inertia caused by a long history of marginalisation and deprivation. Thus, sanitation or water is not the issue. It is a small step towards a larger goal. It is a part of the process that will enable people to decide their own destiny. It is the journey out of a life as victims of circumstances, to one where they are the makers of their own destinies.

CONCLUSION

The foregoing discussion leads to the conclusion that the provision of safe drinking water on a sustainable basis entails coordination of the Government, NGO and the people at large. In most cases, the state would provide a source of water but end up with a failure for want of proper operation and maintenance. Since the policies seldom address the nitty-gritty of the issues concerned, which are eminently important to discern the ground realities. On the other side there are instances, where people collectively organized themselves in creating a community source. The experience of 'Gram Vikas' has shown that once systems are in place and local institutions developed, communities can successfully manage and maintain their facilities and ensure sustainability of the project even after the external assistance is withdrawn. Hence, it is envisaged that a synergized interaction between Government, NGO and people is essential. All the stakeholders should play their due role. Government as the major partner formulates policy, NGOs act as the facilitators but the real player is the 'people'. The active participation and the responsible role of the villagers represent the hallmark of the success of the programme.

REFERENCES

Ama Ganna Jala Jogana Byabastha: Ama Panchayata Hatare, Ministry of Rural Development, Government of Orissa.

Annual Report 2002, Rajiv Gandhi Foundation, GOI, New Delhi.

Economic Survey, 2003-04, GOI, New Delhi.

Jalavani, Vol. 4, No. 2, July-October 2001.

www.gramvikas.org

9

Disaster Management and its Need in Formal Education

S. Paltasingh,[1] S.N.Padhi[2] and S.K. Das[3]

ABSTRACT

Disasters include both natural and man-made disasters. A multi-pronged strategy involving prevention, preparedness, response and recovery are required for disaster management. Early warning and precautionary measures can reduce the risks substantially. Climate change and global warming causes disasters by changing ecology in different areas. Disaster management needs to be incorporated in school curriculum to acquaint the public in vulnerable areas for preparedness from their childhood. Capacity building of selected people can be done through training and distance education to address the situation in susceptible areas. Research works on different

1. Lecturer, SIET, 5/B.R. Dasgupta Road, Kolkata.

2. Reader in Zoology, KBDAV College, Nirakarpur, Khurda, Orissa.

3. Professor & Head, Deptt. Fishery Biology & Resources Management, W.B. University of Animal & Fishery Sciences, Kolkata-94.

aspects of disaster management needs to be strengthened. Public officials must act feeling urgency of situation by understanding the need of people to relieve the stress due to disasters.

INTRODUCTION

Man has been witnessing various natural and man-made disasters on earth since time immemorial. These unwanted events happen suddenly causing enormous loss to society. The natural disasters occurring frequently are earthquakes, volcanic eruption, tsunami, floods, droughts, famines, land slides, cyclones etc. Man-made disasters include pollution, smog, gas and electricity failure, toxic wastes, chemical leakage, fires, bombing, bloodshed, violence etc. According to UNDP report some 75% of world population live in areas affected at least once by earthquake, tropical cyclone, flood, drought between 1980-2000.The consequence of such wide spread exposure to natural hazard for human development is only now beginning to be identified. Billions of people in more than 100 countries are periodically exposed to any of such natural disasters resulting more than 184 deaths per day recorded in different parts of the world. Losses out of it poses severe challenge to development of any nation. The destruction of infrastructure and erosion of livelihood are direct outcomes of it. The disaster loss also lead to financial, political, health and environment shocks to different countries. It upsets social development meant for poverty alleviation, primary education, health care, drinking water, environment upliftment, employment generation etc.

NATURAL DISASTERS

Four mega disasters occurred in India during 1993-2004 are earthquakes of Latur and Bhoj of 1993 and 2001, Supercyclone of Orissa in 1999, Indian Ocean tsunami in December 2004 and each had claimed more than 10,000 lives. The natural disasters used to eat away gains of development with annual deaths of 4350 human beings, 40000 animals, damage of 2.5 million house and 1.5 million ha crops as well as infrastructure of wide magnitude accounting about 2.5% of national GDP. Several countries frequently experience natural disasters and such risks should be kept in minds of planners and they should integrate prospective disaster risk management with sustainable development planning. Four natural types of disasters viz. earthquakes, tropical cyclones, floods and droughts account for 94% deaths caused by natural disasters. For every one person killed, about 3000 people are exposed to natural hazards world wide. Disaster risk is quite low in developed countries in comparison to medium and low income countries. Countries classified as high human development countries represent 15% of exposed population and only 1.8% of deaths.

According to Dhar Chakraborty (2006) nearly 60% of landmass of India are prone to earthquake or landslides of different magnitudes and about 40 million hectares which is about 8% of its geographical area are subjected to riverine and flash floods. Thirty-five important cities with population of more than half million each are located in seismic zone IV and V where magnitude of earthquake of 6 or more in Richter scale may occur. Wide variation of rainfall and climate make many regions of India susceptible to various hazards like drought, flood, hailstorm, heat and cold waves that claim lives, livelihood and property. Sixty per cent of net sown area are prone to drought even after several irrigation projects. Nearly 8000 km coast line of India face threats of cyclone, storms, inundations before and after monsoon. Climatic change due to global warming enhance oceanic disturbances and its result was tsunami in December 2004.

India is a major maritime country and one of the leading fish producers of the world. It produces about 6.5 million tonnes of fish ranking third in world next to China and Peru in recent years. Its 2.02 million square kilometres of Exclusive Economic Zone and vast coast line harbors rich marine biodiversity having importance to food, medicines, export, tourism etc. Marine fish is very cheap and rich in nutrients which enhance nutritional security of poor in coastal belt of India. The coastal region is most vulnerable to disasters like cyclones, tsunami, sea erosion, tornado etc. Other hazards occurring in such zones are oil spills, fires, spills from chemical storage tank, flooding, sinking of fishing crafts, damage to fishing nets etc.

DISASTER DUE TO CLIMATE CHANGE

Climate change is one of the reasons for occurrence of disasters. The enhanced "Green House Effect" due to trapping of long wave radiation emitted from earth's surface in turn changes heat balance on the surface. It results due to increasing concentration of carbon and nitrogen gas (carbon dioxide, methane, nitrous oxide etc.) due to rapid urbanization and industrialization. It can cause irregular rainfall with increase (even up to 50%) in some areas and acute scarcity in other areas. Global warming caused by it leads to tropical cyclone intensification and its increased frequencies. Ramkrishnan (2008) reviewed possible impacts of climate change in Indian context where he cited that increased rainfall in north eastern region of India could result in increased leaching of soil and consequent depletion of soil fertility. Cimatic/edaphic factors can create stress conditions when combined with human pressures on the ecosystems, leading to extreme desertification with rapid breakdown of fragile mountain ecosystems. Reduction of rainfall can lead to degradation of rain forest resulting dominance of few tall grass species and exotic weeds. Such grass lands are highly susceptible to fire hazards.

APPROACHES TO DISASTER MANAGEMENT

Five key elements of disaster management are prevention, mitigation, preparedness, response and relief as well as rehabilitation. The need of the hour is to chuck out multi-pronged strategy for total risk management comprising prevention, preparedness, response and recovery in one hand and initiate development efforts aimed towards risk reduction and mitigation on other hand to proceed forward towards sustainable development.

Many disasters can be prevented if hazards are recognized and precautionary approach is adopted. So early warning system to the public needs to be strengthened. Cyclones, tornados, heavy rains and consequent flooding can be predicted and thus warnings can be made .But some events like tsunami, oil spills, collisions, fires etc. cannot be warned well in advance. The vulnerable community can be made well aware of risks and what actions should be taken in the event of eventuality (Mohan Joseph, 2006).

DISASTER MANAGEMENT THROUGH EDUCATION AND TRAINING

An individual should be made aware of disaster management right from childhood education to meet the challenges in future. Natural disaster may occur at any time, hence every person should be ready to face it and overcome it in right manner. This can be possible provided children can learn details of it from school level. The mankind should learn from each natural disaster. The tsunami of December 2004 taught us on protecting the coast line from tidal waves. The flooding of Mumbai in July 2005 made alert on importance of urban drainage. Earthquakes do not kill people but it is poorly designed and built buildings that kill people. When an earthquake of larger magnitude shook Seattle (USA) after a month of Gujurat earthquake of February 2001, only one person died by heart attack and not a single building collapsed. If USA and Japan can overcome adverse impact, then why not India? There is need to study disaster management lessons of developed countries and apply it in Indian context. It must be incorporated well in school syllabus. Some state Boards and CBSE had already included it realizing the importance which includes measures and procedures for awareness, preparedness, prevention, mitigation, reconstruction, relief, response, and safeguard of people who had fallen as victims of disaster. They had initiated the process of reorientation in school curriculum in order to fight unforeseen calamities right from childhood.

Natural disasters severely damage the crops, horticultural products, animal husbandry, fisheries etc. and thus shake the economy of rural households. So disaster management must be kept as a subject in Under Graduate curriculum in different disciplines such as Agriculture, Veterinary Science, Horticulture, Fisheries, Forestry etc. in Agriculture and Animal Sciences

Universities to meet the challenges arising out of it. Preparedness, mitigation and recovery measures along with integrated planning for sustainable agriculture development must be addressed through education in such universities.

There is need for capacity building on disaster management in vulnerable areas through training and distance education. Identified people may be educated accordingly to address such situations during its occurrence. Development workers and functionaries of NGOs can be imparted necessary training to manage the entire ambit of disasters from warning, rescue to mitigation. Research is important in identifying characteristics of each disaster as well as how to overcome its harmful effects. It should also emphasise on methods of prediction, early warning, decision support, rescue, rehabilitation etc.

CONCLUSION

Disasters mainly cause loss of human and animal life. It results in huge loss of infrastructure like roads and transport, disruption of communication, environmental degradation, incidence of epidemic and other diseases, loss to industry, agriculture, business and other livelihood activities etc. Its social impacts include trauma, depression, poverty, loss of employment etc. Achievement of MLD (Millennium Development Goal) is severely challenged by losses from disasters. Such loss interact with and aggravate other financial, political, health, and environmental shocks which set back social investments meant for education, health, poverty eradication, housing, sanitation, drinking water, protecting environment, employment generation etc. Generally, five types of large scale disasters occur in India. These are cyclones, flood with or without cyclones, earthquakes, tsunami and drought. It is possible to visualize the probable sits of their occurrence by studying the natural conditions. A plan of action can be formulated by imagining the worst situation for immediate rescue efforts. UNDP has begun development of Disaster Risk Index (DRI) in order to improve understanding of the relation between development and disaster risk. It enable to measure and compare relative levels of physical exposure to hazard, vulnerability and risk in different countries. Disaster may occur at any time in vulnerable sites and concerned Government should act effectively to mitigate the loss of life and suffering to relieve the distress.

REFERENCES

Dhar Chakraborty P.G. (2006) Emerging Framework. *Yojana,* 50(5): 4-8.

Mohan Joseph, M. (2006) *Disaster Management in Marine Sector.*

S. Ayyappan (Ed) *Handbook of Fisheries and Aquaculture.* ICAR, New Delhi.

Ramkrishnan, P.S.(2008) *Ecology and Sustainable Development: Working with Knowledge Systems.* National Book Trust, India, New Delhi.

10

Low Cost Production Practices to Prevent Distress Sale of Paddy

H.K. Patro,[1] L.R. Patro[2]
S.C. Mohapatra[3] and S.C. Swain[4]

ABSTRACT

Distress sale of paddy is the main problem in the State of Orissa either due to excess production or excess cost of cultivation, which decreases the profit margin in the paddy production system. A field experiment in paddy was conducted in the farmer's field of north eastern ghat zonc of Orissa under Farmers Participatory Research trials during kharif seasons of 2002-03 and 2003-04 to find out the lowest package of practices

1. Krishi Vigyan Kendra (Gajapati), Rudragiri - 761 016, *E-mail:* pranati_hkp@hotmail.com.

2. Environmental Toxicology Lab. Deptt. of zoology & Bio-technology, KBDAV College, Nirakarpur, 752 019, Orissa, India. *E-mail:* dr.lrpatro@rediffmail.com, dr.lingarajpatro@sify.com

3. Khusi Vigyan Kendra (Subarnopur), Sonpur, Orissa, India.

4. Krishi Vigyan Kendra Rayagada, Gunupur, Orissa, India.

with the use of INM, IPM and the optimum mechanization level. This will ultimately increase the profit margin and thus reduce the distress sale. The present study reveled that the cost of cultivation could be reduced by 27.6 percent over the farmer's practice in the paddy production system due to adoption of low cost practices with an increase in yield to 38 q/ha for farmers practice to 39.5 q/ha in low cost practices.

Key Words: Production, low cost, yield, net return, paddy, distress sale.

INTRODUCTION

Paddy is the predominant crop of Orissa being grown in an area of 42.74 lakh ha with a productivity of less than 2.61 t/ha. Among different districts of Orissa, paddy occupies an area of 2.54 lakh ha with a productivity of 3t/ha in the district of Ganjam. Most of the paddy is grown only in *kharif* season in Ganjam. Paddy cultivation in the district of Ganjam in past few years has become very much un-profitable as well as un-sustainable due to non-adoption of modern technology by the farmers, which is evident from the distress sale of paddy. For sustainability of paddy cultivation there has to be a sea change in the concept of the paddy farmers. Quality, scientific management as well as selective mechanization are the key factors for sustainability (Satheesh *et. al.*, 1995). Excess production or higher cost of cultivation of paddy which reduces the profit margin of the farmers leading to distress sale in the state in general and Ganjam district in particular. Keeping this in view, the present study was undertaken in the farmers field during Kharif seasons of 2002-03 and 2003-04 to find out the low cost package of practices for paddy production system.

MATERIALS AND METHODS

During the kharif Season of 2002-03 and 2003-04, field experiments were conducted in eight different farmers field of three selected villages (Malaspadar, Mudulipalli and Bhaliakhai) with eight farmers from these village having an experimental area of 1.5 ac each. The soil of the experimental field was medium with red loam soil. The paddy variety Swarna (MTU-7029) was taken in all the villages. Three treatments were taken in each of the farmers field. The treatments were:

T_1: Through ploughing by country plough + manual seedling raising + manual transplanting and weeding + fertilizer dose of 100 kg N +10 kg P_2O_2 + 20 kg K_2O + chemical plant protection + harvesting by local sickle + threshing by bullock treading (Farmers practice)

T_2: Once Ploughing by country plough followed by twice pudding by bullock drawn puddler + manual seedling raising + manual transplanting and weeding + fertilizer dose of 80 kg N + 40 kg P_2O_5 + 40kg K_2O + chemical plant protection + harvesting by improved sickle + threshing by pedal thresher (Recommended practice).

T_3: Once ploughing by M.B. Plough followed by twice pudding by bullock drawn puddler + mat type nuesery raising + transplanting by S.P. transplanter and weeding by Cono weeder + green manuring (Dhanicha) + plant proection by light trap + harvesting by KAMCO reaper + threshing by power thrsher (Low cost practice).

All other operation were uniform in all the treatmens.

RESULTS AND DISCUSSION

The cost of cultivation of paddy by farmer's practice (T1), recommended practice (T2) and low cost practice (T3) are given in Table 10.1. From the table it is seen that the cost of land preparation by FP is Rs. 2,400 per ha where as the same for the treatments T2 and T3 are Rs. 1,180 and Rs. 1,102 respectively. By the use of bullock drawn puddler for puddling, the cost of land preparation was reduced drastically by 50.8 and 54% in case of T2 and T3 in comparison to FP respectively. In treatment T3, mat type nursery was raised for transplanter. In this case, seedlings are not uprooted, hence the cost of seedling raising and up rooting is reduced by Rs. 935 per hectrare. By the use of transplanter on hire basis @ Rs. 300 per hour, there was a saving of Rs. 375 per hectare as compared to manual transplanting. By using KAMCO reaper only for harvesting, the harvesting cost has decreased by 66.7 and 58.3% with respect to harvesting by local sickle and improved sickle. Cost of threshing by power thresher is found to be higher than bullock treading but 25% less than pedal thresher. Total cost of cultivation of paddy by farmers' practice, recommended practice and low cost practice were computed to be Rs. 13,688 Rs. 13,134 and Rs. 9,905 respectively (Table 10.1). By use of low cost practice, the cost of cultivation reduces by 27.63% and 24.58 respectively over farmers practice and recommended practice in comparison to farmer's practice. This corroborates with the finding of Patro *et al.* (2005).

Yield of paddy was found to be 38.0, 38.5 and 39.5 q/ha for T1, T2, and T3 respectively (Table 10.2). the gross return @ Rs. 530.00/q comes to be Rs. 20,140 Rs. 20,405 and Rs. 20,935 per hectare in that order. Consequently, highest net return of Rs. 11,030 per has was observed with low cost practice followed by Rs. 7,271 and Rs. 6,452 for recommended and farmer's practice (Table 10.2). The cost of production per quintal of paddy comes out to be Rs. 360, Rs. 341 and Rs. 251 for treatments T1, T2 and T3 respectively. Highest benefit-cost ratio of 1.11 was found in care of treatment T3 followed by T2 (0.55) and T1 (0.47). These findings are in agreement with the observation recorded by Panda et al. 1999.

CONCLUSION

Low cost practice comprising of ploughing with M.B., plough, pudding by bullock drawn puddler, transplanting by S.P. transplanter, mechanical weeding by cono weeder, plant protection by light trap, mechanical harvesting and threshing could reduce the cost of production of paddy by 27.6% over farmers practice and increase the profit of the farmers considerably. The increase in profit margin of the farmers could help preventing the distress sale of paddy in the district.

Table 10.1. Comparison of cost of cultivation of different paddy production practices

Sl. No.	*Operation*	T_1 *(Farmers' Practice)*	*Cost (Rs./ha)*	T_2 *(Recommended practices)*	*Cost (Rs./ha)*	T_3 *(Low cost practice)*	*Cost + (Rs/ha)*
1.	Land preparation	Thrice ploughing bycountry plough	2400	Once ploughting by country plough followed by twice pudding by bullic drawn puddler	1180	Once ploughing by m.b. plough followed by twice pudding by bullock drawn puddler	1102
2.	Seedling raising along with cost of seed and uprooting	Manual	2510	Manual	2610	Mat type nursery	1575
3.	Transplanting	Manual	1875	Manual	1875	S.P. Tranplanter	1500
4.	Weeding	Manual	1250	Manual	875	Cono weeder	750
5.	Fertilizer application including cost of fertilizer	Manual (100 :10:20)	1528	Manual (80:40:40)	2074	Bradcaste 60: 40 : 40 + green manure +	2228
6.	Pant protection	Chemical Control	1500	Chemical Control	1500	Light trap putting wild sugar cane plants in rice field + Bel leaf extract.	1000
7.	Harvesting	Local Sickle	1875	Improved sickle	1500	Self propelled vertical conveyor reaper (KAMCO)	625
8.	Threshing	Bullock treading	750	Pedal operated hold on type thresher	1500	Power thresher	1125
9.	Total cost of cultivation, Rs/ha		13688		13134		9905

Table 10.2: Grain yield (q/ha), net return (Rs/ha) and B : C ratio as affected by different paddy production practices

Parameters	*Treatment*	*Year*		*Mean*
		2002-2003	*2003-2004*	
Grain yield, q/ha	T1	36.5	39.5	38.0
	T2	38.6	38.4	38.5
	T3	39.2	39.8	39.5
Net return, Rs/ha	T1	5657	7247	6452
	T2	7324	7218	7271
	T3	10871	11189	11030
B:C ratio	T1	0.41	0.53	0.47
	T2	0.56	0.55	0.55
	T3	1.09	1.13	1.11

REFERENCES

Panda, S.C. Patro, H. Panda, P.C. and Reddy, G.M.V. 1999 Effect of Integrated Nitrogen Management on Rice Yield and Physico-chemical Properties of Soil. Crop Research 18 (1): 25-28.

Patro, H., Mahapatra, B.S, Sharma, G.L. and Kumar, Ajay 2005, Total Productivity, Nitrogen, Phosphorus and Potassium Removal and Economics of Rice-wheat Cropping System with Integrated Nitrogen Management in Rice. *Indian Journal of Agronomy* 50 (2): 94-97.

Satheesh, A.V. Sharma, B.M. and Sharma, V.KI. 1995 Impact of Diversification and Liberal Credit Policy on Income and Employment of Non-viable Farmers, in Pithapuram Block, Eastern Goadavai District, A.P. *Indian Journal of Agricultural Economics* 19 : 313-29.

11

Environment Management
Sustainable Competitive Advantage

Dr. Suman Kalyan Chaudhury[1]

ABSTRACT

Environmental pollution and degradation have been the bane of the industrialized world. Over the past two centuries, there has risen a world that has been more and more driven by machines and materialistic interests that has led to a fast evolving and changing lifestyle. This, in turn, has made the world population to rapidly use the naturally available resources and convert them into products that are increasingly non-recyclable and polluting to the natural environment. The rapid industrialization and fast growing population in India have been demanding on environment, infrastructure and natural resources. In view of the growing environmental concerns EMS is emerging as the next significant source of competitive edge for businesses. A well developed EMS can help a firm manage,

1. **Faculty Member, Alphia Institute Business Management, Bhubaneswar (Orissa).**

measure, and improve the environmental aspects of its business activities. The EMS has the potential to bring about better compliance with mandatory and voluntary environmental requirements. Also governments around the world have also woken up to the enormity of the problem and several non-governmental organizations (NGOs) and corporate bodies have also taken up the issue and are working to create environmental awareness and devising pollution control strategies that could reduce the enormity and severity of the problem of environmental pollution and degradation.

Keywords: EMS, sewage sludge, deforestation, ozone depletion, industrial pollution, global warming, acid precipitation.

PREAMBLE

Firms have been using different strategies to enhance its ability to gain a competitive advantage over other firms in the industry through differentiation in the product, cost or quality, firms undertake extensive measures to adopt systems intended at enhancing a firm's ability to compete on one or more of these dimensions. However, the benefits offered by them have been short lived as changes in consumers preferences diminishes their importance and as competition gives rise to better systems the above-stated dimensions lose their relevance. In view of the growing environmental concerns EMS is emerging as the next significant source of competitive edge for businesses. A well-developed EMS can help a firm manage, measure, and improve the environmental aspects of its business activities. The EMS has the potential to bring about better compliance with mandatory and voluntary environmental requirements. The aspect of quality brought about a cultural change in the way business was carried out. Similarly, EMS can bring about a cultural change in the environmental business practices when integrated into overall business activities.

ENVIRONMENTAL POLLUTION

Environmental pollution is a problem increasingly faced by both developed and developing countries. It occurs as a combination of a variety of factors. It is neither within the nature's purview to decompose the by-products of the myriad of human activities nor is it possible for humans to break-down each of the contaminants artificially to render them harmless.

There are three dominant types of pollution which have a direct, and often lasting. impact on the environment:

- Air Pollution
- Water Pollution
- Soil Pollution

Air Pollution

The presence of contaminants in the atmosphere in such quality and duration that can harm human health or welfare and other living organism or damages the environment is termed as air pollution. It can occur on account of both natural and man-made factors. Some of the prominent are the following:

Carbon monoxide (CO): This is a poisonous, gaseous product resulting from incomplete burning of frequently used carbon- based fuels such as diesel, petrol and wood.

Carbon dioxide (CO_2): This is a gas emitted as a result of burning of coal , oil and natural gases.

Chloroflorocarbons (CFC): These gases, which are primarily responsible for ozone layer depletion, are released mainly from air – conditioning and refrigeration systems.

Nitrogen Oxide (NO*x*) ; The nitrogen content in fuels like petrol , diesel and coal leads to the formation of this contaminating gaseous product , which causes smog and acid rain.

Sulphur dioxide (SO_2): This is an undesirable by-product of burning of sulphur-containing coals, primarily in thermal power plants.

Suspended Particulate Matter (SPM): Unlike the above gaseous impurities, SPM constitutes solids that remain suspended in the environment in the form of dust , smoke or vapour.

Water Pollution

It refers to the harmful disruption of the ecosystem balance on account of changes in the physical, biological, and chemical conditions of any body of water. Like any other type of pollution, it occurs when large quantities of pollutants let out from different sources which can no longer be supported by the natural ecosystem. Only three per cent of the total amount of water available on earth is potable and all the popular sources of this potable water, which constitute strems, spring, rivers, lakes, and waterfalls, are under constant threat of pollution and contamination. Industrial, agricultural as well as household discharges constitute the main sources of pollution as far as the above water bodies are concerned.

Soil Pollution

It is defined as the build-up of persistent toxic compounds, chemicals, salts, radioactive materials, or disease causing agents , which adversely affect plant growth and animal health and also results in deterioration of the quality of soil. Soil pollution can be primarily traced to one or more of the following:

- Overburdens of mines;
- Effluents from industries;
- Sewage Sludge; and
- Application of pesticides and fertilizers in crop cultivation.

CONSEQUENCES OF ENVIRONMENTAL POLLUTION

Global Warming

Global warning, also called the greenhouse effect because of the gases that accumulate above the earth surface makes it comparable to a greenhouse. By trapping heat near the surface of the earth, the greenhouse effect leads to warming of the lower layer of atmosphere around earth. Among the various reasons causing global warming like overpopulation, deforestation, ozone depletion , garbage dumping, the release of certain gases in the atmosphere are the most important causes for concern. The greenhouse gases CO_2, NO_2, methane, halogens and CFCs are mainly caused by fossil fuel and wood burning. If the chemicals released due to human activities continue, the global temperature will rise.

Acid Precipitation

Acid rain is caused by airborne acidic pollutants present in gases let out from automobiles as well as power plants that burn coal. Most of the sulphur dioxide, around 70 per cent is caused by the power plants that use coal as the primary fuel, and 50 per cent of the worlds nitrogen oxide is produced by automobiles.The above two gases can be carried very far depending upon the prevailing wind pattern and are readily converted into acidic pollutants as a result of their reaction with oxygen , water and other chemicals while in the atmosphere. These acidic pollutants then become part of rain , snow and fog.

Ozone Layer Depletion

The ozone layer, located 10-50 km above the earth's surface, is essential to life on earth as it absorbs the ultraviolet (UV) rays from the sun. The principal cause of ozone layer depletion is increased stratospheric concentration of chloroform , methyl bromide and hydro-chloro -floro-carbons (HCFCs). The above chemicals decompose in the presence of sunlight in the upper stratosphere to release chlorine and bromine.

ENVIRONMENTAL POLLUTION IN INDIA

The rapid industrialization and fast growing population in India have been demanding on environment, infrastructure and natural resources. The process of industrialization has been accompanied by unrestrained exploitation of natural resources like land and water, resulting in environmental degradation on a mammoth scale. Some of the dominant current problems confronting India are industrial pollution, soil erosion, deforestation, urbanization and land degradation. The problems are further worsened by India's overbearing dependence on coal for generating power.Pollution of water bodies mainly occurs on account of dumping untreated sewage and garbage.

BENEFITS OF ADOPTING AN EMS

The benefits of an EMS and registration of the EMS to ISO 14000 are structured in to the following categories:

- Profit Maximization;
- Operation efficiency;
- Marketing;
- Regulatory Compliance; and
- Social Benefits.

PROFIT MAXIMIZATION

An organization can expect increased profits as a result of any one or all of the following:

- An EMS can help reduce occurrence of pollution and the related cost of recovery.
- Recycling waste or by-products generated during production and unused inputs could increase revenues.
- Improved employee health and safety decreases sick days and insurance risks, thereby improving productivity.
- Improved safety measures reduces insurance claims due to which costs of coverage and settlements are brought down.

OPERATION EFFICIENCY

- The EMS standards can establish "best practices" in environmental management and create a basis for the next stage of improvement.
- An EMS integrated with all other business systems in the company helps the management to get an overall idea of the effect of various processes on the company based on which environmental problems can be efficiently resolved.

- Disseminating environmental responsibility and awareness thought the organization can help to improve the effectiveness and efficiency of pollution prevention programmes.

MARKETING

- Creating a strong environmental image through an EMS and ISO 14000 registration can help catch the attention of environmentally conscious customers and build pressure on competitors.
- Community support for a firm could be enhanced by demonstrating concern for the local environment through an EMS.
- An organization with ISO 14001 certification has a positive corporate image as registration to this standard demonstrates that the organization's EMS meets the international standards for all purpose.

REGULATORY COMPLIANCE

An organization with ISO 14000 EMS is an indication to the regulatory agencies that it is committed to reducing pollution and continual improvement. Improved compliance with laws and regulations leads to reduction in penalties and redemption costs and such organizations are favoured by regulators.

SOCIAL BENEFITS

Adopting EMS in an organization can also bring in some social benefits such as cleaner air, water and soil, longer resource life through reduced usage , better waste management and progress toward a sustainable culture. Thus it can be seen that an EMS can prove to be a strategic tool for an organization for promoting a positive corporate image and sustainability. While adopting EMS it may be worthwhile to look into the various determining factors so as to deploy in most efficiently.

ROLE OF EMS IN PROVIDING A COMPETITIVE ADVANTAGE

Some of the exogenous agents like stakeholders, regulations, and industry together affect a firm's response to environmental initiatives while endogenous factors like existing technology and awareness of top management has a major role in the strategic impact of EMS. The firms who are early adopters of EMS have a strategic advantage over others who are yet to adopt it as these firms will be benchmarked as an environmental leader in the future. Investments made by firms in environmental health and safety initiatives not mandatory by regulations may not bring in profits in the short run but it definitely pays in the long run with an increase in stock price. Whenever a firm decides to implement EMS, an evaluation and analysis phase followed by development and improvement phase has to be undertaken. This helps in detecting any lapses that might have occurred in waste generation and consequently make progress towards waste reduction. A firm with an EMS in place projects an image of a socially responsible firm. It further helps in a positive public acceptance resulting in strengthening its competitive position in relation to its industry rivals.

CONCLUSION

The EMS is increasingly recognized as a means to provide a framework for integrating environmental measures into a firm's processes. If environment is saved, the environment shall save us should be the buzz word. It can assist a firm in meeting new environmental objectives, become a distinctive resources of the firm for supporting decision making processes concerning environmental issues and improving accountability for better management of environmental impacts. Sensitivity of eco imagination has also started gaining value and been utilized in all new ventures as has become a new effort and Endeavour. Business across the world are realizing that it is not enough to merely be compliant with environmental regulations but be a means to enhance environmental performance measures to be integrated into various processes so as to be able to compete on a new level and enhance profitability. The long sustainability of nature and its product shall nurture the human kind as well as their living hood. It will protect earth health.

REFERENCES

Robert, P. Sroufe, Steven A Melnyk, Gyula Vastag (1998), *Environmental Management System as a Source of Competitive Advantage.*

Nicole, Darnall, Danial Edwards jr. (2006), Predicting the Cost of Environmental Management System Adoption; The Role of Capabilities, Resources and Ownership Structure.

Environmental Management System and ISO 14000, Pollution Prevention and Abatement Handbook, WORLD BANK GROUP, Effective July 1998.

Edwin, Pinero, P. Charles Mason, Case Study: ISO14000-Benefits to the Bottom line.

Cary, Coglianese (1999), *Policy Implications of Environmental Management Systems.*

Martin, Baxter, (2000), *Environmental Management System.*

USEPA (United States Environmental Protection Agency). 2001a. An Organizational Guide to Pollution Prevention. USEPA, Office and Research and Development, epa-625-R-01-003: Cincinnati, OH.

USEPA (United States Environmental Protection Agency) 2001b. *Action Plan for Promoting the Usage of Environmental Management Systems. USEPA. Washington, DC.*

12

The Pledge for Environmental Protection

Dr. Bhavani Prasad Panda[1]

In this discourse an attempt has been made to provide basic information on 'the pledge of environment protection'; its purpose is to create awareness of the legal aspects and endeavors in India so as to enhance sensitivity to issues of caring and protection of the environment.

The Constitution of India (the mother law of the land), provides in its very preamble We, the People of India having solemnly resolved to constitute India into a Sovereign Socialist Secular Democratic Republic and to secure to all its citizens:

- Justice - social, economic and political;
- Liberty of thought, expression, belief, faith and worship;
- Equality of status and of opportunity and to promote among them all;
- Fraternity assuring the dignity of the individual and the unity and integrity of the nations.

1. P.G. Department of Law, Berhampur University, Orissa.

... hereby Adopt, Enact and Give to ourselves this Constitution'.

[The Preamble of the Constitution of India: 26th November 1949].

Environment and Directive Principles of State Policy

'The State shall endeavor to protect and improve the environment and to safeguard the forests and wild life of the country.' [Article 48-A Constitution of India (Included by1976 Amendment)].

Fundamental Duties

It shall be the duty of every citizen of India:

(a) to value and preserve the right heritage of our composite culture;

(b) to protect and improve the natural environment including forests, lakes, rivers and wild life, and to have compassion for living creature;

(c) to strive towards excellence in all spheres of individual and collective activity so that the nation constantly arises to higher levels of endeavor and achievements.'

[Article 51-A Constitution of India (Included by1976 Amendment)]

Environment includes water, air and land, and the inter-relationship which exists among water, air and land, and human beings, other living creatures, plants, micro-organism and property.

[(Environment (Protection) Act 1986]

VARIOUS STATUTES FOR ENVIRONMENT PROTECTION

- *Air (Prevention and Control of Pollution) Act,* 1981 — This is an Act to provide for the prevention, control and abatement of air pollution, for the establishment, with a view to carrying out the aforesaid purposes, of Boards, for conferring on and assigning to such Boards powers and functions relating thereto and for matters connected therewith. The 1987 amendment empowered the Board to shut down the defaulting industrial plant or may stop its supply of power or water. Air pollution also included noise pollution.

- *Water (Prevention and Control of Pollution) Act,* 1974: This is an Act to provide for the prevention and control of water pollution and the maintaining or restoring of wholesome of water, for the establishment. With a view to carrying out the purposes aforesaid of Boards for the prevention and control of water pollution, for conferring on the assigning to such Boards powers and functions relating thereto and for matters connected wherewith. After 1988 amendment, a Board may close a defaulting industrial plant or withdraw its supply of power· or water by any administrative order; the penalties are more stringent and a citizen's initiative provision bolsters the enforcement machinery.
- *The Water (Prevention and Control of Pollution) Cess Act,* 1977 - The Act creates economic incentives for pollution control through a differential tax structure (with higher rates applicable to defaulting units) and requires local authorities and certain designated industries to pay access for water consumption. These revenues are used to implement the Water Act, 1974.
- *The Indian Forest Act,* 1927: It includes the provisions for hunting restrictions is reserved or protected forests and authorized establishments of sanctuaries. The Act provides both for the public and private forests and facilitates the extraction of timber for profit.
- *Forest (Conservation) Act 1980:* This is an Act to provide for the conservation of forests and for matter connected therewith or ancillary or incidental there to.
- *Wildlife (Protection) Act, 1972:* This Act provides for the statutory framework for protecting wild animals, plants and their habitats. It specifies endangered species, which are

protected regardless of location, and all species protected in designated areas called sanctuaries and national parks. [Under Article 252(1)].

- *Environment (Protection) Act 1986*: This is an Act to provide for the protection and improvement of environment and matters connected there with:
  - Environment (Protection) Rules, 1986;
  - Hazardous Wastes (Management and Handling) Rules 1989;
  - Rules for the Manufacture, Storage and Import of Hazardous Chemicals, 1989;
  - Rules for the Manufacture, Use, Import, Export and Storage of hazardous Micro-Organisms/Genetically Engineered Organisms of Cells, 1989;
  - The Coastal Regulation Zone Notification 1991;
  - Environmental Impact Assessment Regulations 1994;
  - Bio-Medical Wastes (Management & Handling) Rules, 1998;
  - Noise Pollution (Regulation and Control) Rules, 2000; and
  - MSW (Management and Handling) Rules 2000
- *The Public Insurance Act,* 1991 provides for immediate relief to the victims of an accident involving a hazardous substance. To achieve this object, the Act imposes 'no fault liability' upon the *over* of the hazardous substances and requires the over to compensate the victims irrespective of any neglect or default on her part.
- *The National Environmental Tribunal Act* 1995 (NETA) is enacted on the foundation laid down by the PLIA and substantially extends the principle of 'no-fault liability', where statutory compensatory limits can be explored for a just settlement, the Tribunal is empowered to make interim

awards after granting opportunity rot he affected party and may determine its own procedure for processing the compensation claims, consistent with the principles of natural justice.

- *The National Environment Appellate Authority Act,* 1997 – Green bench for resolving litigations of environmental clearance.
- *The Mines into Minerals (Regulation and Development) Act* 1957 - This statute promotes the prospecting of minerals and the development of mines. In 1986 amendment, "Provisions are introduced requiring greater environmental sensitivity whilst conducting mining operations.
- *The Insecticide Act 1968* and *The Insecticide Rule,* 1971 along with Tiwari Committee report mandates for effective monitoring pesticide residues in the environment.
- *The Atomic Energy Act 1962* and *the Radiation Protection Rules 1971:* The regulation of nuclear energy and radioactive substances in India is governed by the Atomic Energy Act, 1962, and *the Radiation Protection Rules,* 1971. The Central Government is in mandate to prevent radiation hazards, guarantee public safety and the safety of workers handling radioactive substances, and the disposal of radioactive wastes.
- *The Factories Act, 1948:* After Bhopal Gas Leak Disaster, special provisions on hazardous industrial activities has been introduced in the year 1987. The Occupier is required to maintain designated "safety" standards and records thereof.

RIGHT TO LIFE AND ENVIRONMENT

A Fundamental Right: 'Enjoyment of life – including (the right to live as under Article 21 of Constitution of India) with human dignity encompasses within its ambit, the protection and preservation of environment, ecological balance free from pollution of air and water, sanitation, without which life cannot be enjoyed . . . Hygienic environment is an integral facet of right to healthy life and . . . there is a constitutional imperative on the State governments and the municipalities, not only ensure and safeguard proper environment but also an imperative duty to take adequate measures to promote, protect and improve both the man-made and the mutual environment.' [Supreme Court of India in *Virendrer Gaur* v. *State of Haryana* 1995 (2)SCC577]

The fundamental right to life and personal liberty as it includes right to livelihood provides a caveat on government actions with an environmental impacts that threatens to dislocate poor people and disrupt their lifestyles. Deprivation of this right to livelihood is deprivation of life the State may by affirmative action, be compatible to provide adequate means of livelihood or work for citizens. But any person, who is deprived of right to livelihood except according to life and fair procedure established by law, can challenge the deprivation as offending the right to life conferred Article 21 [Supreme Court of India in *Olga Tellis* v. *Bombay Municipal Corporation* 1986].

Fundamental Norms Guiding Environment

Ten Commandments of Environmental Practice:

1. Every person enjoys the right to a wholesome environment, which is a facet of the right to life guaranteed under Article 21 of the constitution of India;
2. Enforcement agencies are under all obligations to strictly enforce environmental laws;
3. Government agencies may not plead non-availability of funds, inadequacy of staff or other insufficiencies to justify the non-performance of their obligations under environmental laws;
4. The 'Polluter Pays' principle which is a part of the basic environmental law of the land requires that a polluter bear the remedial or clear up costs as well as the amounts payable to compensate the victim, of pollution;

5. The 'Precautionary Principle' requires government authorities to anticipate and prevent and attack causes of environmental pollution. This principle also imposes the onus of proof of the developer or industrialists to show that his or her action is environmentally benign;

6. Government Development Agencies changed with decision-making ought to give due regard to ecological factors including:

   (a) the environmental policy of the Central or State government;

   (b) the sustainable development and utilization of natural resources; and

   (c) the obligation of the present generation to present natural resources and pass on to future generations an environment as intact as the one who inherited from the previous generation;

7. Stringent action ought to be taken against contumacious defaulters and persons who carry on industrial or development activity for profit without regard to environmental laws;

8. The power conferred under the Environmental Protection Act, 1986 may be exercised only to advance environmental protection not for a purpose that would defeat the object of the law;

9. The State is the trustee of all natural resources which are by nature meant for public use and enjoyment. The public at large is the belldiciary of the sea-shore, running waters, air, forests and ecologically fragile lands. These resources cannot be converted into private ownership;

10. For the purpose of creating an informed citizenry and transparency of information and in order to harmonies any conflicting interests while preserving the democratic idea is the right to information provides a vital tool even with regard to environmental matters under the Right to Information Act, 2005.

[The Supreme Court of India on *Environmental Practice* - Refer Article 141].

Environment

'The Environment is a source of the energy and materials which mankind transforms into goods and services to meet his needs. It also acts as a vast sink for the wastes and polluting substances he generates. It provides a number of basic conditions needed for a successful economy - a stable climate. Environmental resources form the basis of and therefore set limits to economic development. Many environmental problems are rooted in an increased demand for natural resources and in the increased pollution and waste associated with current pattern of economic development' [J Thronton & S Beckwith 1997].

Pollution

'. . . the introduction by man into environment of substances or energy liable to cause hazards to human health, harm to living resources and ecological systems damage to structures or amenity, or interference with legitimate use of environment.' [M W Holdgate 1979].

Environment Pollution

'. . . the direct or indirect introduction as a result of human activity, of substances, vibrations, heat or noise into the air, water or land which may harmful to human health or the quality of the environment, result in damage to' material, property, or impair or interfere with amenities and other legitimate uses of the environment' [European Council 1996].

Harm means: '. . . harm to health of living organisms or other interference with the ecological systems of which they form part and in the case of man includes offence caused to any of his senses or harm to his property'.

Nuisance: means hurt or injury that which annoys or hurts especially if there is a legal remedy; which is offensive to the senses: a person or thing that is troublesome or obtrusive in some way [*Chambers 20th Century Dictionary*].

Public Nuisance: A person is guilty of a public nuisance, who does any act or is guilty of illegal omission which causes any common injury, danger or announce to the public or to the people in general who dwell or occupy property in the vicinity, or which must necessarily cause injury, obstruction, danger or annoyance to persons who may have occasions to use any public right. A common nuisance is not excused on the ground that it causes some convenience or advantage [Section 268 IPC, under chapter - 'Of offences affecting the public health, safety, convenience, decency and morals'].

Environmental Regulation Principles:

- Sustainable Development;
- Preventive Principle;
- Polluter Pays Principle;
- Precautionary Principle.

Sustainable Development Mechanisms

- Effective economic growth for poor nations;
- The participation of citizens in decision making;
- The adoption by the more affluent nations, of life styles within the planet's ecological means, particularly by reducing their use of energy;
- The control of population growth.

Development with regard to Land means

- The carrying out of building operations, engineering operations, minig operations or other operations in, over, or under land; or
- The making of any material change in the use of any buildings If other land.

Urban Development Planning

Local planning authorities should take into account of the environment in the widest sense in plan preparation. They are familiar with the 'traditional' issues of green belt, concern for landscape quality and nature conservation, the built heritage and conservation areas. They are familiar too with pollution control planning for healthier cities. The challenge is to ensure that newer environmental concerns such as global warming and the consumption of non-renewable resources are also reflected in the analysis of policies that form part of plan preparation.'

International Cooperation

The UN Conference on the Human Environment, Stockholm held in June 1972 made a declaration for international cooperation to:

> . . . effectively control, prevent, reduce and eliminate adverse environmental effects from activities conducted in all spheres, in such a way that due account is taken of the sovereignty and interests of all States. [Principle 24].

The World Commission on Environment end Development in 1987 noted that there had been a marked increase in the incidence of environmental crisis of a global nature', such as the drought in Mrica, which triggered an environmental and developmental crisis putting some 35 million people at risk and killing perhaps a million; . . . that if natural resources continued to be used at the current rate, if the plight of the poor was ignored, and if polluter and wasting of resources continued, a decline was to be expected in the quality of life of the world's population . . . Wealthy nations are called upon to make changes in their lifestyle by recycling waste' conserving energy and rehabilitating' damaged landscapes. [The Brundtland Report, *Our Common Future*, 1987]

The UN Conference oil Environment and Development Rio de Janeiro (1992)

It was described as starting the 'environmental revolution' which, if succeeds, will rank with agriculture and industrial revolutions as one of the economic and social transformation in human history.

Agenda 21 the global action plan for all States on development and environment was evolved. Two multi-lateral agreements were opened for signature - the Convention on Biological Diversity 1992 and UN Framework Convention on Climate Change 1992.

Rio de Janeiro Declaration - The right to development must be fulfilled so as to meet equitably developmental and environmental needs of present and future generations (Principle 3).

In order to achieve sustainable development environmental protection shall constitute an integral part of the development process and cannot be considered in isolation from it (Principle 4).

Waste Management

Waste is anything, which the holder discards intends discard or required to discard. Three types of wastes emanates from human activities:

- Waste which need not be produced at all;
- Waste which can be recycled; and
- Waste which must inevitably be produced but which cannot be recycled.

There is a need to:

- Prevention of waste production - 'eco-labelling initiatives'
- Recovery of waste products - 'recycling'
- Safe-disposal of waste - *'stricter standards'*.

Water Pollution

Water, Water Everywhere, Not a Drop to Drink!

[S T Coleridge]

'Human health and development are threatened in many places because of insufficient or poor quality water . . . increased water-use, discharge of wastes, excessive application of fertilizers, and pesticides and accidental spills of harmful substances have led to increasing pollution of many water bodies'.

Water pollution means such contamination of water or such alteration or the physical, chemical, biological properties of water or such discharge of any sewage or trade effluent or any other liquid, gaseous or solid substances into water (whether directly or indirectly) as mayor is likely to, create a nuisance or render such water harmful or injurious to public health or safety, or to domestic, commercial, industrial agricultural or other legitimate uses or to the life and health of animals or of plant organism.

'Trade or Sewage Effluent'

Trade effluent includes any liquid, gaseous or solid substances which is discharged from any premises used for carrying on any industry operation or process or treatment and disposal system other than domestic sewage.

Sewage effluent means effluent from any sewage system or sewage disposal works and includes sulage from open drains.

[Water Act 1974]

There is a need to:

- provide a secure supply of drinking water throughout the community which is safe in quality and sufficient in quantity;
- provide a supply of water which is of sufficient quality and quantity to meet the needs of agriculture and industry;
- maintain and enhance the4 ecological state of the aquatic environment;
- manage the water supply so as to prevent or reduce floods and drought.

Air

Air!- (The Oxygen for Life) The precious lifeline!

Air quality has a continuous and pervasive impact on human well-being and on our environment. As individuals we have little opportunity to pick and choose the air we breathe, still less to contract out, and the invisibility of many of our most significant contemporary air pollutants only further emphasises our dependence.

Air pollution means any solid, liquid or gaseous substance including noise present in the atmosphere in such concentration as may be or tend to be injurious to human beings or other living creatures or plants *ot* property or environment. [The Air Act 1981].

Nuisance Regime:

- Smoke emitted from premises so as to be prejudicial to health or a nuisance;
- Fumes or gases emitted from premises so as to prejudicial to health or a nuisance;
- Any dust, steam, smell, sound or other effluvia arising on industrial trade or business premises and being prejudicial to health or a nuisance.

The Directives are:

- To maintain the quality of air where it is good and to improve it where it is poor;
- To establish objectives for ambient air pollution control through out the community;
- To move closure towards harmonization of national air quality measurement programmes and provides monitoring information to the public.

Supreme Court of India observed

'We are conscious that environmental changes are the inevitable consequences of industrial development in our country, but at the same time the quality of environment cannot be permitted to be damaged by polluting air, water and land to such an extent that it becomes a health hazard for the residents of the area. . . . Needless to say that every citizen has a right to fresh air and live in pollution-free environment.' [*M C Mehta* v.' *Union of India* 1992 (3) SCC 257]

Noise: '. . . Sound which is undesired by the recipient', . . . a number of tonal components disagreeable to man and more or less intolerable to him because of the discomfort, fatigue disturbance and in some cases, pain it causes. Acute exposure to high noise levels prolonged exposure at lower levels are known to adversely affect the health and social development of exposed persons. The direct psychological effects include a loss of hearing, either temporary or permanent. The non-auditory efforts include cardiac ailments, stress and fatigue, and sleep disturbances. Among the psychological effects as documented by experts are a lack of concentration, loss of memory, and an adverse impact on the education of children. Noise is also suspected of aggravating nausea, headache, insomnia and loss of appetite. [*Dr. Y Toke* v. *State of Mahatrashtra* 1985].

Forest Cover

India's forests are in a devastated condition, with less than 18 per cent of India under forest cover as in 1997. To ensure ecological stability, 30 per cent of the nation should be under adequate forest cover. The recorded forest area constitutes about 37.34% of the total geographical area of the State of Orissa, actual forest cover exists over only 31% of the geographical area, and out of this 13% are open degraded forests. National Forest Policy has mandated that 33% of the geographical area should be under forest cover. The department has been constantly endeavouring to protect the forest areas and regenerate the degraded forests. It is heartening to note that according to the the Forest Report of the Forest Survey of India (2003), there has been actually an increase in dense forest cover in the State by 198 sq. km. This is attributed to both protection and successful Joint Forest Management (JFM) efforts. There is reported a decrease in forest cover by 472 sq. km, but overall there has been increased in forest and tree cover combined.

Joint Forest Management

One of the salient features of the National Forest Policy (1988) is to actively associate the people in the protection, conservation and management of the forests. The State Government is wedded to a policy of promoting participation of local village communities in protection and management of degraded forest. In August 1988, the State Government brought out a resolution to formally introduce a scheme of protection of peripheral reserve forests with participation of the people of adjoining villages. These guidelines have been fine-tuned from time to time, ending with September 1996 Resolution. In accordance with the 1993 JFM Resolution of the Government, 7,358 Nos. of Vana Samrakshana Samities (VSS) are functioning in the State for protecting and regenerating an area of about 8,039 Sq. km. of degraded forests through Joint Forest Management as in March 2005. During 2005-06 (up to September 2005) additional 2248 VSS have been formed with assignment of 479 sq. km. of forest area. Thus, the total number of VSS formed in the State as on September 2005 stands at 9,606 and 8,518 sq.km. of forest area is covered under protection of these Van Samrakshana Samitees. All the families of 8,010 villages are members of these VSS so far constituted.

Plantation Programme

According to the Forest Survey of India the forest cover in the State is 31% as against 33% of the total geographical area mandated by the National forest policy, 1988. There is thus an imperative need to accelerate efforts for a forestation and regeneration of the degraded forests for achieving the mandated 33% forest cover and also to reforest the degraded forests with less than 10% crown density in the entire recorded forest area measuring 4,574 sq.km. during 2005-06 the afforestation programmes has been implemented in the State under different State Plan and Central Plan over a total area of 19090 ha. Out of this 10,366 ha has been covered under Revised Long Term Action Plan (RLTAP), 2315 ha under National Afforestation Programme (NAP) and 6409 ha under Economic Plantation. Bulk of plantation is carried out in KBK districts under RLTAP. The department has been implementing Afforestation Programmes in K.B.K. districts under the Revised Long Term Action Plan for past nine years. During 2005, 5265 ha have been covered under Block Plantation, 10lha under Medicinal Plantation and another 5000 ha have been covered by rehabilitation of degraded forests. Fruit bearing and N.T.F.P. species as well as fuel wood, economic species and bamboo has been planted under the scheme. At every plantation site Vana Samrakshana Samities have been formed and people's participation ensured. The Forest and Wildlife Wing has also taken up 81 ha Jagannath Vana Prakalpa plantation and 343 ha mixed plantation from DRDA funding. Further 3642 ha plantation under compensatory afforestation has. also been taken up during the current year out of fund deposited by User Agencies for the purpose. Frangipani seedlings in 7400 number have also been planted at Lalitagiri Heritage site.

Orissa Forest Sector -Elements of a Vision - Principles

1. Forest planning and operations are sustainable, and balance environinental services, local use and commercial extraction;
2. Environmental services from forests are recognized and protected.
3. Local subsistence and forest based livelihood use has the first charge in forests, especially in scheduled areas based on strong incentives for local participation. Customary rights and usage are protected.
4. Operations and procedures are simple, transparent and effective.
5. Regulatory burdens and transaction costs are low.

Air/Water Pollution Problems

In the year 2005-06, 1029 industrial waste water/sewage samples, 330 stack emission samples and 730 ambient air (industrial premises) have been analyzed.

Regulation of Hazardous Wastes Management

The Board has granted authorization to 20 units for Management and Handling of Hazardous Wastes during 2005-06.

Management of Bio-Medical Wastes

The Board has granted authorization to 175 nos. of Health Care units during 2005-06 under the Bio-Medical Wastes (Management and Handling) Rules, 1998, with conditions for appropriate management, handling, treatment and disposal of biomedical wastes.

Management of Municipal Solid Waste

It has been decided to support two model MSW management facilities in two small ULBs of Orissa.

Planning and Monitoring

To plan a comprehensive programme for prevention and control of pollution, the Board has undertaken the following activities during 2005-06.

Water Qualities

In 62 stations of six major rivers of the state (Mahanadi, Brahmani, Baitarani, Rushikulya, Subarnarekha and Nagavali) 32 water quality parameters are being regularly monitored in each of those stations.

Monitoring of Ambient Air Quality

Monitoring of ambient air quality is regularly carried out in eight important towns and industrial areas like, Cuttack, Bhubaneswar, Balasore, Sambalpur, Berhampur, Rayagada, Angul and Rourkela. Air quality is being monitored in 15 stations in the above eight towns in respect of four parameters namely, suspended particulate matter, respirable particular matter, sulphur dioxide and nitrogen oxides.

Monitoring of Noise Pollution Level

Monitoring of noise pollution level on festive occasions like Dushera, Dipavali and Baliyatra and impact of idol immersion (Durga Puja) the water quality have been undertaken.

Preparation of district-wise Zoning Atlas for sitting of industries based on environmental consideration, for the districts of Khurda, Balangir and Sonepur are in progress.

The Board acts as a facilitator for the implementation of the Eco-city programme for Puri town, which has been approved in principle by the Central Pollution Control Board.

13

Conservation Priority of Little Known Endemic Species *Cycas spherica* Roxb. from Eastern Ghats, India

Chiranjibi Pattanaik,[1]
C. Sudhakar Reddy[2] and **P. Manikya Reddy**[3]

ABSTRACT

The gymnosperms are paid little attention in India now-a-days. *Cycas spherica* Roxb. is a rare and endemic species found in the Eastern Ghats of northern Andhra Pradesh and southern part of Orissa. The present article highlights the geographical distribution and detailed description of the species. Proper

1. Salim Ali Centre for Ornithology & Natural History, Deccan Regional Station, 12-13-588/B, Nagarjuna Nagar Colony, Tarnaka, Hyderabad 500 017, Andhra Pradesh.
E-mail: chiranjibipattanaik@gmail.com

2. Forestry & Ecology Division, National Remote Sensing Centre, Hyderabad 500 625, Andhra Pradesh

3. Department of Botany, Osmania University, Hyderabad 500 007, Andhra Pradesh.

assessment of the dwindling species and appropriate conservation measures are to be needed immediately before it wiped out from the world.

INTRODUCTION

The genus *Cycas* is the single genus of the family Cycadaceae, the sole living cycad group occurring in Asia. *Cycas* consists of about 100 species, chiefly Indo-Chinese (about 40 species) and Australian (27 species) (Lindstrom and Hill, 2007). The genus also occurs in the Malesian region, Japan and India, extending to Micronesia and Polynesia, Madagascar and East Africa. A total of six species are found in India (Hill, 1995; Muniappan and Viraktamath, 2006; Prathapan, 2006). But the survey done by Lindstorm and Hill suggested nine species of *Cycas* are present in India including sub-species *C. rumphii* (Lindstrom and Hill, 2007). *Cycas rumphii* found only in Andaman and Nicobar Islands. *C. revoluta*, *C. siamensis* and *Zamia* sp. have been introduced to India by the landscape industry under ornamental horticulture. The type species of this genus, *Cycas spherica* is distributed in Eastern Ghats of Orissa and found only in some forest patches of Orissa and Andhra Pradesh (Fig. 13.1). The taxon is described as *Cycas circinalis* var. *orixensis* by Haines (1924) and generally treated as *Cycas circinalis* earlier, differs markedly in its megasporophylls. The distinguishing characters of C. spherical in which it has been separated from *C. circinalis* are mentioned in Table 13.1.

Cycas spherica was first mentioned by Roxburgh in 1814, and formally described by him in 1832 (Roxburgh, 1832). No type was cited, although reference was made in the description to plants in cultivation in the botanic gardens in Calcutta. Roxburgh had evidently confused plants of *C. spherica* and *C. rumphii* with *C. circinalis*. Two Roxburgh collections from the Calcutta gardens were identified as *C. spherica* and *C. rumphii* respectively. The latter is annotated '*C. circinalis*', and the former bears only the annotation '*C. planifolia* Solander MS.' This taxon was redescribed in 1924 as a variety of the closely related *C. circinalis* by English

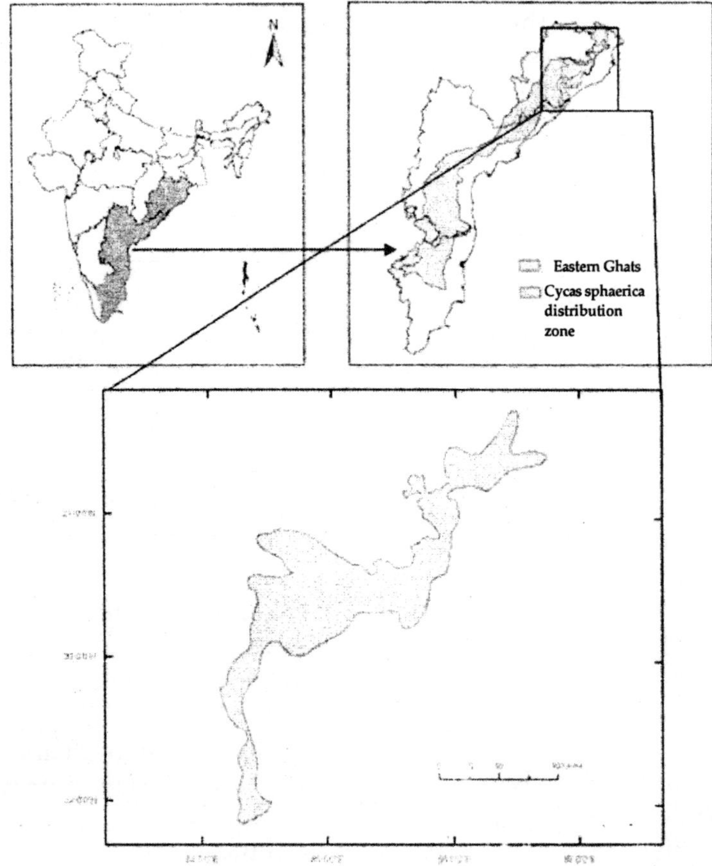

Fig. 13.1: **Location map of the study area**

forester Henry Haselfoot Haines (1867-1945). No type was cited, but Haines stated 'Wild in the hill forests of the Mals of Puri, especially on the tops of ridges with heavy rainfall extending to Angul, in open forest, where it is less common Fl. July-August'. Haines' practise was to add the '!' when he had seen the plant in the wild in that locality. Later, this species is added in Haines flora and Flora of Orissa (Saxena and Brahmam, 1996).

Table 13.1: Distinguishing characters of two *Cycas* species

	Cycas circinalis L.	*Cycas spherica* Roxb.
Stem Leaves	up to 7 m 150-270 cm long; 54-110 leaflets	up to 5 m 95-185 cm long; 55-130 leaflets
Petiole	34-70 cm long	27-50 cm long
Median leaflets	220-360 cm long	180-270 cm long
Cataphyll Pollen cones	50 mm long light brown to brown in colour; 24-48 cm long	50-70 mm long orange in colour; 45 cm long
Microsporophyll	45-60 mm long	28-34 mm long
Megasporophyll	20-35 cm long	20-25 cm long
Ovule	4-12 in number	2-5 in number
Seeds	elongted; 30-39 mm long	subglobose; 25 mm long
Lateral teeth of megasporophyll	less than 6 mm long	more than 6 mm long
Megasporophyll lamina	7.4 to 10 cm long	3.5 to 5.5 cm long
Microsporophyll lamina	3.8 to 5 cm long	3.2 to 3.8 cm long
Female cone	6-12 carpophylls	more than 50 carpophylls
Endemic	Western Ghats (Kerala, Karnataka, Tamil Nadu, south of Maharashtra)	Eastern Ghats (Orissa and Srikakulam of Andhra Pradesh)

* modified after Reddy *et al.*, 2007; Lindstorm and Hill, 2007.

The species has botanical, economic, ornamental and distributional interest. Young leaves of the plant are edible. The pithy hearts of cycad trunk is the source of starchy material 'Sago' which is used by tribal people (Reddy et al., 2006). It is often planted in home gardens for landscaping purpose. The fronds of this plant are used extensively in bouquets by floriculture industry. A paste of seeds with coconut oil is used for the treatment of skin complaints, wounds, ulcers, sores and boils. We are able to find this species in moist and dry deciduous forests in most of our field visits to the Eastern Ghats of Orissa. A detailed description with additional notes is provided.

DESCRIPTION

Cycas spherica Roxb., Fl. Ind.: 747 (1832). TYPE: ex hort. Calcutta, *Roxburgh s.n.*, 1808 (lecto BM, fide Hill 1995).

Cycas circinalis var. *orixensis* Haines, Bot. Bihar Orissa 6: 1228 (1924). TYPE: India, Orissa, Mals of Puri, *Haines 5876*, June 1917 (syn. K); Angul, *Haines 5877*, July 1917 (syn.K).

Stems arborescent, to 5 m. tall, 9-27 cm diameter (Fig. 13.2); growing in soil or humus; base not strongly swollen; bark thick with persistent leaf bases and cataphylls. Leaves dark green, semiglossy, 95-185 cm long, flat (not keeled) in section, (opposing leaflets inserted at 180° on rachis), with 55-130 leaflets, with newly emerging leaves light green and lacking tomentum because tomentum sheds very early as leaf expands. Petiole 27-50 cm long (15-30% of total leaf length), glabrous, spinescent for 20-100% of length. Basal leaflets not gradually reducing to spines. Median leaflets simple, weakly discolorous, 180-270 mm long, 7-12 mm wide, narrowed to 3-4 mm at base (25-60% of maximum width), spaced at 12-22 mm on rachis; section flat; margins flat or slightly decurved, not undulate; apex softly acuminate, not spinescent; midrib raised above, raised below, narrow. Cataphylls narrowly triangular soft, thinly sericeous or lacking tomentum, 50-70 mm long. Pollen cones narrowly ovoid, orange, c. 45 cm long, c. 10 cm dia., microsporophyll lamina firm, not dorsiventrally thickened, 32–38 mm long; fertile zone 28-34 mm long, sterile apex c. 4 mm long, merging with apical spine; apical spine prominent, gradually raised, c. 17 mm long. Seed cones open at pollination, open at seed set. Megasporophylls 20-25 cm long, persistently orange-tomentose; ovules 3-8, glabrous; lamina lanceolate, 28-43 mm long, 18-20 mm wide, shallowly pectinate or regularly dentate, with 21-25 pungent lateral spines 5-10 mm long; apical spine distinct from lateral spines, 17-29 mm long, 4-5 m wide at base. Seeds subglobose, 25 mm long, c. 25 mm wide; sarcotesta yellow, fibrous layer absent; sclerotesta smooth; spongy endotesta absent (Haines, 1921-25; Roxburgh, 1814).

Fig. 13.2. (a) *Cycas spherica* plant; (b) Megasporophyll; (c) Leaf; (d) Young leaf buds

DISTRIBUTION

Cycas spherica is found in the Eastern Ghats of Orissa in north-eastern and eastern peninsular India (Fig. 13.1). It grows in dry and moist mixed deciduous forest and also in woodlands on hills. From our field reports, we could confirmed the species from Mahendragiri hills (Gajapati district), Ganjam district, Chandaka Wildlife Sanctuary (Khurda), Cuttack and Dhenkanal districts; sparse in moist deciduous forests of Phulbani, Boudh (Khondmals), Nayagarh, Angul, Hadgarh Wildlife Sanctuary (Keonjhar), Kuldiha Wildlife Sanctuary (Balasore) and southern part of Similipal Biosphere Reserve (Mayurbhanj district) of Orissa. This species is also reported from northern most part of Srikakulam district in deciduous forests and woodlands of Palakonda, Donubayi and Seetampeta areas (Rao and Sreeramulu, 1986).

ASSESSMENT AND CONSERVATION MEASURES

Proper and adequate information regarding the taxa, its ecological requirements and population dynamics are essential for the conservation and preservation of the species. Out of nine *Cycas* species found in India, only three are listed in IUCN 2007 Red List Category (IUCN, 2007). This is because of inadequacy of data and improper assessment of other taxa in India. *Cycas spherica* is already in endemic list because of exclusively native to Eastern Ghats of Orissa and northern Eastern Ghats of Andhra Pradesh. But in IUCN 2007 Red List Category, the threat status is mentioned as Data Deficient (DD). It is also included in the CITES Appendix II category list which indicates the species are not necessarily now threatened with extinction but that may become so unless trade is closely controlled (UNEP-WCMC, 2008). It has first included in the CITES Appendix II category in CITES species database in the year 1977. Since then, it has not been upgraded to CITES Appendix I category after 31 years due to lack of information on the species. A consistent assessment and taxonomic survey is essential on total population demography (age profiles, sex ratios, mortality and regeneration rates), which allow upgrading the threat status in IUCN Red List Category. Conservation status of all cycad species is summerised in Table 13.2.

The species should be accorded the highest conservation priority to protect from rampant habitat destruction. In Orissa, most of the tribal people are practising the shifting cultivation, locally known as *Podu* cultivation. In this practice, all the virgin forests are cut down, burnt and the land is used for rice cultivation for two to three years. Later, the tribal people abandoned the cultivated field and search out for some other forest areas for the same purpose. The bulk of the shifting cultivation takes place along the roads and nearby areas, as they are the most accessible. Due to this practice many virgin forests of the Eastern Ghats of Orissa which includes *Cycas* habitat also, has disappeared (Reddy *et al.*, 2008). Forest fire is also one of the threats to this species because when fire occurs, along with other

Table 13.2: Conservation status of *cycad* species in India

Species	*Habitat*	*Wild locality*	*Other countries*	*Estimated No. of matured population**	*IUCN 2007 threat status*	*Status in India*	*CITES Appendix*
1	2	3	4	5	6	7	8
C. *annakailensis*	Steep slopes of	Annaikal hills near palghat	–	<100	DD	E	–
Rita Singh and P.Radha Rita Singh Radha, 2006)	evergreen forests	district of Kerala (Western Ghats)					
C. *beddomei* Dyer	dry open hill slopes, open woodland or grassland	Cuddapah hills (Eastern Ghats of Andhra Pradesh)	–	500	CR	E	I
C. *circinalis* L.	Dense seasonally dry scrubby woodlands in hilly areas	Andhra Pradesh, Karnataka, Kerala and South Maharashtra	–	7500	DD	E	II
C. *indica* A.Lindstrom and K.D. Hill	Flat land	East of Tamil Nadu	–	–	–	–	–
C. *nathorstii* J. Schust	Flat sandstone or on quartzite-dominated areas	Hassan district of Karnataka	North Sri Lanka	–	DD	–	II

(*Contd…*)

1	2	3	4	5	6	7	8
C. *pectiata* Buch.-Ham.	Hill forests	Northeast India	Vietnam, China, Thailand, Bangaladesh	>10000	VU	E	II
C. *rumphii* Miq.	Dense evergreen forests	Andaman & Nicobar Islands	Indonesia, papua New Guinea	–	NT	–	II
C. *spherica* Roxb.	Moist and dry deciduous forests and woodlands on hills	Hilly areas of Eastern Ghats of Orissa	–	–	DD	–	II
C. *zeylanica* (J.Schust) A.Lindstrom & K.D.Hill	Littoral forest near · sea in sandy soil	Andaman Islands	South Sri Lanka	–	DD	–	II

N.B. *Osborne, 1995; Lindstorm and Hill, 2007.

vegetation *Cycas* is also burnt and destroyed. Large-scale deforestation, drying of streams, plantation programmes by State Forest Department has become common phenomena, which adversely affect the regeneration of *Cycas* species. Probability of dispersal of spores of *Cycas* sp. in adverse/dry habitats has increased many folds due to logging and thinning operations in forest areas. Understanding the mechanisms of pollination in *Cycas* is important, as their regeneration is crippled by slow growth and reproduction. That is why a very few seedlings and saplings were observed in the forest areas during our field visits. This indicates the failure of regeneration. Attack of invasive alien species like *Eupatorium, Lantana, Parthenium* species on deforested areas hampers the regeneration capacity. Any natural disaster like diseases, pest attack, etc. may eventually wipe out the remaining populations of this species. The killing of several cycad species by the Asian *cycas* scale, *Aulacaspis yasumatsui*, a native of Southeast Asia has been already illustrated (Muniappan and Viraktamath, 2006).

This species needs *in situ* as well as *ex-situ* conservation by establishing arboreta and gene banks in suitable locations. Advanced technology like tissue culture, biochemical and molecular tool techniques need to be implemented to surmount the regeneration problem of the species. More research efforts are required to coordinate between different research organizations, universities for identification and mapping of those critical cycad areas using advanced geospatial tools like remote sensing (RS) and geographic information system (GIS). Other components like to study the behaviour of pollinators, seed dispersers and diseases of *Cycas* also need to be studied thoroughly. Large-scale harvesting of leaves for decorative purpose in urban areas should be banned. Many of the private and government organizations are planted this species in the gardens for beautification. This practice should not be encouraged. Collection of male cones before pollen shed for the use in traditional medicine prevents the flow from male to female leading to loss of reproduction (Prathapan, 2006). Emphasis will be given on creating awareness on the scientific and cultural importance of the species to the tribal people who are in frequent contact to forest areas and harvesting it for their needs. Last but not least, habitat loss and selective removal of mature plants from the wild for trade or utilization are major threats for existence of the species. The high demand for *C. spherica* pith, cones and leaves, combined with the slow growing nature of this species, suggest that conservation will require the combined efforts of cultivation inside and outside of the forests, pressure on the floriculture industry to use leaves of substitute species, and better protection of the remaining wild populations.

REFERENCES

Haines, H.H. 1921-25. *The Botany of Bihar and Orissa,* Adlard & Son Ltd., London.

Hill, K.D. 1995. The Genus *Cycas* (Cycadaceae) in the Indian Region, with Notes on the Application and Typification of the Name *Cycas circinalis*. *Taxon*, 44: 23-31.

IUCN 2007. *2007 IUCN Red List of Threatened Species,* www.iucnredlist.org, Downloaded on 12 August 2008.

Lindstrom, A. J. and Hill, K.D. 2007. The genus *Cycas* (Cycadaceae) in India. *Telopea,* 11: 463-489.

Muniappan, R. and Viraktamath, C. A. 2006. The Asian Cycad Scale *Aulocaspis yasumatsui,* A Threat to Native Cycads in India. *Current Science,* 91: 868-870.

Osborne, R. 1995. The World Cycad Census and a Proposed Revision of the Threatened Species Status for Cycad Taxa. *Biological Conservation,* 71: 1-12.

Prathapan, K. D. 2006. Conservation of Cycads in India. *Current Science,* 91: 862-863.

Rao, S. S. and Sreeramulu, S. H. 1986. *Flora of Srikakulam District, Andhra Pradesh,* Meerut University, Meerut.

Reddy, C.S., Rao, K.R.M., Pattanaik Chiranjibi and Joshi, P. K. 2008. Assessment of Large-scale Deforestation of Nawarangpur District, Orissa, India: A Remote Sensing Based Study. *Environment Monitoring and Assessment*, DOI 10.1007/s10661-008-0400-9.

Reddy, C.S., Reddy, K.N., Pattanaik Chiranjibi and Raju, V. S. 2006. Ethnobotanical Observations on Some Endemic Plants of Eastern Ghats, India. *Ethnobotanical Leaflets,* 10: 82-91.

Reddy. C.S., Rao, K.S., Pattanaik Chiranjibi, Reddy, K. N. and Raju, V. S. 2007. *Cycas spherica* Roxb: A Little Known Endemic Species from Eastern Ghats, India. *Journal of Plant Sciences*, 2: 362-365.

Roxburgh, W. 1832. *Flora Indica and Descriptions of Indian Plants*, Calcutta.

Roxburgh, W. 1814. *Hortus Bengalensis*, Mission Press, Serampore.

Saxena, H.O. and Brahmam, M. 1996. *The Flora of Orissa*, vol-3, Orissa Forest Development Corporation Ltd., Bhubaneswar.

Singh, R. and Radha, P. 2006. A New Species of *Cycas* from the Malabar Coast, Western Ghats, India. *Brittonia*, 58: 119-123.

UNEP-WCMC, *UNEP-WCMC Species Database: CITES-Listed Species* On the World Wide Web : http://www.unep-wcmc.org/isdb/CITES/Taxonomy/, accessed on 12 August 2008.

14

Lymphatic Filariasis
A Major Public Health Problem

Surajit Das[1]
Soumendranath Chatterjee[2]

INTRODUCTION

Vector-borne diseases such as malaria, dengue, yellow fever, plague, filariasis, louse-borne typhus, trypanosomiasis, and leishmaniasis are responsible for more human diseases and death than all other causes. However, the benefits of vector-borne disease control programs were short-lived, and in the last thirty years, there has been a dramatic global resurgence of infectious diseases. In recent years, vector-borne diseases (VBD) have emerged as a serious public health problem in countries of the South-East Asia Region, including India. Many of these, particularly dengue fever, Japanese Encephalitis (JE) and malaria now occur in epidemic form almost on an annual basis causing

1. Department of Zoology, Kabi Nazrul College, Murarai, Birbhum-731219, West Bengal, India.

2. Microbiology Research Unit, Department of Zoology, The University of Burdwan, Burdwan- 713104, West Bengal, India.

considerable morbidity and mortality. Dengue is spreading rapidly to newer areas, with outbreaks occurring more frequently and explosively. Chikungunya has re-emerged in India after a gap of more than three decades affecting many States. The risk factors, which play a key role in the spread and transmission of mosquito-borne diseases, include globalization, unplanned and uncontrolled urbanization, developmental activities, poor environmental sanitation, human behaviour relating to water collection, lifestyles, widespread travel and human migration, both within the country and across borders. Lymphatic filariasis is infection caused by the filarial worms, *Wuchereria bancrofti*, *Brugia malayi* or *B. timori*. These parasites are transmitted to humans through the bite of infective mosquitoes and develop into adult worms in the lymphatic vessels, causing severe damage and swelling (lymphoedema). Elephantiasis – painful, disfiguring swelling of the legs and genital organs – is a classic sign of late-stage disease (Fig. 14.1). The infection can be treated with drugs. However, chronic conditions may not be curable by anti-filarial drugs and require other measures, e.g. surgery for hydrocele, care of the skin and exercise to increase lymphatic drainage in lymphoedema. Annual treatment of all individuals at risk (individuals living in endemic areas) with recommended anti-filarial drugs combination of either diethyl-carbamazine citrate (DEC) and albendazole, or ivermectin and albendazole; or the regular use of DEC fortified salt can prevent occurrence of new infection and disease.

DISTRIBUTION

Human lymphatic filariasis occurs in humid tropical foci in Africa, the Americas, Asia, and numerous islands in the Pacific Ocean. Local epidemiology of the disease is strongly influenced by the behaviour and ecology of the various species of mosquito vectors, so that seven principal epidemiological zones of Bancroftian filariasis distribution are based on regional variations of the vectors. Brugian filariasis is restricted to parts of Southeast Asia and Australasia. Unlike malaria or arboviruses, which may be transmitted by the bite of a single infective vector, filarial

Indian vector: *Culex quinquefasciatus*

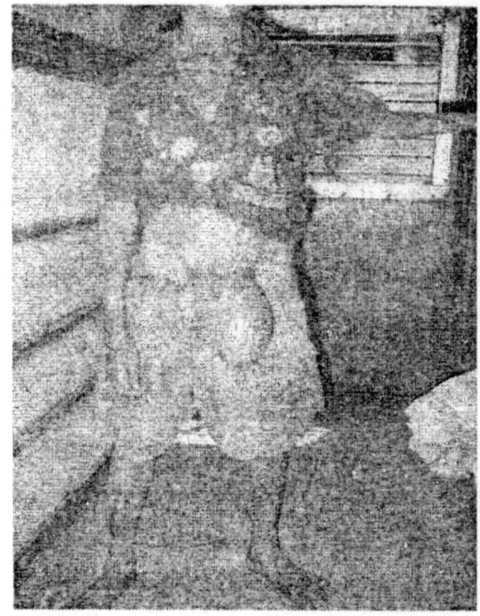

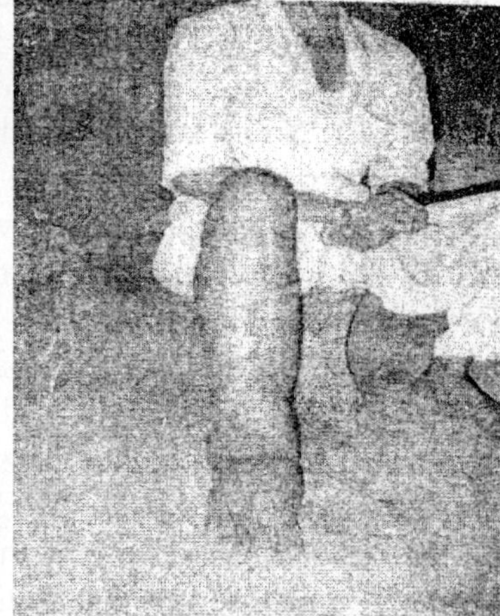

Fig. 14.1: **Patients of filariasis**

infections require repeated inoculation of infective larvae - perhaps hundreds per year - in order for the worms to reproduce successfully and produce microfilaraemia. Often the disease is asymptomatic initially with subsequent episodes of acute inflammation of the lymphatic system and fever, with the chronic stage of "elephantiasis" developing only after many years, if at all, by which time the microfilariae have usually disappeared from the bloodstream of the patient.

Bancroftian Filariasis

In urban situations, *W. bancrofti* is becoming increasingly prevalent in warm countries due to transmission by *Culex quinquefasciatus* and *C. pipiens*, which prefer to breed in polluted water.

Brugian Filariasis

Brugia malayi occurs only in South Asia, where its distribution and prevalence have been reduced by control of vector *Mansonia* spp. by the simple method of removal of the host-plants from their breeding-places. Sub periodic strains occur in swamp-forest habitats, transmitted mainly by the *M. bonneaedives* group as a zoonotic cycle. The sub periodic forms are transmitted by the *Mansonia* spp. and by *Coquillettidia crassipes*. *Brugia timori* is restricted to Indonesian islands of Flores and Timor and of others nearby. It is apparently not zoonotic, and the only known vector is *Anopheles barbirostris*. It is interesting that *B. timori* can apparently not be transmitted by various other mosquito species such as *A. subpictus*, which is a vector of both malaria and *W. bancrofti* among people in that area.

EARLY HISTORY OF FILARIASIS

The famous physician Sushruta recorded human filariasis in Indian sub-continent in *Sushruta Samhita* as early as sixth century B.C. He described the two varieties of disease as *vridhi* (scrotal tumour) and *slipadam* (elephantiasis of the leg). Sushruta described *slipadam* as the disease giving rise to swelling form inguinal region to thigh, knee and finally foot, accompanied with pain at intervals, fever and burning sensation. According to him the disease used to be continued to legs and hands and sometimes extended to ear, nose, lips and from scrotum to penis. He stated that extensive swelling of the affected part, exudation and knotty growths were incurable (Harnle, 1877; Ray, 1902; Vishagaratna, 1907; Seal, 1915; Garrison, 1917).

The clinical features of filariasis presently differ very little from the description of Sushruta, described more than 2500 years ago. Modern therapeutic knowledge supports the prognosis of the disease as predicted by that famous physician.

The clinical features produced in brancroftian filariasis were observed and described by ancient Hindu savants and by Persian physicians like Rhazes, Avicenna who referred to this disease as *Elephantiasis arabicum* (Faust and Russel, 1964).For past 25 centuries no further knowledge of this disease was added. Only in the middle of nineteenth century, a series of events occurred focusing this disease.

In 1863, French surgeon, Demarquay discovered the embryo of a nematode from chylous hydrocele fluid of a patient in

Havana, Cuba. He observed the same nematode larvae in 1868 and 1869 in Chyluria patients. Wucherer of Brazil found the embryo in the Chylus urine of man in August 1866; but these particulars were not published till 1868.

In 1872 Timothy Lewis found this microscopic nematode larva in the peripheral blood and urine of a patient in Calcutta for the first time.

Bancroft (1899) found the adult female parasite in an abscess from the arm of a Chinese in Brisbane in December 1876 and sent the same to Cobbold who named it *Filaria bancrofti* and published the news in July 1877 in the Lancet, about a month before finding of this parasite by Lewis in Calcutta (Lewis, 1877).

Alfred Gibbs Bourne, in Madras, described the male parasite in May 1888, from a specimen sent to him by Sibthrope (1888), through in August 1877, Lewis could isolate portions of male and female worm from a lymph scrotum in Calcutta.

The discovery of the mosquito as the intermediate host and biological vector of the falarial parasite was made by Sir Patrick Manson and was communicated through Cobbold to the Linnean Society in October 1878. He pointed out the necessity of a blood sucking arthropod for intermediation and development of filarial worm.

Manson (1883) gave the description of the dramatic metamorphosis of the filarial embryo to the adult from in his book *The Filaria Sanguinis Hominis*. Cobbold accepted the work of Manson in March 1878 and wrote unreservedly "Manson's remarkable discovery of the intermediate host" (Manson Bahr and Alcock, 1927). Bancroft (1899) of Brisbane provide conclusively that the infective embroys of the filarial worms entered into human system through the skin when they were deposited on it during their act of biting by the mosquitoes bearing them. He also noticed that the microfilariae required 16-17 days in the mosquito to reach infective stage (Bancroft, 1899).

This view was corroborated by Low (1900) in England and James (1900) in India. Since Wucherer was the first to discover the embryo, now known as microfilaria and Bancroft (Joseph) (1899) the adult, this filarial worm later received the new nomenclature *Wuchereria bancrofti* (Cobbold, 1877).

Microfilariae of *W. bancrofti* are nocturnally periodic. This observation was supported by many scientists from different tropical countries. Several theories have been put forward to explain the different factors involved for norturnal periodicity, but none of these was adequate to clear off the phenomenon (Manson, 1883; Korke, 1928; Iyenger, 1933; Raghaban and Krishnan, 1949; Hawking and Thurston, 1951).

In 1956, Mc Fadzean and Hawking proved that the periodicity of *W. bancrofti* may depend on changes in the difference of oxygen tension between venous and arterial blood by day and night. During day-time, the microfilariae accumulate in the lungs where the oxygen tension is increased by rise in oxygen tension and decreased by its fall. Masuya *et al.* (1887) suggested that the mircrofilariae possess a photosensitive substance containing a Vitamin-A like carotenoid similar to visual pigments in fluorescent granules in the epidermis which causes them to leave the peripheral circulation in day light and collected in the lungs. Periodic microfilariae possess numerous granules in contrast to sub periodic and aperiodic forms which have few or none. A high infection rate has also been recorded by several workers during their study on experimental transmission of *W. brancrofti* to *Cx. quinquefasciatus* (Rao and Iyenger, 1932; Raghavan and Krishnan, 1949). Available records on certain epidemiological and entomological aspects of bancroftian filariasis and its vector, *Cx. quinquefasciatus* in relation to the present study are mentioned below under separate headings.

Infection Rate

World Scenario

Dissanayake S (1989) made a sero-epidemiological survey of bancroftian filariasis in two townships of Sri Lanka with the objectives of determining the microfilaria rates, dependence of age and sex etc. The mean microfilaria rate was 5.4%. Microfilariaemia was not sex-dependent but a marginally elevated incidence was seen in the 6 to 35 years of age. Cartel *et al.* (1992) reported that in French Polynesia, lymphatic filariasis was due to subperiodic *W. bancrofti* var. *pacifica*, transmitted by the vector mosquito, *Aedes polynesiensis*. Microfilariaemia was determined with 571 samples (314 males and 280 females); 122 subjects were microfilaria positive, which gave a microfilaria carrier prevalence rate of 21.4%. The percentage of carriers was significantly higher in males than females.

In 1993, Desowitz *et al.* surveyed bancroftian filariasis in an isolated hunter gatherer, shifting horiticulturist group in Papua New Guinea. Adult men had a significantly higher microfilariaemia rate than women. The microfilaria rates were 68.8% in males and 30.5% in females, although the average microfilarial density was approximately the same for adults of both sexes.

In 1993, Harb *et al.* made a survey of 3,25,000 residents of 314 villages in six governorates of the Nile delta area of Egypt and revealed that the prevalence of lymphatic filariasis increased from <1% in 1965 to >20% in 1991, especially in the governorates of Qulynbiya, Monufiya, Dakhalilya and Giza.

In 1993, Marzhuki *et al.* described that in Malaysia during 1988 to 1990 a decreasing trend was appeared in the number of filariasis cases detected countrywide.

In 1991, brugian filariasis accounted for 92% of the cases detected. The microfilaria rate also showed a decreasing trend countrywide for the years 1988 (0.57%) to 1990 (0.35%), but there was an increase in 1991. Gyapong *et al.* (1993) made a preliminary study regarding bancroftian filariasis in the Kassena Nankana district of the Upper East region of Ghana and found microfilaria rate 41.1% of *W. bancrofti*. In case of clinical manifestations, hydrocele was 30.8% and elephantiasis was 3.6%. Go VM, in the year 1993, studied lymphatic filariasis in a recently described endemic area in Marinduque, Philippines and microfilaria rate was found 16%. Among positive cases, 68% were males.

Mohamed *et al.* (1994) studied the present status of filariasis in an endemic area in Giza Governorate, Egypt. In Kafr Ghataty, clinical cases were found. In Azizya village, microfilaria cases were 8% but there was no clinical case.

In 1994, Anosike *et al.* conducted a filariasis survey was made in Bauchi State, Nigeria II and found 1.9% microfilaria rate of *W. bancrofti.*

Zhang *et al.* (1988) reported that in Hubei, China, before 1979, the microfilaria rate in some villages was as high as 30.69%. Up to 1988 the microfilaria rate in all endemic villages decreased to below 1%. Kimura *et al.* (1994) performed parasitological and clinical studies on *W. bancrofti* infection in Chunk State, Federated States of Micronesia. A total of 2193 people in 14 villages of nine islands were examined. Average microfilaria rate was 2.6%. High microfilaria rate of 7-10% were obtained in three villages of three islands.

Estambale *et al.* (1994) conducted a cross-sectional parasitological and clinical survey for *W. bancrofti* infection in an endemic community of South-Eastern Kenya, revealing circulating microfilariae at the rate of 13.7%. Mircrofilaria rate was higher in males (15.9%) than in female (11.6%).

Meyrowitch *et al.* (1995) carried out a clinical and parasitological survey of bancroftian filariasis in five endemic communities in North-Eastern Tanzania, covering a population of 3086 individuals. High microfilarial prevalences (17.7%-34.7%) and geometric mean intensities (251-1122 mf/ml) were observed in the communities.

Jemanch and Kebede (1995) made a clinico-epidemiological study of lymphatic filariasis in South-Western Ethiopia. The survey covered more than 90% of the population in Tektak and Ketch. The overall microfilaria prevalence was 20.7% (males-23.7%, females-18.5%). In males 20.3% had hydeoceles and this condition was noted in the age group of above 35 years. About 40% of those with hydrocoele had microfilariaemia. Mean microfilarial density was 309 mf/ml of blood. No elephantiasis was found.

Albuquerque *et al.* (1995) studied bancroftian filariasis in two urban areas of Recife, Brazil. In some areas microfilariaemia prevalence reached 14%. Overall microfilariaemia prevalence was 10% and males had higher prevalences of infection and disease than females.

Simonsen *et al.* (1995) made a filariasis survey in 3 endemic communities of North-Eastern Tanzania. Microfilaria rate of *W. bancrofti* was ranged from 22.2% to 37.6% and GMI (Geometric Mean Intensity) was 546-535 mf/ml blood. Hydrocele cases were found in 14.5% to 21.3% for all males and 52.9% to 62.1% for males aged 45 years and above. Elephantiasis cases were found 0.6% to 3.3%. In 1996, Gbakima and Sahr reported filariasis in the Kaiyamba Chiefdom, Moyamba district Sierra Leone 64 (10.2%) of the total 630 individuals examined were found positive for *W. bancrofti* microfilaria, 71.3% clinical cases due to *W. bancrofti* were inflammatory in nature, 36.5% were chronic of which 26.6% had hydroceles and 0.4% involve elephantiasis of both the scrotum and the lower legs.Omar (1996) surveyed bancroftian filariasis among South-East Asian expatriate workers in Saudi Arabia. Microfilaria rate and mean microfilarial density were found as 3.5% and 6.0%/20 mm3 blood respectively.

Holly and Hartman (1996) performed a study on Egyptian man that *Wuchereria bancrofti* is a mosquito-borne filarial nematode that commonly invades lymphatic vessels.

In 1998, World Health Organization reported in Geneva that in India accounts for 42.8% of global burden of lymphatic filariasis caused by *Wuchereria bancrofti*.Ivoke (2000) reported that a clinical and parasitological study was conduct in North Western Cameroon, Prevalence of microfilaria (mf) was statistically significant. In all ages mf rate of males (7.8%) were more significant than females (6.7%).

In Triteeraprapab *et al.* (2000) conducted a study regarding the prevalence of patient of *Wuchereria bancrofti* infection in the immigrants (2-5%) which has prompted concern in the public health community that the potential now exists for a re-emergence of bancroftian filariasis in Thailand.

Weill *et al.* (2000) conducted a study regarding quantitative polymerase chain reaction to estimate the number of amplified esterase genes in insecticide-resistant mosquitoes in France.

Weerasooriya *et al.* (2001) described that in Sri Lanka, the overall prevalence of microfilariaemia and mean microfilariaemia density were 4.4% and 20.6% respectively. Prevalence was significantly lower in the female subjects than male, and in males aged <20 years than in older males overall, 9.5% of the subjects had the clinical manifestations of bancroftian filariasis.

INDIAN SCENARIO

Kar (1993) conducted a filariasis survey in two villages namely Patrapara and Bhagabanpur of Puri district, Orissa. Clinical manifestations of lymphatic filariasis, microfilariaemia and filarial abscesses were observed in 37.2%, 15.8% and 11.8% of subjects respectively. Mean microfilarial density was 41.06.

Sarma *et al.* (1987) surveyed two villages in Chingleput district of Tamil Nadu for filariasis. In Valama Kandigai and Thomur, clinical disease and mircrofilaria rate were 20% and 12% respectively.

Jain *et al.* (1989) carried out an epidemiological survey of brugian filariasis in a rural community of Kerala State. Out of the total (11,604) examined population, 8.1% had microfilariaemia and 7.6% had filarial disease. The filarial disease rate showed no significant difference between two sexes while the microfilaria rate was significantly higher in males than females.

Srividya *et al.* (1991) made a survey in Pondicherry, examined 6493 individuals for filarial disease and 34,615 individuals for night blood microfilariaemia. The prevalence of chronic disease increased with age in both sexes, whereas acute episodic lymphangitis was independent of age. Clinical manifestations occurred in 14% of males and 2% of females, with the reference due to the high prevalence of hydrocele in males.

Raina *et al.* (1992) described status of lymphatic filariasis in some selected slum clusters of Delhi. Five thousand slum dwellers from three areas namely Harinagar, Yamuna Pushta and Vijay Ghat were surveyed. Microfilaria and disease rates in these three areas were in order of 6.3%, 2.2%, 3.7% and 1.4%, 0.5% and 0.1% respectively.

In 1993, Kar *et al.* studied 591 main landers and 106 tribals in an endemic village of Orissa.

The overall prevalences of clinical disease and infection in both mainlanders and tribals were 34.18%, 14.4% and 25.47%, 17.9% respectively. No true elephantiasis was observed in Tribals.

Kumar *et al.* (1994) conducted a survey for prevalence of filariasis in 8 randomly selected villages of Puri district and 782 persons were examined. The prevalence of microfilaria rate was found to be 7.3% and the disease rate was 9.5%. The microfilaria rate was higher in males (8.8%) than females (5.7%) and similarly the disease rates were 10.6% and 8.3% respectively in two sexes.

Dutta *et al.* (1995) surveyed the labour population of a tea estate in upper Assam and microfilaria rate was found as 8.3%. The microfilaria rate was high in males (10.8%) as compared to females (6.03%). Mean microfilaria count in males was 36.8% and in females 26.7% and overall disease rate was 0.50% (males 0.82%, females 0.22%).

Tiwari *et al.* (1989) reported diurnally subperiodic filariasis among tribal population in the Nancowry group of islands in the Andaman and Nicobar islands due to *W. bancrofti* and microfilaria rate was ranged from 1.2% to 18.7% with a low disease rate (mean-1.9%). Incidence of microfilariaemia was low in children less than 10 years old (3.5%), but increased with increasing age.

Chand *et al.* (1996) conducted a study regarding prevalence of *W. bancrofti* infection among the tribals of Panna district of Madhya Pradesh. The overall microfilaria rate in the area was 3.8% and the males had higher microfilaria rate (4.5%) than the females (2.8%).

Shriram *et al.* (1996) reported that a survey was carried out for the first time in the Little Andaman island, covering a population of 12,247 in 12 of the 13 villages. Infection due to nocturnally periodic *W. bancrofti* was found only in three villages with microfilaria rate ranging from 1.02% to 6.35%.

Norman *et al.* (2000) reported that the effects of control options against filariasis by incorporating the impact of age structure of human community. This was tested for *Wuchereria bancrofti* transmitted by *Cx. quinquefasciatus* in Pondicherry, South India.

In 2001, Chhotray *et al.* conducted a study on lymphatic filariasis in the coastal district of Orissa. The clinical and epidemiological status of the diseases in Puri district, known to be endemic for filariasis.

In 2002 Srividya *et al.* reported that in Southern India, the spatial population structural of infection agent is increasingly recognized as being key to their more effective mapping and to improving knowledge of their overall population dynamics and control.

Beuria *et al.* (2003) reported that in Orissa, India, the prevalence of uninfected individuals was highest in the younger age groups (aged less than or equal to 15 years), decreased rapidly in those aged >15 to 40 years, and then stabilized in those aged >40 years conducted a study.

Suma *et al.* (2003) assessed the perceptions, practices and socio-psychological problems of 127 patients with brugian filariasis in Kerala.

Ramaiah *et al.* (2005) conducted a study on filariasis. According to them the main strategy now adopted for the elimination of lymphatic filariasis (LF) is based on mass drug administrations (MDA). Annual administration of antifilarial drugs to 65%-80% of the population at risk of the disease is believed to be necessary if LF is to be eliminated, at least as a public-health problem, within a reasonable time-frame.

To facilitate the development of drug-delivery strategies that are sufficient to ensure such high treatment coverages in large urban areas, a situation analysis was undertaken in the Indian city of Chennai.

The subjects interviewed came from households with high, moderate, low or very low incomes. A lack of information on the prevalence and socio-economic impact of the disease meant that LF was not viewed as a major pubic-health problem in the study area, even though cases of elephantiasis and hydrocele were detected in 2%-8% and 7%-20% of the households investigated. Overall, 40% of the interviewees from very-low-income households and 78% of those from middle-income households knew that (the parasite causing) elephantiasis was transmitted by mosquitoes.

Only 4% of the subjects from high-income areas and 1% of those from low-income areas were aware that filarial infection was a major cause of hydrocele. Most of the subjects (>55% of each of the four socio- economic groups considered) felt that they were not at risk of developing elephantiasis.

When specifically asked, only 35% of the subjects from high-income households but 84% of those from low-income households said that they would be willing to consume tablets of an antifilarial drug (diethylcarbamazine) in MDA to eliminate LF.

It is therefore unclear whether high-income households in urban areas should be included in MDA programmes.The interviewees felt that an intensive campaign of information, education, communication and advocacy would be necessary if an effective MDA-based programme were to be implemented. Drug distribution through the health services was the most preferred option.

Clearly, factors such as a lack of appreciation of the socio-economic impact of LF, a general belief that the risk of elephantiasis is low, doubts about the need to include all sectors of the eligible population in MDA, and a common dependence on private practitioners make successful MDA against LF in urban areas a challenging task. On the positive side, however, an urban population is often covered by a huge network of colleges, private practitioners, non-governmental organizations and residents' associations, and such networks provide new opportunities in the development of effective drug-delivery strategies (Ramaiah *et al.* 2005).

WEST BENGAL SCENARIO

First report about filarial endemicity in West Bengal was recorded back in 1930 by Acton and Rao. Microfilaria rate was 9.6% during that time on Calcutta.

Knowles and Basu (1934) reported microfilaria rate as 9.5% in Calcutta. Basu and Rao supported the findings in 1939. Rao and Sukhatme (1941) recorded that during 1929 and 1938, average microfilaria rate in Calcutta was 9.0%. Iyenger (1941) surveyed 2 rural villages of Birbhum district and found microfilariaemia in 17% of the villagers examined and cases of elephantiasis were in evidence.

In 1954, Chernin surveyed the workers at a jute mill near Calcutta for finding prevalence of filariasis in the labour force with a note on its transmission and found microfilaria rate of 6.8% (7.7% in males and 4.1% in females).

Bhattacharyya and Gubler (1973) carried out a survey and reported that microfilaria rates were 13.6% and 7.8% in Howrah and M.G. Road, Calcutta respectively.

Dondero *et al.* (1976) recorded a high microfilaria rate of 15.0% (18% in males and 10.0% in females) among the people of suburb of Calcutta. He also found lypmhoedema in 1.5% (1.0% in males, 3.0% in females), lymph scrotum in 1.0% and chyluria in 0.5% male and 0.1% female members.

Hati *et al.* (1989) reported that microfilaria rate, mean microfilarial density, disease rate and endemicity rate of bancroftian filariasis were 2.5%, 5.1%, 3.7% and 6.1% respectively in the central Calcutta (Dharmatala).

Chandra *et al.* (1994) completed a filariasis survey in Narkeldanga, Sealdah and Bowbazar areas of Calcutta.

Microfilaria rates and disease rates were 2.27% and 3.98%, 4.06% and 6.2% and 3.22% and 4.81% in Narkeldanga, Sealdah and Bowbazar areas respectively. Collectively in these three areas of Calcutta, microfilaria rate, disease rate, mean microfilarial density and endemicity rate were 3.2%, 5.0%, 5.7% and 8.2% respectively. Both microfilaria rate and disease rate were highest in the age group of 31-40 yrs. Males were preferred victims than females. De and Chandra (1994) reported that a parasitological study was conducted at Kanchrapara of North 24-Parganas between December 1991 to August 1992. Microfilaria rate among the human population was found 1.9% (35 out of 1200 persons).

Adhikari *et al.* (1994) made a comparative study between colliery and non-colliery and non-colliery areas of Burdwan district. The clinicopositivity, endemicity, microfilaria positively and microfilaria density were determined to be 68.4%, 11.51%, 7.44% and 27 in colliery areas and 2.13%, 4.42%, 3.16% and 0.84 in non-colliery areas respectively.

Rudra and Chandra (2000) reported that the little information on the epidemiology of lymphatic filariaisis, caused by infection with *Wuchereria bancrofti,* in West Bengal. Filariasis endemicity, measured as the percentage of subjects with microfilariaemia and/or disease, was therefore much lower among the tribal subjects (8.95%) than the non-tribal (22.12%).

Chandra, Chatterjee, Das and Sarkar studied on filariasis at Digha, West Bengal. According to their report the state of West Bengal, India, has a long coastline with the Bay of Bengal. No information exists regarding filarial epidemiology and its vector in these coastal areas.

The present study was designed to assess the epidemiology of lymphatic filariasis and the role of available mosquitoes as its vector in eight coastal villages around Digha, West Bengal. Night blood samples of 4016 individuals were collected and each of them was examined clinically for any manifestations of the disease. Overall, microfilaria rate, mean microfilarial density and disease rate were 9.06%, 8.63% and 7.72%, respectively. The causative parasite was identified as *Wuchereria bancrofti* and *Culex quinquefasciatus* was incriminated as the vector responsible. Vector infection and infectivity rates were assessed to be 12.5% and 0.73%, respectively. The human blood index of human-house-frequenting vector population was 70%. Vector density, vector infection, infectivity rates and human blood index were higher in the rainy season in the study area. Overall, the filarial situation was bad and, as a measure, single-dose diethylcarbamazine citrate (6 mg/kg body weight) treatment was given to all the microfilariaemic patients. Night blood samples of the treated individuals were tested for microfilariae on days 10 and 365, which revealed interesting results.

Vector Incrimination

World Picture

In 1927, Mansfield-Aders reported that in the towns and villages of Zanzibar Protectorate, *Cx. fatigans* was the vector of bancroftian filariasis and their natural infection rate was found to be as high as 20.3%. In 1940, Hawking found that *Cx. fatigans* was common in Tanzanyka territory of East Africa. Natural infection and infectivity rates of the vector were 22.3% and 0.6% respectively during November 1937 to May 1938.

Byrd and Bromberg (1945), during their studies in American Samoa, dissected 1063 wild caught *Cx. fatigans* and obtained an infection rate of 7.4%. No infective mosquito was detected during the study period.

Carter (1948) recorded that in the suburbs of Colombo, *Cx. fatigans* was the dominant mosquito (90%) of the houses. Natural infection rate of the vector varied from 2.2% to 21% in different areas, with a mean rate of 8.8% during 1937 to 1940.

In the same year Giglioli reported that *Cx. fatigans* comprised 91.5% of the total mosquitoes in Lodge village, British Guiana. Infection rate of mosquitoes varied from 0.83% to 1.29%

but in delayed dissection, it varied from 4.1% to 7.2%. Iyenger (1952) reported that *Cx. fatigans* constituted 92% of the mosquitoes caught in habitations of Maldive islands.

Out of 1729 mosquitoes examined, 429 (24.8%) were naturally infected with all stages of *W. bancrofti* during January to March 1951.Symes (1955) found that natural infection and infectivity rates of *Cx. fatigans*, collected from houses and bushes in Fiji were 4.8% and 0.34% respectively.

Kessel (1957) reported that infectivity rate of natural population of *Cx. quinquefasciatus* was 0.38% in Tahiti. In 1958, Dobbin *et al* found in Fernando Noronha island of Brazil that in the houses, inhabited by microfilariaemic patients 15% of the *Cx. p. fatigans* were infected with Wuchererian larvae.

In 1959, Chow *et al.* examined 24,271 mosquitoes collected from Rawasari district of Djakarta during 1956-57. Natural infection and infectivity rates were 1.8% and 0.3% respectively.

Density of all stage larvae and matured larvae was 0.12 and 0.014 respectively. Heisch *et al.* (1959) reported that *Cx. p. fatigans* was more prevalent in the semi-urban areas of Faza on the island of Pate, Kenya with a high natural infection and infectivity rates of 24.7% and 7.1% respectively, among 154 mosquitoes examined during July 1957 to September 1957.

In 1960, Symes noted that *Cx. fatigans* was the most common mosquito in houses of Fiji. Natural infection and infectivity rates were 3.6% and 0.9% respectively. Load of microfilariae, 1st, 2nd and 3rd stage larvae of *W. bancrofti* per infected mosquito was 11.8, 4.2, 2.0 and 1.9 respectively during 1954 to 1956.

In southern Tiwan, Wu and Chen (1960) dissected 95 *Cx. fatigans* during their survey and found that 5 (5.3%) and 2 (2.1%) were infected and infective respectively with filarial larvae. Out of 31 *Cx. vishnui* dissected only 1 (3.2%) was found infected.

Joe *et al* (1960) reported that 17,247 vector mosquitoes were collected from Rawasari district of Djakarta and dissected. It was found 3.5% harbour all stage larvae and only 0.1% to harbour infective stage larvae of *W. bancrofti*.

In 1962, Hawking reported that in Brazil natural infection rate of *Cx. fatigans* was 10.8% before 1953. But in 1954, 1955 and 1956, it was reduced to 1.1%, 0.6% and 0.6% respectively for adopting controlling measures. Before 1953, infectivity rate was 0.7% but in later years the corresponding figures were 0.8%, 0 and 0 respectively.

Kessel and Massal (1962) during their work in Pacific found that natural infection and infectivity rates of *Cx. quinquefasciatus* were 14.3% and 0.8% respectively in Inanwatan of Netharlands New Guinea, 8% and 1.7% respectively in Tiwan and 2.4% and 0.13% respectively in Philippines.

In 1962, Nelson *et al.* found an infectivity rate of 1.5%, dissecting 14,153 *Cx. p. fatigans* in Kenya Coast.

Sasa (1963) reported that most important natural vector of bancroftian filariasis in Japan was *Cx. pipiens,* whose infection and infectivity rates were 5.7% and 1.5% respectively during 1958-1961.

In 1965, Abdul Cader *et al.* reported that in Ja Ela, Ceylon, (Bow Sri Lanka) density of *Cx. p. fatigans* per house was 0.69. Out of 998 mosquitoes dissected, 1.3% were infected and 0.4% contained infective larvae of *W. bancrofti.*

Abdul Cader and Sasa (1966) recorded that *Cx. p. fatigans* comparised 84.6% of the total resting mosquito population in human dwellings in Ceylon during 1959-64. Natural infection and infectivity rates were worked out to be 1.7% and 0.7% respectively. Transmission was found to occur in all the seasons of the year.

In 1967, Abdul Cader reported that among the *Cx. p. fatigans,* collected from cattle sheds in Ceylon, 4.1% were infected with *W. bancrofti.* Natural infection rate of the resting mosquitoes in human dwellings was 24.1% in 1949, 15.5% in 1956, 1.1% in 1958 and 0.7% in 1962 in some areas of Ceylon.

Burton (1967) dissected altogether 15,622 female *Cx. fatigans* collected from Guyana, of which 9.6% contained all stages larvae and 0.5% had infective larvae of *W. bancrofti* during 1961-63.

In 1967, Franco and Lima reported that in Belem (Pare State) of Brazil, 82% of the mosquitoes, caught in houses were *Cx. p. fatigans*, of which 7.3% were infected and 1% were infective with filarial worm during 1954-55.

But in Savadove (Bahia State), during 1954-55, out of 6000 *Cx. p. fatigans* examined, 6 (0.1%) were infected and 2 (0.03%) were infective.

Meillon, *et al.* (1967), during their survey at two stations of Kemmendine, Rangoon found natural infection rate of the filarial vector was 2% and 66% respectively in May 1964.

Meillon and Sebastian (1967) in an another experiment recorded that average infection and infectivity rates of both resting and biting population of *Cx. p. fatigans* were 4.8% and 0.36% in a few stations of Kemmendine, Rangoon during March to August 1964.

Sherlock and Sarafim (1967) found during 1954-66 that in the districts of Salvadore, Castro Alves and Uruguai of Brazil, the filarial vector was found in 90% houses and out of 633 mosquitoes examined, 26 (3.0%) contained microfilariae of *W. bancrofti*.

In 1968, Dobbins and Cruz reported that in the city of Sao Lourenco de mata in Pernambuco, out of 356 houses searched, 79.8% were positive for *Cx. p. fatigans*. Among 754 vector mosquitoes examined, 1.06% harboured *W. bancrofti*.

In the same year i.e. in 1968, Ramlingam dissected and examined 145 *Cx. p. fatigans*, collected from Samoa and Tonga but none of them was infected. According to him, the role of *Cx. p. fatigans* as vector of filariasis was insignificant in those area.

In 1971, Ogunba dissected 2128 *Cx. p. fatigans* collected form Ibadan of West Nigeria during November 1968 to March 1970 but none contained developing larvae of *W. bancrofti;* therefore the role of *Cx. p. fatigans* as a vector could not be properly assessed.

White (1971) recorded an infectivity rate of 0.23% of *Cx. p. fatigans* in the urban parts of Tonga, a coastal town of North-

Eastern Tanzania. In the rural area around Muheza, the infectivity rate was 0.54% during November 1968 to June 1970.

Aslamkhan and Wolfe (1972) reported that natural infection and infectivity rates of houses resting *Cx. p. fatigans* were 10.8% and 1.1% respectively in Dinajpur district, East Pakistan during August 1968 to July 1969.

Colbourne and Neg (1972) during their survey of Singapore, examined 2895 *Cx. fatigans* of which 49 (1.7%) contained all stages larvae and 2 (0.07%) had infective forms of *W. bancrofti*.

In 1973, Jung reported that *Cx. p. fatigans* was common both in rural and urban areas of Nepal and in some areas up to 14% of the mosquito population were found to be infected by Wuchererian larvae.

Fan *et al.* (1975) during his control operation of bancroftian filariasis in Liehyn district, Kinmen islands, China, found that before control measure, out of 844 *Cx. p. fatigans* dissected, 77 (9.1%) were infected, 31 (3.7%) were infective and average larval density per infected mosquito was 6.2.

But after control measure, the corresponding figures were worked out to be 4 (0.8%), 1 (0.2%) and 1.3, out of 504 *Cx. p. fatigans* examined during July to December 1974.

Hawking (1976b) reported that *Cx. p. fatigans* was the chief vector of filariasis in South China.

In Furkien, infective rate was 4.9% and the corresponding figure was 12.6% in Kwantung.

Raccurt and Hodges (1977) noted that *Cx. p. fatigans* was the most abundant in Haiti and their natural infection and infectivity rates were recorded to be 20% and 1% respectively.

Weinstock *et al.* (1977) reported that in Purerto Limon, Costa Rica, out of 663 *Cx. p. fatigans* dissected, 25 (3.7%) were infected. Average load of all stage larvae per positive mosquito was 1.8. In the year 1983, they dissected 2714 mosquitoes from the same region, of which 162 (6.0%) contained 1st and 2nd stage larvae and 2 (0.07%) had 3rd stage larvae.

In 1977, Wijers and Kiilu reported that *Cx. p. fatigans* was an efficient vector of filariasis in East Africa. At Mamburi in Kenya, natural infection and infectivity rates of the vector species were 5.7% and 0.97% respectively. Average number of infective larvae per positive mosquito was 3.4 during May 1973 to January 1975.

Self *et al.* (1978) found that in Kepu district of Djakarta, *Cx. p. fatigans* comprised 99% of the total mosquitoes caught. Natural infection and infectivity rates among the biting population were 1.1% and 0.29% respectively. The corresponding figures among the wild resting population were 1.6% and 0.38% respectively in one year study during 1974-1975.

In the year 1979, Valeza and Grove studied the transmission of *W. bancrofti* in an isolated village on a small island of Philippines, where *Cx. quinquefasciatus* was less common. Eleven per cent of them had microfilariae or 1st stage larvae but none had later stages. *Aedes poicilius* was the main vector of filariasis there.

Nathan (1981) reported that in Blanchisseuse village of Trinidad, among the indoor biting population of *Cx. quinquefasciatus*, 43(2.1%) were infected and only 2(0.1%) were infective with Wuchererian larvae, out of 2024 mosquitoes examined during September 1978-79.

Wijers and Kaleli (1984) dissected 814 *Cx. p. fatigans* from Mamburi, Kenya in which 41 (5%) and 15 (1.8%) were found to be infected and infective respectively. They also examined 548 mosquitoes after DEC treatment and found 4 (0.7%) infected and 1 (0.2%) infective.

Nathan *et al.* (1987) reported that in North Trinidad, after a mass treatment with DEC, the filarial infection rate in the vector from randomly sampled houses fell from 6.4% to 0.

Vincent *et al.* (1987) found that in Santo Domingo of Dominican Republic, most of the mosquito collected in filaria affected areas were *Cx. quinquefasciatus* and out of 543 mosquitoes examined, 147 (27%) harboured microfilariae of *W. bancrofti.*

Zhang *et al.* (1988) reported that in Hubei, China, *W. bancrofti* was transmitted by *Cx. quinquefasciatus* mainly in mountain areas.

Abeyewickreme and Wanniarachchi (1991) reported that in Sri Lanka, *Anopheles jamesii* was incriminated as a potential natural vector of bancroftian filariasis.

Samarawickrema *et al.* (1992) described that in Samoa, *Cx. quinquefasciatus* was an inefficient vector of subperiodic *W. bancrofti*.

Cartel *et al.* (1992) reported that in French Polynesia, during the three week entomological survey, 387 mosquito collections were performed and 1748 female *Aedes polynesiensis* were dissected, of which 1176 were parous. Among the latter, 114 (9.7%) were infected with *W. bancrofti* larvae at L1, L2 or L3 stages. The mean number of Larvae per mosquito was 2.46.

Marzhuki *et al.* (1993) described that in Malaysia, two species of filarial worms, namely *Brugia malayi* and *W. bancrofti* and the mosquito vectors belongings to the *Mansonia* and *Anopheles* genera, involved in the transmission of filariasis.

Bryan *et al.* (1995) reported that entomological studies were undertaken in three villages in the East Sepik province of Papua New Guinea. In Yanatong, infection rates in *Anopheles* vectors (*An. punctulatus and An. koliensis*) varied from 20.5 to 46.6% with infectivity rates of 0-1.4%, while these rates were 10.9-13.3% and 0-1.1% respectively in *Cx. quinquefasciatus*.

Bockarie *et al.* (1996) reported that in East Sepik province, Papua New Guinea, a total of 1735 Culicine mosquitoes including *Culex* and *Mansonia* species were dissected, but none were infected with filarial larvae. In contrast, *Anopheles punctulatus* and *An. koliensis* were found to be potential vectors, 7.3% of *Anopheles* were infected and infectivity rate was 2.1%.

INDIAN SCENARIO

Korke (1928) reported that *Cx. fatigans* was the prevalent species in Gaya district of Bihar and Puri district of Orissa. He found that 15% of the species showed developmental stages of microfilaria bancrofti in Gaya during February-March but in the Puri town 12% of the mosquitoes, carried developmental stages of *W. bancrofti*. In the same year, during his work in Balasore area, Orissa, it was noted that 8.3% of mosquitoes, species not confined, but mostly *Culex* showed developmental stages larvae of the parasite.

Iyenger in (1933) reported that *Cx. fatigans* was the main vector of filaria bancrofti in Trivandrum and its surroundings. The natural infection rate of the vector varies in different parts, the average being 20.6%.

Raghavan (1951) dissected a total of 995 *Cx. fatigans*, of which 138 (14.6%) were found to be naturally infected by different stages of the parasite in Porbandar, Saurashtra during November-December, 1949.

Krishnaswami (1955) during his work in Mangalore, South India, found a natural infection rate of 13.9%, among the vectors in March-April 1954.

Basu (1957) dissected 1725 *Cx. fatigans*, collected from Chabua village of Assam during February to April 1957 and found 45 (2.6%) infected with all stages larvae of *W. bancrofti*. He also examined 1908 mosquitoes from Bokakhat village, Assam and found nil infection rate.

Rahaman *et al.* (1957) examined 365 *Cx. fatigans* collected from Ballia town of U.P. during November 1955 to May 1956, of which 17 (4.6%) were infected and 5 (1.4%) were infective with filarial larvae.

Subramanium *et al.* (1958) estimated the natural infection rate of filarial vector in Laccadive, Minicoy and Aminidive group of islands. Infection rates were 0, 10.8%, 8.6% 15.4%, 16.8%, 18.2%, 0, 0 and 0 in Kalpeni, Androth, Agathi, Chetlat, Kilton, Kadamath, Minicoy, Karavathi and Amini islands respectively. *Cx. fatigans* constituted an average of over 95% of the total catch in those islands in the study period during December 1954 to February 1955.

Nair *et al.* (1960) during their survey in Fort Cochin Municipality Kerala, found that *Cx. p. fatigans* was the most prevalent and out of 348 mosquitoes dissected, 13.7% were infected by all stages larvae and 13.4% were infective. They also found 14 species of mosquitoes, *Cx. p. fatigans* was the vector of filariasis and their infection and infectivity rates were 8.96% and 1.4% respectively, out of 435 mosquitoes dissected.

Sinha (1960) reported that in Basti, U.P., from 30 catching stations, ten each of human habitations, cattlesheds and mixed dwellings, altogether 4471 mosquitoes were collected of which 2931(65.5%) were Culicine. Out of 822 mosquitoes dissected 10% of *Cx. fatigans* were found infected and in the check areas the infection rate was 9.2%.

Verma *et al.* (1960) found in Sultanganj and its suburbs of Bihar that 10.1% of the *Cx. fatigans* population were infected with different stages of filarial worms and this was the only species found to be infected. In the next year (1961) they reported that infection rate of *Cx. fatigans* in Bhagalpur town of Bihar was 10.1% and monthwise range being 5.2% to 23.9%. Infectivity rate was varied from 2.2% to 17.7% in different months between December 1957 and December 1958. But in the rural areas around Bhagalpur, out of 224 *Cx. quinquefasciatus* dissected 11 (4.9%) were infected during March 1958. In an another piece of work, they found that out of 185 mosquitoes 9 (4.8%) were infected with all stage larvae in the same areas.Nair reported in 1960 that average infection rate of *Cx. fatigans* collected from Laccadive, Minicoy and Aminidive group of islands was 16.7%, ranging from 8.7% to 24.3% in different islands.

Chand *et al.* (1961) recorded that *Cx. fatigans*, was the only vector in both rural and urban areas of Ghazipur district, U.P. and their infection and infectivity rates were 6.5% and 0.3% respectively during 1956-1958. In Deoria district of the same province they found that out of 2517 mosquitoes, collected in human habitations, cattlesheds and mixed dwellings, 1482 (58.9%) were *Cx. fatigans* and the natural infection and infectivity rates were 15.7% and 2.8% respectively during 1955-56. In Bahraich district, U.P., out of 4690 *Cx. fatigans* dissected 411 (8.8%) were naturally infected and 23 (0.5%) were infective. During their survey in Gonda town of U.P. they collected 2548 mosquitoes, of which 2253 (87.2%) were *Cx. fatigans* which was the only vector. Natural infection and infectivity rates were 1.3% and 3.7% respectively, out of 536 mosquitoes examined during 1958-1959. In 1962 they reported that in Gorakhpur district of U.P., among all the species, 64.4% were *Cx. fatigans* and their natural infection and infectivity rates were 7.5% and 3.5% respectively during 1957 to 1960.

In Ponani of Kerala, Nair (1962) found that natural infection and infectivity rates of *Cx. fatigans* were 16.4% and 4.5% respectively. Average load of 3rd stage larvae per infective mosquito was 1.2 during the year 1957.

Verma *et al.* (1962) reported that natural infection rate of *Cx. fatigans* was as high as 32.5% in Monghyr district of Bihar during May 1957 to 1958.

Joseph and Peethambaran (1963) recorded that during a filariasis survey in Trichur, Kerala between December 1960 to October 1961, natural infection and infectivity rates of *Cx. fatigans* were 0.5% and 0.3% respectively. The maximum number of larvae of *W. bancrofti* found in single mosquito was 6.

Pattanayak and Chandrasekhar (1963) reported natural infection and infectivity rates of *Cx. quinquefasciatus* was 1.3% and 0.3% respectively in Kottayam Municipality of Kerala during February 1961 to February 1962.

Laurence (1963) reported that in Vellore, Tamil Nadu, 15.7% of the *Cx. fatigans* population contained all stages larvae and 1.5% carried infective stage larvae of *W. bancrofti* during October to December 1961.

In Sitapur district of U.P., Singh *et al.* (1963) captured 4385 mosquitoes in one year during 1961-1962, of which 2674 (60.1%) were *Cx. fatigans*. Out of 1005 mosquitoes dissected 12 (1.2%) were infected and 9 (0.9%) were infective.

The report of filariasis survey by Nair (1966) in Palghat town of Kerala revealed that out of 141 *Cx. fatigans* dissected, 6 (4.1%) contained developing larvae and 1 (0.7%) contained 2 matured larvae of *W. bancrofti.*

Singh (1967) recorded that in the urban areas of Orissa state the range of infection and infectivity rates of *Cx. fatigans* were 0.9% to 1.2% and 0.15% to 0.2% respectively. But in the rural areas of the State, the corresponding figures were 2.7% to 3.5% and 0.08% to 0.3% respectively.

Dhar *et al.* (1968) reported that annual infection rate of *Cx. fatigans* was 11.5% ranging from 10.2% to 13% in different months of Rajamundry town in Andhra Pradesh. Infectivity rate varied from 2.1% to 2.4% in different months with an average of 2.2%.

Power and Mittal (1968) reported from Jamnagar, Gujarat that *Cx. fatigans* was the only vector, incriminated in the transmission of filariasis. In the urban area, density was higher than the rural area. The infection and infectivity rates of the vectors were 3.4% and 0.5% respectively in the urban area and the corresponding figures in the rural surroundings were 0.7% and 0 respectively during the study period between July and September 1964.

Rao *et al.* (1980) surveyed four villages of East Godavari district, Andhara Pradesh during July 1975 to June 1976 and recorded that vector infection and infectivity rates were 7.7% and 1.4% respectively out of 2679 *Cx. fatigans* examined. Average number of infective larvae per infective mosquito was 2.1.

Rajagopalan *et al.* (1981) reported that in Pondicherry, out of 3415 mosquitoes collected 47.9% were *Cx. p. fatigans*. They examined 1545 mosquitoes during August 1979 to July 1980, of which 5.6% were naturally infected and 0.97% were infective with filarial larvae. In an another piece of work, they obtained natural infection and infectivity rates of 1.9% and 0.4% respectively in Pondicherry villages.

Sarma *et al.* (1987) observed that natural infection, infectivity rates of *Cx. quinquefasciatus* in Thomar village of Chengliput district, Tamil Nadu were 20% and 6% respectively.

Dash *et al.* in 1988, reported that in Puri district, Orissa out of 18 species of mosquitoes, *Cx. quinquefasciatus* was the most dominating species (76.9%). Annual infection rate was 7.8 varying from 2.6% to 25% in different months. Infectivity rates ranged from 1.29% to 12.5% in different months in one year study period.

Jain *et al.* (1989) described that in rural Kerala, the infection rate of *Mansonia annulifera* was between 0 to 5.7%, while the infectivity rate ranged from 0 to 4.9%.

Tiwari *et al.* (1989) reported that in the Nancowry group of islands in the Andaman and Nicobar islands, *Cx. quinquefasciatus* was present at a very low density. *Aedes niveus* and *Ae. malayensis* were the only species commonly biting man. The former was incriminated as a vector and found naturally with *W. bancrofti*. Infection and infectivity rates were found as 1.1% and 0.9% respectively.

Raina *et al.* (1992) studied the status of lymphatic filariasis in three selected slum areas i.e. Harinagar, Yamuna Pushta and Vijay Ghat of Delhi. Harinagar accounted for least 10 man hour density of *Cx. quinquefasciatus*, because the collection was made during winter months. The dissection of mosquitoes did not reveal any human filarial infection except in Yamuna Pusht where out of 139, only one *Cx. quinquefasciatus* was found to be infective.

Dutta *et al.* (1995) reported that in upper Assam *Cx. quinquefasciatus* was incriminated as a vector with man-hour density of 68.5 in human dwellings. A total of 186 live mosquitoes were dissected and different stages of filarial larvae were detected from the thoracic region of 14 mosquitoes, the infectivity rate being 3.8.

Shriram *et al.* (1996) dissected a total of 442 mosquitoes belonging to 8 species collected from houses of Little Andaman island and natural infection was found only in *Cx. quinquefasciatus,* the rate being 0.24%.

Chand *et al.* (1996) described that in tribal areas of Panna district of MP, the overall per man-hour density of vector *Cx. quinquefasciatus* was 10.33, which varied from tehsil to tehsil. The infection and infectivity rate of 4.9% and 1.03% respectively were observed only in the tehsil with lowest tribal concentration.

Kumar (1997) made a survey in 40 villages of Khurda district, Orissa, India. The observed proportions of infected mosquitoes were found to correlate well with the estimated infectivity levels ($r = 0.8$, $p < 0.05$).

Kumar and Singh (1999) reported that, on the basis of survey randomly in 40 villages of Khurda district, Orissa during 1993-94, the prevalence of mf and disease was found to be 10.5% and 18.6% respectively. The infection rate (mf and/or diseases) was 27.3% in the district.

Hoti *et al.* (2003) worked that in different geographical regions in India to assess their presence in parasites from areas endemic for lymphatic filariasis.

Subramanian *et al.* (2004) reported that the intensity of *Wuchereria bancrofti* infection in Pondicherry, India. Explanation of the large variation in mf-density required considerable variation between individuals in exposure and immune responsiveness.

REFERENCES

Abdul Cader MHM (1967). The Significance of the *Culex Pipiens Fatigans* Wiedemann Problem in Ceylon. *Bull. Wid. Hlth. Org.*, 37: 245-249.

Abdul Cader MHM, Rajakone P, Fernando WB and Siriwardene S (1965). Control of Bancroftian Filariasis in Ja Ela, Ceylon. *Ceylon J. Med. Sci*, 14: 49-58.

Abeywickrema, W and Wanniarechachi P (1991). *Anopheles jamesi*-A Potential Natural Vector of Bancroftian Filariasis in Sri Lanka. *Trans. Roy. Soc. Trop. Med. Hyg.*, 85(5): 644-646.

Acton HW and Rao SS (1930). Factors which Determine the Differences in the Types of Lesions Produced by Filaria Bancrofti. *Ind. Med. Gaz.*, 65: 620-629.

Adhikari P, Halder S, Ghosh N R, Mondal MM and Halder JP (1994). Prevalence of Bancroftian Filariasis in Burdwan District, W.B.: A Comparative Study Between Colliery and Non-colliery Areas, *J. commun. Dis.*, 26(1): 6-13.

Akiba Y (1991). Assessment of Rainwater Mediated Dispersion of Field-sprayed *Bacillus Thuringiensis* in the Soil. *Appl. Ent. Zool.*, 26(4): 477-483.

Albuquerque MF, Marzochi MC, Sabroza PC, Braga MC, Padilha T, Silva MC, Silva MK, Schindler HC, Maciel MA and Souza W (1995). Bancroftian Filariasis in Two Urban Areas of Recife, Brazil: Pre-control Observations on Infection and Disease. *Trans. Roy. Soc. Trop. Med. Hyg.*, 89(4): 373-377.

Anosike JC and Onwuliri CD (1994). Studies on Filariasis in Bauchi State. Nigeria II. *Appl. parasit.*, 35(4): 242-250.

Aslamkhan M and Wolfe MS (1972). Bancroftian Filariasis in Two Villages in Dinajpur District, East Pakistan II Entomological Investigations. *Am. J. Trop. Med. Hyg.*, 21: 30-37.

Bancroft TL (1899). *J. Proc. Roy. Soc.* New South Wales, 82: p. 62.

Basu PCR (1957). Filariasis in Assam State. *Ind. J. Mala.*, 11: 293-308.

Beuria MK, Bal MS, Mandal NN and Das MK (2003). Age-dependent Prevalence of Asymptomatic Amicrofilariaemic Individuals in a *Wuchereria Bancrofti* Endemic Region of India. *Trans. Roy. Soc. Trop. Med. Hyg.*, 97(3): 297-298.

Bhattacharyya B, Das Dalal AK and Sukul NC (1988). Infection of *Cx. Quinquefasciatus* with *W. bancrofti* Larvae in Natural Populations in Filaria Endemic Village of W.B., India. *Environ. Ecol.*, 6: 377-380.

Bhattacharyya NC and Gubler DJ (1973). A Survey for Bancroftian Filariasis in the Calcutta Area. *Ind. J. Med. Res.*, 61: 8-11.

Bockarie M, Kazura J, Alexander N, Dagoro H, Bockarie F, Perry R and Alpers M (1996). Transmission Dynamics of *W. Bancrofti* in East Sepik Province, Papua New Guinea. *Am. J. Trop. Med. Hyg.*, 54(6): 577-581.

Bryan JH, Dagoro H and Southgate BA (1995). Filarial Vector Studies in a DEC-treated and Untreated Villages in Pupua New Guinea. *Am. J. Trop. Med. Hyg.*, 98(B): 445-451.

Burnhes J (1975). La bilariose de Banbcrof dans la sous Region Malgache (Comores-Madagascar-Reunion) *Mem. Ors.* Paris, 81: 212-216.

Burton GJ (1967). Observations on the Habits and Control of *Culex pipiens Fatigans* in Guyana. *Bull. Wld. Hlth. Org.*, 37: 317-322.

Byrd EE and Bromberg L (1945). Studies on Filariasis in the Samoan Area. *Nav. Med. Bull.*, 44: 1-6.

Cartel JL, Mguyen NL, Spiegel A, Moulia-Pelatg P, Plicharat R, Martin PMV, Manuellan AB and Lardeux F (1992). *Wuchereria bancrofti* Infection in Human and Mosquito Populations of a Polynesian Village Ten Years After Innterruption of Mass Chemoprophylaxis with Diethyl Carbamazine. *Trans. Roy. Soc. Trop. Med. Hyg.*, 86: 414-416.

Carter HF (1948). Records of Filaria Infections in Mosquitoes in Ceylon. *Ann. Trop. Med. Parasit.*, 42: 312-321.

Chand D, Singh MV, Gupta BB and Srivastava RN (1961). A Note on Filariasis in Gonda Town (Uttar Pradesh). *Ind. J. Malar.*, 15: 39-47.

Chand G, Pandey GD, Tiwary RS (1996). Prevalence of *W. Bancrofti* Infection Among the Tribals of Panna District of Madhya Pradesh. *J. Commun. Dis.*, 28(4): 304-307.

Chandra G (1996). Filariasis Survey in a Rural Area of W.B. *J. Commun. Dis.*, 28(3): 206-208.

Chandra G (1998). Studies on Transmission Dynamics of Lymphatic Filariasis in Rural Areas of West Bengal. *Proc. Zool. Soc. Cal.*, 51(2): 116-128.

Chandra G, Banerjee A and Hati AK (1993). Seasonal Prevalence of *Culex Quinquefasciatus* in An Urban and a Rural Area of West Bengal. *Bull. Cal. Sch. Trop. Med.*, 41: 10-11.

Chandra G, Chatterjee SN and Hati AK (1996). *Wuchereria* Infection in the Natural Population of *Culex quinquefasciatus* in a Rural Area of West Bengal. *Environ. & Ecol.*, 14: 774-776.

Chandra G, Das SK, Ghosh A and Behera MK (2003). Studies on Vector of Bancroftian Filariasis at Katwa, West Bengal, *J. Parasit. Appl. Anim. Biol.*, 12: 1-2.

Chandra G, Majumdar G and Hati AK (1995). An Alternative Approach for Assessing Filarial Endemicity. In Hati, A.K. (Ed.) *Studies on Some Vectors of Public Health Importance* Edited by Dr. A K Hati, Department of Medical Entomology, Calcutta School of Tropical Medicine.

Chandra G, Banerjee A and Hati AK (1994). Current Filariasis Situation in some Pockets of Calcutta. *Bull. Cal. Sch. Trop. Med.*, 42: 4-7.

Chandra G, Chatterjee S.N, Das S and Sarkar N (2007). Lymphatic Filariasis in the Coastal Areas of Digha,West Bengal, India. *Tropical Doctor*, 37: 136-139.

Chernin E (1954). Problems in Tropical Public Health Among Workers at a Jute Mill Near Calcutta. *Ind. J. Malar.*, 8: 77-83.

Chhotray GP, Mahapatra M, Acharya AS and Ranjit MR (2001). A Clinico-epidemiological Perspective of Lymphatic Filariasis in Satyabadi Block of Puri District, Orissa. *Ind. J. Med. Res.*, 114: 65-71

Chow CY, Joe LK, Winoto RMP, Rusad M and Soegiarto (1959). The Vector of Filariasis in Djakarta and its Bionomics. *Bull. Wld. Hlth. Org.*, 20: 667-676.

Cobbold TS (1877). On Filaria Bancrofti. *Lancet* (II).

Das S.C, Nath D.R, Sarkar P.K, Bhuyan M, Chakraborty B.C, Rao KM, Taran N.G and Misra J.N (1988). Records of Manbiting Mosquitoes of Tezpur (Assam)-A Preliminary Investigation. *Ind. J. Publ. Hlth.*, XXXI: 231-234.

Das UP, Hati AK and Chowdhury AB (1971). Nocturnal Man-biting Mosquitoes of Urban and Rural Areas. *Bull. Cal. Sch. Trop. Med.* XIX: 80-83.

Dash AP, Tripathy N and Hazra RK (1988). Bionomics and Vectorial Capacity of Mosquitoes in Puri District, Orissa. Proc. 2nd Sym. Vectors & Vector Borne Diseases. 90-100.

De SK and Chandra G (1994). Studies on the Filariasis Vector *Culex Quinqnefasciatus* at Kancharapara, West Bengal (India). *Ind. J. Med. Res.*, 99: 255-258.

Desowitz RS, Jankins C and Anian G (1993). Bancroftian Filariasis in an Isolated Hunter-gatherer Shifting Horticulturist Group in Papua New Guinea. *Bull. Wld. Hlth. Org.*, 71(1): 55-58.

Dhar SK, Das M, Srivastava BN, Menon PKM and Basu PC (1968). Seasonal Prevalence, Resting Habits, Host Preference and Filarial Infection of *Culex Quinquefasciatus* in Rajamundry Town, Andhra Pradesh. *Bull. Ind. Soc. Malar. Commun. Dis.*, 5: 74-87.

Dissanayake S (1989). Microfilariaemia, Serum-antibody and Development of Clinical Disease in Microfilariaemic Subjects Infected with *Wuchereria Bancrofti* and Treated with Diethyl Carbamazine Citrate. *Trans. Roy. Soc. Trop. Med. Hyg.*, 83: 384-388.

Dobbin JE, Coelho MV and Cruz AE (1958). Filariasis in Fernando Noronha Island, Brazil. *Rev. Bras. Malariologia.*, 10: 133-136.

Dobbins JE (Jr.) and Cruz AE (1968). Bancroftian Filariasis Survey in Sao Lourenco da Mata Pernambuco. *Revta. Soc. Bras. Med. Trop.*, 2: 9-12.

Dondero (Jr.) TJ, Bhattacharyya NC, Black HR, Chowdhury AB, Gubler DJ, Inui TS and Mukherjee MS (1976). Clinical Manifestations of Bancroftian Filariasis in a Suburb of Calcutta, India. *Am. J. Trop. Med. Hyg.*, 25: 64-73.

Drobniewski FA (1994). A Review: The Safety of *Bacillus* Species as Insect Vector Control Agents. *Bacteriol*, 76: 101-109.

Dutta P, Gogoi BK, Chelleng PK, Bhattacharyya DR, Khan SA, Goswmi BK and Mahanta J (1995). Filariasis in the Labour Population of a Tea Estate in Urban Assam. *Ind. J. Med. Res.*, 101: 245-246.

Dutta SN (1977). Evidence of *Culex Fatigans* Mosquito Breeding in Underground Pits of a Coal Mine in India. *Trans. Roy. Soc. Trop. Med. Hyg.*, 71: 180-184.

Ellis R (1991). BTK, Unpublished Report Winnipeg-MB, Canada, Prairie Pest Management.

Entwistle PF, *et al.* (eds.) (1993). *Bacillus thuringiensis*, An Environmental Biopesticide: Theory and Practice. New York: John Wiley & Sons.

Estambale BBA, Simonsen PE, Knight R and Bwayo JJ (1994). Bancroftian Filariasis in Kwale District of Kenya. 1. Clinical and Parasitological Survey in an Endemic Community. *Ann. Trop. Med. Parasit.*, 88(2): 145-151.

Fan PC, Wang YC, Liu JC, Lo HS and King ML (1975). Control of Bancroftian Filariasis by Common Salt Medicated with DEC in Liehyu District (Little Kinmen), Kinmen (Quemoy) Islands, Republic of China. *Ann. Trop. Med. Parasit.*, 69: 515-516.

Farm Chemicals Hand Book (1992). Willoughby, OH: Meister Publishing Company.

Faust EC and Russel PF (1964). *Clinical Parasitology*. Lea and Febiger, Philadelphia, p. 53.

Feitelson JS, Payne J and Kim L (1992). *Bacillus Thuringiensis* Insects and beyond. *Bio/Technology*, 10: 271-275.

Franco O and Lima DM da S (1967). Some Aspects of the Activities Against Bancroftian Filariasis in Brazil. *Revta. Bras. Malar. Doenc. Trop.*, 19: 73-89.

Garrison FH (1917). *An Introduction to the History of Medicine*, W.B. Saunders Co., Philadelphia, p. 59.

Gbakima AA and Sahr F (1996). Filariasis in the Kaiyamba Chiefdom, Moyomba District Sierra Leone; an Epidemiological and Clinical Study. *Publ. Hlth.*, 110(3): 169-174.

Ghosh SM and Hati AK (1966). House Frequenting Mosquitoes of West Bengal and Calcutta: Detection of Filaria Parasites in *Anopheles* and *Culex* species. *Bull. Cal. Sch. Trop. Med.*, XIV: 9-10.

Go VM (1993). Lymphatic Filariasis in Recently Described Endemic Area in Marinduque, Philippines. *Southeast Asian J. Trop. Med. Publ. Hlth.*, 24(2): 19-22.

Gubler DJ and Bhattacharyya NC (1974). A quantitative Approach to the Study of Bancroftian Filariasis. *Am. J. Trop. Med. Hyg.*, 22: 1027-1036.

Gyapong JO, Babu JK, Adjei S and, Binka F (1993). Bancroftian Filariasis in the Kassena Nankana District of the Upper East Region of Ghana; A Preliminary Study. *Am. J. Trop. Med. Hyg.*, 96(5): 317-322.

Harb M, Faris R, Gad AM, Hafez ON, Ramzy R and Buck AA (1993). The Resurgence of Lymphatic Filariasis in the Nile Delta. *Bull. Wld. Hlth. Org.*, 71(1): 49-54.

Hariston NG and Meillon BDE (1968). On the Inefficiency of Transmission of *Wuchereria Bancrofti* from Mosquito to Human Host. *Bull. Wld. Hlth. Org.*, 38: 935-941.

Harnle AFR (1877): *The Sushrata Samhita*. Calcutta.

Hati AK, Chandra G, Bhattacharya A, Bishwas D, Chatterjee KK and Dwibedi HN (1989). Annual Transmission Potential of Bancroftian Filariasis in an Urban and a Rural area of WB, India. *Am. J. Trop. Med. Hyg.*, 40(4): 365-367.

Hawking F (1940). Distribution of Filariasis in Tanganyika Territory, East Africa. *Ann. Trop. Med. Parasit.*, 34: 107-119.

Hawking F (1962). A Review of Progress in the Chemotherapy and Control of Filariasis Since 1955. *Bull. Wld. Hlth. Org.*, 27: 555-568.

Hawking F (1976b). The Distribution of Human Filariasis Throughout the World Part II Asia. *Trop. Dis. Bull.*, 73: 967-1016.

Hawking F and Thurston JP (1951). The Periodicity of Mocrofilariae 1. The Distribution of Microfilariae in the Body. *Trans. Roy. Soc. Trop. Med. Hyg.*, 45: 307-340.

Hayes J and Downs TD (1980). Seasonal Changes in an Isolated Population of *Culex Pipiens Quinquefasciatus* (Diptera: Culicidae), A Time Series Analysis. *J. Med. Ent.*, 17: 63-69.

Heisch RB, Nelson GS and Furlng M (1959). Studies on Filariasis in East Africa I. Filariasis on the Island of Pate, Kenya. *Trans. Roy. Soc. Trop. Med. Hyg.*, 53: 41-53.

Holly M Gilbert and Barry J Hartman (1996). Short Report: A Case of Fibrosing Mediastinitis Caused by *Wuchereria Bancrofti*. *Am. J. Trop. Med. Hyg.*, 54(6): 596-599.

Hoti SL and Balaraman K (1991). Changes in the Populations of *Bacillus Thuringeinsis* H-14 and *Bacillus Sphaericus* Applied to Vector Breeding Sites. *The Environmentalist*, 11(1): 39-44.

Hoti SL, Subramaniyan K and Das PK (2003). Detection of Codon for Amino Acid 200 in Isotype 1 Beta-tubulin Gene of *Wuchereria bancrofti* Isolates, Implicated in Resistance to Benzimidazoles in Other Nematodes. *Acta. Tropica.*, 88(1): 77-81.

Ivoke N (2000). Rural Bancroftian Filariasis in North-Western Cameroon; Parasitological and Clinical Studies. *J. Commun. Dis.*, 32(4): 254-263.

Iyenger MOT (1933). Filariaisis in Trivandrum. *Ind. J. Med. Res.*, 20: 921-937.

Iyenger MOT (1952). Filariasis in the Maldive Islands. *Bull. Wld. Hlth. Org.*, 7: 375-403.

Jain DC, Chandrasekharan A, Sethumadhavan KVP, Johny VM, Cherian C and Ghosh TK (1989). Epidemiology of Brugian Filariasis in a Rural Community of Kerala State. *J. Commun. Dis.*, 21(1): 27-33.

James SP (1900). On the Metamorphosis of the Filaria *Sanguinis Hominis* in Mosquito. *Brit. Med. J.*, 11: 533-537.

Jemanch L and Kebede D (1995). Periodicity of *W. bancrofti* Microfilariae in South Western Ethiopia. *Eithop. Med. J.*, 33(2): 125-128.

Joe LK, Hudojok, Wijono and Maliah SA (1960). Filariasis Survey in Rawasari district, Djakarta. *Ind. J. Malar.*, 14: 339-352.

Joseph C and Peethambaran P (1963). A Filariasis Survey of Trichur (Kerala State). *Ind. J. Malar.*, 17: 33-36.

Jung RK (1973). A Brief Study on the Epidemiology of Filariasis in Nepal. *J. Nepal Med. As.*, 11: 155-168.

Kar SK, Mania J and Kar PK (1993). Clinical Filarial Disease in Two Ethnic Endemic Communities of Orissa, India. *Am. J. Trop. Med. Hyg.*, 96(5): 311-316.

Kessel JF (1957). An Effective Programme for the Control of Filariasis in Tahiti. *Bull. Wld. Hlth. Org.*, 16: 633-634.

Kessel JF and Massal E (1962). Control of Bancroftian Filariasis in the Pacific. *Bull. Wld. Hlth. Org.*, 27: 543-554.

Kimura E, Remit K, Fujiwara M, Aniol K and Siren N (1994). Parasitological and Clinical Studies on *W. bancrofti* Infection in Chunk State, Federated States of Micronesia. *Ann. Trop. Med. Parasit.*, 45(4): 344-346.

Knowles R and Basu BC (1934). Mosquito Prevalence and Mosquito Borne Disease in Calcutta city. *Rec. Mal. Surv. India*, 4: 291-319.

Korke VT (1928). Observations on Filariasis in some Areas in British Indian Part II. *Ind. J. Med. Res.*, 16: 187-198.

Korke VT (1928). Observations on Filariasis in some Areas in British Indian Part III. *Ind. J. Med. Res.*, 16: 695-715.

Krishnaswami AK (1955). Filariasis in Mangalore (South India). *Ind. J. Malar.*, 9: 1-16.

Krishnaswami AK, Nair CP, Singh D, Bhatnagar VN, Mammen ML and Sharma HL (1963). Fresh Local Filaria Transmission Resulting from Urbanisation. *Ind. J. Malar.*, 17: 65-69.

Kshirsagar NA, Gogtay NJ, Garg BS, Deshymukh PR, Rajgor DD, Kadam VS, Kirodian BG, Ingole NS, Mehendale AM, Fleckenstein L, Karbwang J and Lazdins-Helds JK (2004). Safety, Tolerability, Efficacy and Plasma Concentrations of Diethylcarbamazine and Albendazole Co-administration in a Field Study in An Area Endemic for Lymphatic Filariasis in India. *Trans. Roy. Soc. Trop. Med. Hyg.*, 98(4): 205-217.

Kumar A (1997). Epidemiology of Filariasis Transmission: Estimation of Infectivity Index in Vector Population from mf data. *J. Parasit. Dis.*, 21: 182-184.

Kumar A and Singh P (1999). Epidemiology of Bancroftian Filariasis in Khurda District, Orissa. *J. Parasit. Dis.*, 23: 1-10.

Kumar A, Dash AP and Mansing GD (1994). Prevalence of Filariasis in Rural Puri, Orissa. *J. Commun. Dis.*, 26(4): 215-226.

Lambert B and Peferoen M (1992). Insecticidal Promise of *Bacillus Thuringiensis*. *Bio. Sc.*, 42(2): 112-122.

Laurence BR (1963). Natural Mortality in Two Filarial Vectors. *Bull. Wld. Hlth. Org.*, 28: 229-234.

Lewis TR (1877). The Microscopic Organisms Found in the Blood of Man and Animal and Their Relation to Disease. 14th Ann. Rep. Sanitary Commissioner, Government of India, Appendix B, p. 157.

Low GC (1900). A Recent Observation on Filariasis Nocturna in *Culex* Probable Mode of Infection of Man. *Brit. Med. J.*, 1: 1456-1457.

Mansfield-Aders W (1927). Notes on Malaria and Filariasis in the Zanibar Protectorate. *Trans. Roy. Soc. Trop. Med. Hyg.*, 21: 207-214.

Manson P (1883). Filariasis Sanguinis Hominis, H.K. Lewis, London; p. 32.

Marzhuki MI, Tham AS and Pooraneswari S (1993). Current Status of Filariasis in Malaysia, *Southeast Asian J. Trop. Med. Publ. Hlth.*, 24(2): 10-14.

Masuya T, cited in Manson-Bahr PEC and Bell DR (1987). *Manson's Tropical Disease*. 19th Eds, ELBS Pub, p. 1366.

Mc Fadzean JS and Hawking F (1956). The Periodicity of Microfilariae *V. stimuli* Affecting the Periodic Migration of the Microfilariae of *W. bancrofti* and of Loa loa in Man. *Trans. Roy. Soc. Trop. Hyg.*, 50: 543-562.

Mc Mahon JE, Magayuka SA and Kolstrup N (1981). Studies on the Transmission and Prevalence of Bancroftian Filariasis in Four Coastal Villages of Tanzania. *Ann. Trop. Med. Parasit.*, 75: 415-431.

Meillon B de and Sebastian A (1967). The Biting Cycle of *Culex Pipiens Fatigans* on Man in Rangoon Burma and the Microfilarial Periodicity. *Bull. Wld. Hlth. Org.*, 36: 174-176.

Meillon B de, Sebastian A and Khan ZH (1967). Outdoor Resting of *Culex Pipiens Fatigans* in Rangoon, Burma. *Bull. Wld. Hlth. Org*. 36: 67-73.

Meyrowitsch DW, Simonsen PE and Makunde WH (1995). Bancroftian Filariasis Analysis of Infection and Disease in Five Endemic Communities of North Eastern Tanzania. *Ann. Trop. Med. Parasit.*, 89(6): 653-663.

Mohamed NH, Safar EH, Fawzy AF, Kamel AM and Abdel Wahab MM (1994). Study of Present Status of Filariasis in an Endemic Area in Giza Governorate, Egypt. *J. Egypt. Soc. Parasit.*, 24(1): 127-135.

Nair CP (1960). Filariasis in Centrally Administered Areas Part II. Survey of Laccadive, Minicoy and Amindive Island. *Ind. J. Malar.*, 15: 233-252.

Nair CP (1962). Filariasis in Kerala State. Part VII Survey of Ponai (Palghat district). *Ind. J. Malar.*, 16: 47-62.

Nair CP (1966). Filariasis Survey of Palghat Town Kerala State. *Bull. Ind. Soc. Mal. Com. Dis.*, 3: 198-206.

Nair CP and Samanta KG (1967). A Note on Urban Malaria, Broach Town, Gujarat State, India. *Bull. Ind. Soc. Mal Commun. Dis.*, 4: 285-995.

Nanda DK, Singh MV and Chand D (1962). Study of the Effect of Climate on the Density of *Culex Fatigans* and the Development of Filarial Parasite in it. *Ind. J. Malar.*, 16: 313-320.

Nathan MB (1981). Bancroftian Filariasis in Coastal North Trinidad, West Indies: Intensity of Transmission by *Culex Quinquefasciatus. Trans. Roy. Soc. Trop. Med. Hyg.*, 75: 721-730.

Nathan MB, Hamilton PJS, Montell S and Tikasingh ES (1987). Bancroftian Filariasis in Coastal North Trinidad; the Effect of Mass Chemotherapy using Spaced doses of Diethyl Carbamazine Citrate on Human Microfilariaemias and Vector Infection rates. *Trans. Roy. Soc. Trop. Med. Hyg.*, 81: 663-668.

Nelson GS, Heisch RB and Furlong M (1962). Studies on Filariasis in East Africa II. Filarial Infections in Man, Animals and Mosquitoes on the Kenya Coast. *Trans. Roy. Soc. Trop. Med. Hyg.*, 56: 202-217.

Norman RA, Chan MS, Srividya A, Pani SP, Ramaiah KD, Vanamail P, Michael E, Das PK and Bundy DAP (2000). The Development of an Age-structured Model for Describing the Transmission Dynamics and Control of Lymphatic Filariasis. *Epidem. Infec.*, 124(3): 529-541.

Ogunba EO (1971). Observations on *Culex pipiens Fatigans* in Ibadan, Western Nigeria. *Ann. Trop. Med. Parasit.*, 65: 399-402.

Ohana B, Margalit J and Barak Z (1987). Fate of *Bacillus Thuringiensis* subsp. *Israelensis* under Simulated Field Conditions. *Appl. Environ. Microbiol.*, 57(4): 828-831.

Omar MS (1996). A Survey of Bancroftian Filariasis Among South East Asian Expatriate Workers in Soudi Arabia. *Trop. Med. Int. Hlth.*, 1(2): 155-160.

Pattanayak S and Chandrasekhar A (1963). Filariasis in Kerala State; Filaria Survey of Kottayam Municipality. *Ind. J. Malar.*, 17: 273-277.

Petras SF and Casida (Jr.) LE (1985). Survival of *Bacillus Thuringiensis* Spores is Soil. *Appl. Environ. Microbiol.*, 50: 1496-1501.

Power RC and Mittal MC (1968). Filariasis in Jamnagar. *Ind. J. Med. Res.*, 56: 370-376.

Prasad RN, Das MK, Sharma T and Dutta GDP (1993). Prevalence of Filariasis in Rural Areas of Shahjahanpur District (Uttar Pradesh): *Ind. J. Med. Res.*, 97: 112-114.

Raccurt C and Hodges W (1977). Filariasis due to *Wuchereria bancrofti* in Haiti. *Trans. Roy. Soc. Trop. Med. Hyg.*, 71: 452-453.

Raghavan NGS (1951). Filariasis in Porbander, Sourashtra. *Ind. J. Malar.*, 5: 203-207.

Raghavan NGS and Krishnan KS (1949). A Note on Microfilaria of Malayi (Brug) in *Cx. fatigans* and *An. stephensi. Ind. J. Malar.*, 3: 249-252.

Rahaman J, Singh MV and Gujral JS (1957). Investigation of Filariasis Problem in Ballia Town (Uttar Pradesh). *Ind. J. Malar.*, 11: 163-167.

Raina VK, Tripathi VC, Ram R, Kumar A and Verghese T (1992). Status of Lymphatic Filariasis in some Selected Clusters of Delhi. *J. Commun. Dis.*, 24(2): 92-96.

Rajagopalan PK, Brooks GD, Menon PKB, Rao B and Mani TR (1977). Observations on the Biting Activity and Flight Periodicity of *Cx. pipiens Fatigans* in an Urban Area. *J. Commun. Dis.*, 9: 22-31.

Rajagopalan PK, Shetty PS and Arunachalam N (1981). A Filariasis Survey in Pondicherry Villages. *Ind. J. Med. Res.*, 73: 73-77.

Rajendran R, Sunish IP, Mani TR, Munirathinam A, Abdulla SM, Arunachalam N and Satyanarayana K (2004). Impact of Two Annual Single-dose Mass Drug Administrations with Diethylcarbamazine Alone or in Combination with Albendazole on *Wuchereria bancrofti* Microfilariaemia and Antigenaemia in South India. *Trans. Roy. Soc. Trop. Med. Hyg.*, 98(3): 174-181.

Rajendran R, Sunish IP, Mani TR, Munirathinam A, Abdullah SM, Angustin DJ and Satyanarayana K (2002). The Influence of the Mass Administration of Diethylecarbamazine, Alone or with Albendazole, on the Prevalence of Filarial Antigenaemia. *Ann. Trop. Med. Parasit.*, 96(6): 595-602.

Ramaiah KD, Vanamail P, Pani SP and Das PK (2003). The Prevalences of *Wuchereria bancrofti* Antigenaemia in Communities given Six Rounds of Treatment with Diethylcarbamazine, Ivermectin or Placebo Tablets. *Ann. Trop. Med. Parasit*, 97(7): 737-741.

Ramaiah KD, Vijay Kumar KN, Ravi R, Das PK. (2005). Situation Analysis in a Large Urban Area of India, Prior to Launching a Programme of Mass Drug Administrations to Eliminate Lymphatic Filariasis. *Ann Trop Med Parasitol.* 99(3): 243-52.

Rao CK, Dutta RK, Sunderam RM, Ram Prasad K, Rao JS, Venkatanarayana M, Nath VVN, Rao PK, Rao Ch K, Das M and Sharma SP (1980). Epidemio-logical Studies on Bancroftian Filariasis in East Godavari District (A.P.) Baseline Filariometric Indices. *Ind. J. Med. Res.*, 71: 712-720.

Rao SS and Iyenger MOT (1932). Experimental Infection of some Indian Mosquitoes with *Wuchereria* (Filaria) *bancrofti*. *Ind. J. Med. Res.*, 20: 25-34.

Rao SS and Sukhatme PV (1941). Seasonal Variations in the Incidence of Filarial Lymphangitis. *Ind. J. Med. Res.*, 29: 209-223.

Rao TR and Rajagopalan PK (1957). Observations on Mosquitoes of Poona District, India: With Special Reference to Their Distribution, Seasonal Prevalence and the Biology of Adults. *Ind. J. Malar.*, 11: 1-54.

Ray PC (1902). A history of the Hindu Chemistry. Bengal Chemical and Pharmaceutical Works, Calcutta, p. 26.

Reisen WK and Milby MM (1986). Population Dynamics of some Pakistan Mosquitoes; Changes in Adult Relative Abundance over Time and Space. *Ann. Trop. Med. Parasit.*, 80: 53-68.

Rozeboom LE, Bhattacharya NC and Gilotra SK (1968). Observations on the Transmission of Filariasis in Urban Calcutta. *Am. J. Epidem.*, 87: 616-632.

Rudra SK and Chandra G (1998). Bancrofitian Filariasis in Tribal Population of Bankura District, West Bengal India. *Japanese J. Trop. Med. Hyg.*, 26: 109-112.

Rudra SK and Chandra G (2000). Comparative Epidemiological Studies on Lymphatic Filariasis Between Tribal and Non-tribal Populations of Bankura District, West Bengal, India. *Annal. Trop. Med. Parasit.*, 94: 365-372.

Samarawickrema WA, Sone F, Paulson GS, Kimura E, Uchida K and Cummings RF (1992). Observation on *Cx. Quinquefasciatus* say in Relation to Subperiodic *W. bancrofti* in Samoa. *Ann. Trop. Med. Parasit.*, 86(5): 517-522.

Sarma RVSN, Vallishayee RS, Mayurnath S, Narayanan PR, Radhamani MP and Tripathy SP (1987). Prevalence Survey of Filariasis in Two Villages in Chengliput District of Tamil Nadu. *Ind. J. Med. Res.*, 85: 522-530.

Sasa M (1963). Pilot Experiments in the Control of Bancroftian Filariasis in Japan and Ryukyu. *Bull. Wld. Hlth. Org.*, 28: 437-454.

Sasa M, Kurihara T and Harinasuta C (1965). Studies on Mosquitoes and Their Natural Enemies in Bangkok. Part-1 Observations on the Bionomics of *Culex Pipiens Fatigans* (Wiedemann). *Jap. J. Exper. Med.*, 35: 23-49.

Seal BN (1915). *The Positive Sciences of the Ancient Hindus*. Longman's Green and Co., London, p. 61.

Self LS, Abdul Cader MHM and Tun MM (1969). Preferred Biting Sites of *Culex Pipiens Fatigans* on Adult Burmes males. *Bull. Wld. Hlth. Org.*, 40: 324-327.

Self LS, Usman S, Sajidiman H, Partonss F, Nelson MJ, Parit CP, Suzuki T and Mc Chfudin H (1978). A Multidisciplinary Study on Bancroftian Filarisis in Djakarta. *Trans. Roy. Soc. Trop. Med. Hyg.*, 72: 581-587.

Service MW (1963). The Ecology of the Mosquitoes of Northern Guinea Savannan of Nigeria. *Bull. Ent. Res.*, 54: 601-630.

Shenoy RK, Suma TK, John A, Arun SR, Kumaraswami V, Fleckenstein LL and Na-bangchang K (2002). The Pharmacokinetics, Safety and Tolerability of the Co-administration of Diethyl Carbamazine and Albendzole. *Ann. Trop. Med. Parasit.*, 96(6): 603-614.

Sherlock (1) A and Sarafim EM (1967). Filariasis in Bahia, Brazil. *Revta. Bras. Malar. Doenc. Trop.*, 19: 395.

Shriram AN, Sugunan AP, Murhekar MV and Sengal SC (1996). Little Andaman Island, a New Focus of Infection with Nocturnally Periodic *W. bancrofti*. *Ind. J. Mal. Res.*, (104).

Sibthrope (1888). Filaria Sanguinis Hominis. *Brit. Med. J.*, 1: 860.

Simonsen PE, Meyrowitsch DW, Makunde WH, Magunssen P (1995). Bancroftian Filariasis, the Pattern of Microfilaraemia and Clinical Manifestations in 3 Endemic Communities of North Eastern Tanzania. *Acta. Tropica.*, 60(3): 179-187.

Singh D (1967). The *Culex Pipen Fatigans* Problem in South East Asia. *Bull. Wld. Hlth. Org.*, 37: 239-243.

Singh MV, Agarwala RS, Nanda DK and Singh N (1963). House Frequenting Behaviour of *Culex Fatigans*. *Ind. J. Malar.*, 17: 297-301.

Sinha HP (1960). Filariasis Survey in Basti (Uttar Pradesh). *Ind. J. Publ. Hlth.*, 4: 146-151.

Smith A (1961). Observations on the Man Biting Habits of some Mosquitoes in the South Pare Area of Tanganyika. *E. Afr. Med. J.*, 38: 246-248.

Someren Van ECC, Heisch RB and Furlong M (1958). Observations on the Behaviour of some Mosquitoes of the Kenya Coast. *Bull. Ent. Res.*, 49: 643-660.

Srivastava RN and Prasad BG (1989). An Epidemiological Study of Filariasis in the Villages of the Rural Health Training Centre, Sarojini Nagar, Lucknow.

Srividya A, Michael E, Palaniyandi M, Pani SP and Das PK (2002). A Geostatistical Analysis of the Geographic Distribution of Lymphatic Filariasis Prevalence in Southern India. *Am. J. Trop. Med. Hyg.*, 67(5): 480-489.

Srividya A, Pani SP, Rajagopalan PK, Bundy DAP and Grenfell BT (1991). Clinical Epidemiology of Bancroftian Filariasis: Effect of Age and Gender. *Trans. Roy. Soc. Trop. Med. Hyg.*, 85(2): 260-264.

Stolk WA, Swaminathan S, Van Oortmarssen GJ, Das PK and Habbema JDF (2003). Prospects for Elimination of Bancroftian Filariasis by Mass Drug Treatment in Pondicherry, India: A Simulation Study. *J. Infec. Dis.*, 188(9): 1317-1381.

Subra R (1972). Etudes ecologiques Sur *Culex Pipiens Fatigans* Wiedemann, 1828 (Diptera, Culicidae) dans uno zone Urbaine de Savanne soudaninenne ovest africaine. Tandence endo exophages et cycle d' agressirite. *Cah. Ser. Ent. Med. Parasit.*, 10: 335-345.

Subramaniam H, Ramoo H and Sumanam SD (1958). Filariasis survey in the Laccadive, Minicoy and Amindive Islands Madras State. *Ind. J. Malar.*, 12: 45-127.

Subramanian S, Stolk WA, Ramaiah KD, Plaisier AP, Krishnamoorthy K, Van Oortmarssen GJ, Amalraj DD, Habbema JDF and Das PK (2004). The Dynamics of *Wuchereria bancrofti* infection: A Model-based Analysis of Logitudinal Data from Pondicherry, India. *Parasit.*, 128(5): 467-482

Sucharit S, Harinesuta C, Surathin K, Deesin T, Vatikes S and Rongsriyam Y (1981). Some Aspects on Biting Cycles of *Culex Quinquefasciatus* in Bangkok. *Southeast Asian J. Trop. Med. Publ. Hlth.*, 12: 74-78.

Suma TK, Shenoy RK and Kumaraswami V (2003). A Qualitative Study of the Perceptions, Practices and Socio-psycho Logical Suffering Related to Chronic Brugian Filariasis in Kerala, Southern India. *Ann. Trop. Med. Parasit.*, **97**(8): 839-845.

Symes CB (1955). Filarial Infections in Mosquitoes in Fiji. *Trans. Roy. Soc. Trop. Med. Hyg.*, 49: 280-284.

Symes CB (1960). Observations on the Epidemiology of Filariasis in Fiji Part I. *Am. J. Trop. Med. Hyg.*, 63: 1-14.

Teesdale C (1959). Observations on the Mosquito Fauna of Mombasa. *Bull. Ent. Res.*, 50: 191-208.

Tiwari SC, Hiriyan J and Ruben R (1989). Epidemiology of subperiodic *W. bancrofti* infection in the Nicobar islands, India. *J. Commun. Dis.*, 89(2): 163-166.

Triteeraprapab S, Kanjanopas K, Suwannadabba S, Sangprakran S, Poovorawan Y and Scott AL (2000). Transmission of the Nocturnal Periodic Strain of *Wuchereria bancrofti* by *Culex quinquefasciatus*: Establishing the Potential for Urban Filariasis in Thailand. *Epidem. Infect.*, 125(1): 207-212.

Valeza FS and Grove DI (1979). Bancroftian Filariasis in a Philippine village: Entomological Findings. *Southeast Asian J. Trop. Med. Publ. Hlth.*, 10: 51-61.

Verma BK, Das NL and Sinha VP (1961). Filariasis in the Rural Population Around Bhagalpur Town, Part II. *Ind. J. Malar.*, 15: 293-299.

Verma BK, Prasad RM, Das NL and Sinha VP (1962). Studies on the Incidence and Transmission of Filariasis in Monghyr (Bihar). *Ind. J. Malar.*, 16: 17-26.

Verma BK, Sinha VP and Das NL (1960). Filariasis in Sultanganj and Its Suburbs (Bihar). *Bull. Nat. Soc.*, 8: 149-152.

Vincent AL, Gonzalvo A, Cowell BC, Nayar JK and Uribe L (1987). A Survey of Bancroftian Filariasis in Dominican Republic. *J. Parasit.*, 73: 839-840.

Vishagaratna KL (1907). *Susrata Samhita*, English translation.

Weerasooriya MV, Weerasooriya TR, Gunawardena NK and Samarawickrema W (2001). Epidemiology of Bancroftian Filariasis in Three Suburban Areas of Matara, Sri Lanka. *Ann. Trop. Med. Parasit.*, 95(3): 263-273.

Weill M, Berticat C, Raymond N and Chevillon C (2000). Quantitative Polymerase Chain Reaction of Estimate the Number of Amplified Esterase Genes in Insecticide-resistant Mosquitoes. *Anal. Biochem.*, 285(2): 267-270.

Weinstock H, Paniagua F, Graces JL, Zuniga A, Granados C and Hernandez E (1977). Bancroftian Filariasis in Puerto Limon, Costa Rica. *Am. J. Trop. Med. Hyg.*, 26: 1148-1152.

White GB (1971). Studies on Transmission of Bancroftian Filariasis in North Eastern Tanzania. *Trans. Roy. Soc. Trop. Med. Hyg.*, 65: 819-829.

WHO (1998). *Life in the 21st Century a Vision for all*, Geneva: World Health Organization: 24.

Wijers DJB and Kiilu G (1977). Bancroftian Filariasis in Kenya. 111. Entomological Investigations in Mumburi, a Small Coastal Town and Jarbuni, a Rural Area more Inland (Coastal Province). *Ann. Trop. Med. Parasit.*, 71: 347-359.

Wizers DJB and Kaleli N (1984). Bancroftian Filariasis in Kenya. V. Mass Treatment given by Member of the Local Community. *Ann. Trop. Med. Parasit.*, 78: 383-394.

Wu YT and Chen CT (1960). Filariasis Endemic Areas in the Taiwan Proper. Part I. Incidence of Bancroftian Microfilarial Infection Among the Native People in Southern Tiwan. *J. Formosan Med. Ass.*, 59: 262-271.

Zhang S, Cheng F and Webber R (1988). A Successful Control Programme for Lymphatic Filariasis in Hubei, China. *Trans. Roy. Soc. Trop. Med. Hyg.*, 88(5): 510-512.

Index

D

E

F

G

N

Q

R

S

T

❑❑❑